# The Battle of
# Camden

# THE BATTLE OF CAMDEN

## A DOCUMENTARY HISTORY

JIM PIECUCH

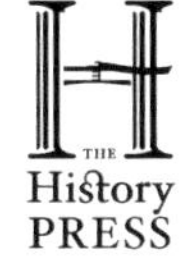
THE History PRESS

Published by The History Press
Charleston, SC 29403
www.historypress.net



Cover painting by Werner Willis.

First published 2006
Second printing 2013
Third printing 2014

Manufactured in the United States

ISBN 978.1.59629.144.7

Library of Congress Cataloging-in-Publication Data

Piecuch, Jim.
The Battle of Camden : a documentary history / Jim Piecuch.
p. cm.
ISBN 978.1-59629-144-7 (alk. paper)
1. Camden, Battle of, Camden, S.C., 1780--Personal narratives. 2. Camden, Battle of, Camden, S.C., 1780--Sources. 3. Generals--United States--Biography. 4. Generals--Great Britain Biography. 5. Soldiers--United States--Biography. 6. Soldiers--Great Britain--Biography. 7. United States--History--Revolution, 1775-1783--Personal narratives. 8. United States--History--Revolution, 1775-1783--Personal narratives, British. I. Title.
E241.C17P54 2006
973.3'36--dc22
2006020459

# Contents

# Acknowledgements

Many people assisted in the process of preparing this book for publication and deserve special thanks. Joanna Craig of Historic Camden provided many of the illustrations; Mike Coker, John Robertson and Werner Willis also supplied maps and pictures; Charles Baxley and David Reuwer gave valuable advice; my son Joey Piecuch did excellent work in tracking down and transcribing some of the documents. I also want to thank my wife, Lori, for her constant support, the staffs at the many archives where I searched for material and Jenny Kaemmerlen and The History Press for their assistance.

# INTRODUCTION

SUNRISE ON the morning of August 16, 1780, found two armies arrayed on a mist-shrouded plain eight miles north of Camden, South Carolina. At the northern end of the field, on open ground beneath the tall pines, stood the American forces of Major General Horatio Gates, numbering over three thousand men. To the west, holding the right flank of the line, were the Continental soldiers, professionals from Maryland and Delaware in their blue uniform coats. On their left, militia units from North Carolina and Virginia stood in battle array, clad in the homespun clothing of civilians. Interspersed among the infantry, artillerists readied their cannon and awaited the order to fire. Behind the center of the first line, another brigade of Continentals formed the reserve.

Deployed in line some two hundred yards south of the Americans, the veteran soldiers of the British army provided a more colorful display. Most wore the red coats issued to British Regular regiments and provincial units, the latter composed of Americans who had enlisted for long-term service against their rebellious countrymen. Among the scarlet clad troops on the left or western flank were about one hundred men wearing the green coats of the British Legion, while many of the two hundred North Carolina provincials and all of the three hundred South Carolina militiamen wore civilian garb. In the rear of these men were more redcoated Regulars as well as the mounted troops of the British Legion cavalry in green jackets.

Of the approximately 2,200 enlisted men commanded by Lieutenant General Charles, Earl Cornwallis, over 1,100, or more than half of the British force, were American Loyalists. Their presence demonstrated the fact that the American Revolution was not just a contest between Americans and Britons, but a civil war between those Americans who desired independence and others who wished the colonies to remain part of the British empire.

The train of events that had brought the two armies to the pine barrens north of Camden had been set in motion in the fall of 1775. Realizing that the growing rebellion in America would have to be subdued by force, British officials in London debated where to strike. New England presented an appealing target. The revolt was centered there, and the newly formed Continental army under George Washington was besieging British troops in Boston, Massachusetts. If a British force captured New York City and the king's soldiers gained control of the Hudson River Valley, New England would be isolated, its troublesome inhabitants could be defeated and then the other colonies might again accept British rule.

Some royal officials, however, proposed an alternate plan that would come to be known as the "Southern strategy." The wisest course, these people insisted, would be to strike at the soft underbelly of rebellion in the Southern colonies. The provinces of East and West Florida remained loyal to King George III and could serve as an anchor for the British position. Georgia was still wavering. The governors of North and South Carolina reported that thousands of Loyalists in those colonies would take up arms if supported by British troops. The powerful Creek and Cherokee Indian nations on the frontier supported Britain and might provide assistance against the rebels. In addition, the large numbers of slaves in the South (South Carolina's slaves outnumbered whites, 100,000 to 70,000) could be a valuable resource. If offered freedom, large numbers would fight against their masters. Even if left alone, the need to keep them under control would divert a significant portion of the rebel militia.

Lord Dartmouth, secretary of state for the American Department, had responsibility for devising and executing the military campaign against the colonists. He chose to undertake a two-pronged offensive against the Americans in 1776. The major British effort would target New York City and a smaller expedition would be sent to aid the Loyalists in North Carolina. Rejecting the advice of more aggressive officers and politicians who wanted to unleash Indians and armed slaves in the South, Dartmouth decided to rely only on Loyalist assistance. Lord George Germain, who replaced Dartmouth in November 1775, allowed the plan to go ahead unchanged.

This first effort to put the Southern strategy into effect ended disastrously. The rebels, or Whigs, dispersed South Carolina's Loyalists and imprisoned their leaders in the fall of 1775. North Carolina's Loyalists took up arms prematurely and were defeated at the battle of Moore's Creek Bridge on February 27, 1776. Shortly afterward, a small British force under General Henry Clinton arrived off the North Carolina coast, but found neither Loyalists nor the larger expedition en route from Cork in Ireland. Various problems assembling the troops and ships at Cork had delayed the expedition's departure and then severe storms scattered the ships. By the time Admiral Sir Peter Parker's fleet arrived, Clinton was ready to give up and join the main army in attacking New York. Parker, however, convinced Clinton that they should mount an attack on Charleston, South Carolina.

The attempt to take Charleston on June 28 was a fiasco. Clinton's troops landed on Long Island (present-day Isle of Palms) with the intention of crossing a shallow channel and attacking the northern tip of Sullivan's Island while Parker's ships struck at Fort Moultrie on the island's southern end. To his dismay, Clinton found that the "shallow" channel was seven feet deep, so his soldiers remained idle while Parker's ships bombarded Fort Moultrie. While British cannonballs embedded themselves harmlessly in the palmetto log walls of the fort, the defenders poured an effective fire into the fleet. Parker finally withdrew with the loss of a frigate and heavy casualties among his crews. The British sailed north, leaving the Whigs in firm control of the Southern colonies.

Sporadic warfare continued, however. The Americans invaded East Florida once each year from 1776 to 1778. Every time hot weather, disease and squabbling between officers forced them to turn back. Loyalist refugees based in East Florida, assisted by Indians and sometimes by British Regulars, retaliated by launching raids into Georgia. But the overall strategic situation remained unchanged.

Meanwhile, the campaigns in the North were not going as the British had planned. In the late summer of 1776, a large army under General Sir William Howe repeatedly defeated Washington's forces, seized Long Island and the region around New York City and then overran most of New Jersey. General George Washington struck back in late December and early January 1777, defeating the British at Trenton and Princeton, New Jersey, and forcing Howe to abandon most of that province. In the summer of 1777, General John Burgoyne advanced southward from Canada to the Hudson River to carry out the plan to isolate New England. He was met by an American army under Horatio Gates, which stopped the British advance, defeated Burgoyne's attempts to break through the American lines and forced Burgoyne to surrender his entire army. Gates's victory in the Saratoga campaign introduced a new word into the American vocabulary: "burgoyned," meaning surrounded and captured. More importantly, the success at Saratoga convinced France to enter the war in 1778 as an ally of the Americans. Since Spain was a close ally of France, French intervention meant that Spanish forces were likely to enter the war against Britain in a short time.

Germain now had to rethink his entire strategy. First, he ordered Henry Clinton, who had replaced Howe as commander-in-chief in North America, to send five thousand men to Canada to replace Burgoyne's army, another five thousand to the West Indies to protect the valuable sugar plantations from the French and two thousand to West Florida to guard against the Spanish in Louisiana. Shorn of one-third of his troops, Clinton's options were limited. He withdrew from Philadelphia, which Howe had captured the previous autumn, and concentrated his army at New York. But Germain knew the British could not subdue the Rebels by remaining passive. With resources in America limited by the need to fight the French, Germain decided it was time to take advantage of Loyalist manpower in the South. He therefore revived the Southern strategy and ordered Clinton to attack Georgia as soon as possible.

In November 1778, Clinton dispatched 2,500 men from New York under Lieutenant Colonel Archibald Campbell to seize Savannah. Campbell put his troops ashore in late December, and with the help of information provided by a slave outflanked and routed Savannah's defenders. After being reinforced by a detachment that had marched overland from East Florida, Campbell advanced into Georgia's interior (the "Backcountry"), occupied Augusta without resistance and enrolled 1,500 men in the Loyalist militia. He expected to meet a large force of Creek Indians, but slow communications and the long distance from the Indians' towns delayed the Creeks. While Campbell waited, American Major General Benjamin Lincoln gathered a large force of Continentals and militia north of the Savannah River. Fearing that he would be cut off from Savannah by Lincoln's army, which greatly outnumbered the British, Campbell withdrew from the Backcountry.

Several battles were fought in the following months, and in May 1779 the British marched to the gates of Charleston, but neither side gained a permanent advantage. The situation seemed about to change in the fall, however, when a French fleet and army arrived in Georgia and joined Lincoln's troops in besieging Savannah. Unwilling to wait the many weeks it would take for the siege to force the British garrison to surrender, the French commander, the Comte D'Estaing, decided to attack. The French and Americans stormed Savannah's defenses on October 9, only to be repulsed with heavy losses. The French sailed away, and Lincoln retreated to South Carolina.

Encouraged by the victory at Savannah, Clinton decided to attack Charleston. A British expedition from New York landed south of the town in February 1780 and soon trapped Lincoln's army within its defensive lines. On May 12, Lincoln surrendered six thousand Continentals and militia in the worst defeat the Americans suffered during the war. British columns fanned out across the South Carolina and Georgia Backcountry. Thousands of people took the oath of allegiance to King George and British officers began organizing a militia to secure their conquests while the army invaded North Carolina. Clinton returned to New York with most of his troops in early June, leaving Cornwallis to command in the South.

American leaders had watched Clinton's progress in South Carolina with growing concern. Washington dispatched the Maryland and Delaware troops from his army to relieve Charleston, putting them under the command of Major General Baron Johann De Kalb. Before these reinforcements arrived, Congress learned of Charleston's surrender. In that emergency, they turned to the general who had won the most important victory of the war thus far. The representatives named Horatio Gates commander of the Southern Department and ordered him to take command of De Kalb's detachment and whatever militia was available and restore the situation before the Southern colonies were permanently lost. With

Gates in command, many in Congress confidently predicted, Cornwallis's army would soon be burgoyned.

Born in England in 1727, Gates looked much older than his fifty-three years and had affectionately been nicknamed "granny Gates" by his troops in the North. With few career options open to a man of humble origins, he entered the British army and joined the expedition that founded Halifax, Nova Scotia, in 1749. Ironically, the expedition's commander and governor of Nova Scotia, Colonel Edward Cornwallis, was the uncle of Charles Cornwallis. Edward Cornwallis considered Gates a capable officer and assisted his rise to the rank of captain. Gates served in America during the Seven Years' War (also known as the French and Indian War), where he saw little action but acquired a reputation as a good administrator. After the war Gates, then a major, returned to England.

Peacetime reductions in the British army blocked any hope Gates had for further advancement, so he retired from the army. As the Americans' dispute with Britain over the issue of taxation intensified, Gates vocally supported the colonists. In 1772, he moved to Virginia. When the war broke out, Congress appointed him a brigadier general in the Continental army, and as Washington's adjutant general he did an excellent job recruiting, organizing and training the troops besieging Boston. Congress promoted him to major general in May 1776. He then reported to General Philip Schuyler's army in New York, where his administrative skills contributed greatly to halting the advance of a British army from Canada.

When Burgoyne renewed the offensive from Canada in 1777 and captured strategic Fort Ticonderoga in July, Congress replaced Schuyler with Gates. Schuyler's troops were demoralized; the New Englanders resented the pretentious New York aristocrat and militia officers felt that he did not respect them or their men. Gates restored the army's morale and discipline and won the affection and confidence of both his Regulars and militia. He chose an ideal defensive position north of Saratoga, which blocked Burgoyne's advance. Gates left tactical matters in the hands of his capable subordinates, Daniel Morgan and Benedict Arnold, who defeated both of Burgoyne's attempts to break through the American lines. On October 17, while Washington was being beaten and driven from Philadelphia, Gates accepted the surrender of Burgoyne's army, instantly becoming America's new hero.

Gates's success also created problems for him. He reported his victory directly to Congress, angering Washington, who thought that the letter should have gone to him first as commander-in-chief. Some army officers and members of Congress thought that Gates should succeed Washington, which convinced some of Washington's supporters that Gates was conspiring against his commander. With Gates's relationship with Washington severely strained, Congress named Gates president of the Board of War, another administrative post. Gates later commanded forces in New York and Massachusetts, but with the war in the North at a stalemate, in late

1779 he asked for leave and returned to his Virginia home. There he remained until Congress appointed him to command the Southern army in June 1780.

Gates's second-in-command, Baron Johann De Kalb, was likewise a man of humble origins. Born into a family of peasants in Bavaria in 1721, De Kalb also sought advancement through military service in the French army. He served in the War of the Austrian Succession and the Seven Years' War, earning promotions and the Order of Military Merit along with the title "baron" for his distinguished service. De Kalb left the army in 1764, but four years later French officials sent him to America on a covert mission to assess the status of the colonists' dispute with Britain. In 1777, De Kalb came to America with his friend, the Marquis de Lafayette, and after some dispute, Congress appointed him a major general. De Kalb commanded a division of two brigades under Washington during the army's agonizing encampment at Valley Forge, Pennsylvania, in the winter of 1777–78, then served with Washington in New Jersey. He saw little action before Congress placed him in command of the troops sent to assist the Southern states in the spring of 1780.

The highest-ranking officer in the Maryland line, Brigadier General William Smallwood, had seen more combat in the Revolution than either Gates or De Kalb. Smallwood was born in 1732, the son of a wealthy Maryland tobacco planter. He had fought in the Seven Years' War, served in the Maryland legislature and taken command of the First Maryland Regiment with the rank of colonel when that unit was organized at the start of the war. He fought under Washington in 1776 at the battles of Long Island and White Plains, and was wounded in the latter engagement. Promoted to brigadier general, he alternately served in Washington's army and at home in Maryland until he was ordered southward with his brigade.

The other Maryland general, Mordecai Gist, was also an experienced veteran. A Maryland native born in 1743, Gist had been engaged in trade when the revolutionaries began to organize armed forces, and in December 1774 he was elected captain of the Baltimore Independent Company. When his state organized its first Continental units in 1776, he became major of the First Maryland under Smallwood. He served with distinction at Long Island and at White Plains, where he took command of the regiment after Smallwood was wounded. At the end of 1776, Gist took command of the Third Maryland Regiment with the rank of colonel and served in the Philadelphia campaign. In January 1779, he was promoted to brigadier general commanding the Second Maryland Brigade.

Otho Holland Williams, another Marylander, had an undistinguished prewar career. He was born in 1749 and worked as a clerk and merchant until 1775, when he joined a Maryland unit as a lieutenant. He participated in the siege of Boston and the campaign in New York, and had attained the rank of major by November 1776. That month he was wounded and captured when the British overwhelmed Fort Washington on the Hudson River. He was promoted colonel of the Sixth

Maryland while still a prisoner of war. Upon his exchange after fifteen months of captivity, Williams assumed command of his troops and led them at the battle of Monmouth, New Jersey, in June 1778. When Gates took command of the Southern army, he appointed Williams deputy adjutant general, a staff position.

Unlike the Continental officers, North Carolina's militia generals had no experience fighting against British Regulars. Major General Richard Caswell, born in Maryland in 1729, had moved to North Carolina in 1746. A lawyer and politician, Caswell was a member of the provincial legislature and represented North Carolina in the Continental Congress. He later accepted a colonel's commission in the militia and led the Whig troops at the battle of Moore's Creek Bridge. His victory earned him promotion to brigadier general and helped him win election to the governor's office later in 1776. His term ended in 1780 and, with the rank of major general, he took command of the militia assembling to defend North Carolina after the fall of Charleston.

Brigadier General Griffith Rutherford had more military experience than Caswell, yet he, too, had seen limited service. Rutherford had been born in Ireland, probably in 1721, immigrated to New Jersey at the age of eighteen and then moved to North Carolina and took up farming. As a representative in the colony's legislature, he was in the forefront of the revolutionary movement. Appointed a colonel in the militia, his regiment helped disperse and disarm Loyalists in the South Carolina Backcountry in 1775. Rutherford was promoted to brigadier general in May 1776, and two months later led his militia in a campaign against the Cherokees in retaliation for their attack on the Southern frontier. Afterwards, Rutherford's chief responsibility was to keep North Carolina's Loyalists in check; he had dispersed one band before joining Caswell and advancing into South Carolina in the summer of 1780.

Virginia's militia commander at Camden, Brigadier General Edward Stevens, was a more experienced officer than Caswell or Rutherford. As a lieutenant colonel of militia, he had led his troops to victory in the battle of Great Bridge, Virginia, on December 9, 1775. Late in 1776, he joined the Continental army as colonel of the Tenth Virginia Regiment. Stevens fought in the 1777 Philadelphia campaign before resigning his commission in January 1778. The following year, Virginia officials appointed him brigadier general of militia and, in 1780, at the age of thirty-five, he led the troops sent to the aid of his state's southern neighbors.

The American commanders needed all the skill and experience they could muster, for arrayed against them were several of the finest officers in the British army.

Ambitious and confident, Lieutenant General Charles, Earl Cornwallis, brought twenty-two years of military experience and training to the battlefield at Camden. Born in 1738 to a prominent noble family, the Eton-educated Cornwallis entered the army in 1758. He took his duties seriously in an age when officers received no formal training, studying strategy and tactics with a Prussian officer and attending a military academy at Turin, Italy. He put his knowledge to use during the Seven Years' War, fighting in several battles in Europe and winning praise for his courage. His combination of military skill and family connections elevated him to the rank of colonel commanding the Thirty-third Regiment in 1766. He was also active in politics, holding various government appointments as well as a seat in Parliament.

When the Revolution broke out, Cornwallis sailed to America with the expedition from Cork that failed to capture Charleston. He then served with distinction in the various battles in New York and led the force that swept the Rebels from New Jersey in the fall of 1776, but was criticized for allowing Washington's army to escape after the battle of Trenton. As William Howe's second-in-command during the 1777 Philadelphia campaign, Cornwallis led the flanking column that defeated Washington at the battle of Brandywine in September. He fought at Monmouth the following summer in what proved to be the last major battle in the North. Learning that his wife was seriously ill and frustrated with the army's inactivity, he returned to England in November 1778.

Cornwallis had not intended to serve again in America, but his wife's death in February 1779 devastated him and he sought distraction from his grief by a return to duty. He accompanied Clinton to Charleston in 1780, but during the siege their relationship, already strained, suffered a complete rupture. As Clinton's second-in-command, Cornwallis had initially joined Clinton in planning operations. Cornwallis had more in mind than being a good subordinate; he knew Clinton had recently sent his resignation to the king, and the earl expected to be elevated to the supreme command in Clinton's place. However, Clinton received word from London during the siege that the king had refused his request to resign. Inexplicably, Cornwallis blamed Clinton for this blow to his ambitions. He refused to give further advice on the army's operations and demanded an independent command.

Before leaving South Carolina in June, Clinton appointed Cornwallis commander of the Southern Department and gave him a free hand in managing military and civil affairs. Cornwallis had been dealing with administrative matters in Charleston when he learned of Gates's approach, and eagerly rode to Camden to take command of the army.

As he disposed his army for battle, Cornwallis assigned command of his left wing to the young but capable Lieutenant Colonel Francis, Lord Rawdon. The son of the Earl of Moira, an Irish nobleman, Rawdon was born in 1754. He joined the Fifteenth Regiment as an ensign in 1771, but obtained leave to pursue his studies at Oxford. In 1774, Rawdon went to America to join the garrison in Boston, and the following year won recognition for his valor at the battle of Bunker Hill. Clinton appointed Rawdon his aide-de-camp, and Rawdon participated in the ill-fated Charleston expedition in 1776. Two years later, Clinton appointed him adjutant general of the army with the rank of lieutenant colonel. During the occupation of

Philadelphia, Rawdon enlisted many of his Irish countrymen into a new provincial regiment, the Volunteers of Ireland. After a dispute with Clinton in the fall of 1779, Rawdon resigned the adjutant general's post and devoted his full attention to his regiment. Rawdon and his troops served in the Charleston campaign, and although he was more experienced at staff work than field operations, Cornwallis recognized his talents and entrusted him with command of the army while the earl tended to government affairs in Charleston. As Gates approached, Rawdon concentrated his forces and conducted a skillful delaying action until Cornwallis arrived at Camden.

Lieutenant Colonel James Webster commanded the right wing of the British army. A Scot, Webster was born in 1743, the son of a minister. He entered the army in 1760 as a lieutenant in the Thirty-third Regiment, the unit Cornwallis commanded, and by 1774 had risen to the rank of lieutenant colonel. Because Cornwallis had higher command responsibilities, Webster actually led the Thirty-third Regiment throughout the war. He took part in the Charleston expedition and New York campaigns in 1776, the Philadelphia campaign in 1777 and distinguished himself at the battle of Monmouth in 1778. The following year, Clinton made Webster a brigade commander, giving him additional responsibility but no promotion. Webster served in this capacity during the siege of Charleston, performing with his usual reliability.

Of all the officers in Cornwallis's army, none inspired more fear and hatred in the Rebels than Lieutenant Colonel Banastre Tarleton. Like Rawdon, Tarleton had been born in 1754 and attained high rank at a young age. The son of a wealthy slave trader who had become mayor of Liverpool, Tarleton attended Oxford before joining the army in 1775 as a cornet (the cavalry equivalent of ensign, the lowest officer rank) in the King's Dragoon Guards. He volunteered for service in America and sailed from Cork with the expedition that attacked Charleston in 1776. In December of that year he participated in the raid that captured American General Charles Lee. He served in the Philadelphia campaign and was afterward promoted to captain in the Sixteenth Light Dragoons. During the army's stay in southeastern Pennsylvania, Loyalist recruits were organized into a mixed force of infantry and cavalry called the British Legion; Tarleton became the unit's lieutenant colonel. At the head of the Legion cavalry during the operations against Charleston in 1780, Tarleton won devastating victories over American mounted troops at Monck's Corner and Lenud's Ferry, earning a reputation as a fast-moving, hard-hitting commander.

After Charleston's surrender, Cornwallis detached Tarleton in pursuit of a regiment of Virginia Continentals that had been en route to Charleston but began to retreat after the town fell. Pushing his men and horses to their limits, Tarleton caught up with the Virginians at the Waxhaws, close to the North Carolina border, on May 29. When the Americans refused to surrender, Tarleton led a mounted charge that overran the Continentals. Over one hundred Americans died in the ensuing melee, which led many Whigs to assert that Tarleton had massacred his opponents after they tried to surrender. Although the evidence for this accusation was sketchy, most Americans accepted it as fact. "Tarleton's quarter," meaning to give no quarter to surrendering enemies, became a common phrase and practice of the war in the South. Tarleton sat astride his horse at the head of his green-coated dragoons, waiting for the infantry ahead of him to breach the American lines so that his horsemen could strike the finishing blow.

If the British infantry failed to break the American line and Gates's larger army triumphed, Tarleton would instead have to protect the British army's rear as it withdrew to Camden. But Cornwallis could not stay there long. The army did not have enough supplies on hand for a protracted campaign, and it was difficult to procure sufficient food and ammunition with Rebel partisans harassing the long supply route from Charleston. Partisan leaders Thomas Sumter and Francis Marion had already struck damaging blows against Cornwallis's line of communications; an American victory would inspire more Whigs to join their ranks, and make Camden untenable.

Camden was the key to the British position in South Carolina. In their hands, it formed a link with their post at Ninety Six and the Backcountry, and a springboard from which to invade North Carolina. Its loss would mean the evacuation of the South Carolina and Georgia interior, the end of the effort to organize the Backcountry Loyalists and confinement to the vicinity of Charleston and Savannah. For the British, defeat at Camden meant the failure of the Southern strategy and, for all practical purposes, the end of the whole effort to subdue the rebellion. For the Americans, victory at Camden would protect North Carolina from invasion, regain most of South Carolina and Georgia and bring independence within a hairsbreadth of reality.

Gates and Cornwallis knew what was at stake. Perhaps many of the soldiers in the ranks did too, but their more pressing concern was surviving the next hour. Waiting for commands from their officers, they jostled one another as they anxiously checked their muskets and cartridge boxes and watched their enemies across the pine-studded field. As the generals made last minute adjustments in the lines, American artillery in the road opened fire, the booming of cannon echoing through the trees. Smoke rose from the guns, thickening the morning fog that already enshrouded the battlefield. The contest had begun, and what followed is best described by those who experienced it.

1

# American Commanders' Accounts

General Horatio Gates was swept from the field early in the battle by the mob of fleeing militia, and was therefore unable to give a detailed description of the engagement. He eventually rode all the way to Hillsborough, North Carolina, covering the 180 miles in three days. Gates was clearly still upset when he composed this report to Samuel Huntington, President of the Continental Congress, on August 20, 1780.[1]

*In the deepest Distress and Anxiety of Mind, I am obliged to acquaint your Excellency with the Total Defeat of the Troops under my Command.—I arrived with the Maryland Line,[2] the Artillery, and North Carolina Militia on the 13th Instant at Rugely's,[3] 13 miles from Camden, took post there, and was the next Day joined by Genl Stevens with 700 Militia from Virginia—Colonel Sumpter,[4] who was at the Waxhaws, had the Sunday before, with 400 So Carolinians killd and taken 300 of the Enemy, who were posted at Hanging Rocks; this and other Strokes upon the Enemy's Advanced posts occasioned their calling all their Outposts to Camden.—The 15th, at Daybreak, I reinforced Colonel Sumpter with 300 North Carolina Militia, 100 of the Maryd Line and two Three-pounders[5] from the Artillery…and directed, as soon as the Reinforcements joined him he should proceed down the Wateree opposite to Camden, intercept any Stores coming to the Enemy, and particularly their Troops from 96[6]—who were likewise withdrawn from that Post.—This was well executed by Colonel Sumpter…*

*Having communicated my plans to the General Officers in the Afternoon of the 15th Instant, it was resolved to march at 10 at Night, to take post in an Advantageous Situation, with a Deep Creek in front, Seven Miles from Camden.—The Heavy Baggage, &c, being ordered to march immediately by the Waxhaws Road—At Ten the Army began their march in the following Order—Colonel Armand's Legion[7] in Front, supported on both Flanks by Colo Porterfield's Regiment,[8] and the Light Infantry[9] of the Militia.—The Advanced Guard of Infantry. The Maryland Line with their Artillery in Front of the Brigades.—The North-Carolina Militia—The Virginia Militia—The Artillery Stores, &c, and the Rear Guard—Having marched about Five Miles, the Legion was charged by the Enemy's Cavalry, and well supported on the Flanks as they were ordered by Colonel Porterfield, who beat back the Enemy's Horse*[10]*, and was himself unfortunately wounded; but the Enemy's Infantry advancing with a heavy fire—the Troops in Front gave way, even to the Front of the First Maryland Brigade, and a Confusion ensued, which took some time to regulate. At Length the Army was ranged in Line of Battle in the following Order—General Gist's Brigade upon the Right—with His Right close to a Swamp—The North Carolina Militia in the Centre,—and the Virginia Militia, with the Light infantry and Porterfield's Corps, upon the Left.—The Artillery divided to the Brigades—and the First Maryland Brigade as a Corps de Reserve, and to cover the Cannon on the Road at a proper distance in the Rear—Colonel Armand's Corps were Ordered to the Left to support the Left Flank and oppose the enemy's Cavalry.—At day Light the Enemy attacked, and drove in our Light Parties in Front, when I ordered our Left to advance and attack the Enemy—but, to my Astonishment, the Left Wing and North Carolina Militia gave Way. General Caswell and Myself, assisted by a number of Officers did all in our Power to rally the broken Troops, but to no purpose; for the Enemy's Cavalry, coming round the Left Flank of the Maryland Division, Completed the Rout of the Whole of the Militia, who left the Continentals alone, to oppose the Enemy's Whole Force.—I then endeavored with General Caswell to rally the Militia at some Distance, on an advantageous piece of ground, but the Enemy's Cavalry continuing to harass their Rear, they ran like a Torrent, and bore all before them. This being the situation of General Caswell and myself at a pass; the Militia pressing us forward, and the Enemy's Cavalry pursuing, we were obliged to Retreat with them—hoping yet that a few miles in the Rear they might recover from their panic, and again be brought into order;—but this likewise provd in vain—and the Firing in a Manner ceasing in the Rear—there was no hopes that the Maryland Division, had any longer sustained the Attack of the Enemy's Whole Infantry.—Though overpowered by numbers their bravery is highly to be commended and honoured, as they made as great an opposition as it was possible so small a Force could make against one so vastly superior.*

*By this time the Militia had taken the Woods in all directions, and I concluded with General Caswell to retire towards Charlotte, I got there late in the night—but reflecting that there was neither Army, Ammunition, nor any prospect of collecting any Force at that Place, adequate to the Defence of the Country I proceeded with all possible Despatch hither:—to endeavor to fall upon some Plan, in conjunction with the Legislature of this State, for the Defense of so much thereof as it is yet possible to save from the Enemy—I shall immediately Despatch a Flag*[11] *to Lord Cornwallis to know the Situation of our wounded—the number of Prisoners and Condition in his Hands—I send this Letter open to the Governor of Virginia*[12] *that he may take proper measures in the present Emergency. He will Seale and forward it immediately by the Bearers Colo Senf and Major Magill my Aid de Camp—who are well acquainted with all the Circumstances of my march, from where I joined General de Kalb, to the unfortunate Hour of the Defeat. The Distresses of the Campaign previous thereto, almost exceed Description, Famine, Want of Tents for the Militia, and of every Comfort necessary for the Troops in this unwholesome Climate has no doubt, in a Degree, contributed to our Ruin. Had it been practicable to have rallied the Militia at any given Distance from the Field of Battle, and could I have even Collected Ammunition and a Magazine; there was no making a Post properly defencible; as I had not any Intrenching Tools—a Want which I so long represented. We lost only Eight Pieces of Cannon in the Action...but most assuredly the small arms are gone, for those that the Enemy did not take are carried off by the Militia. I mention this that proper Measures may be taken to supply Arms. It is a considerable Consolation to my Mind, that I never made any Movement of Importance... without the consent and approbation of all the General officers, and particular in the Night of the 15th, after the First attack of the Enemy—they gave their unanimous opinions, that there was no retreating with Safety, and that a Battle must be fought at all Events.—Seized with a violent Disorder, occasioned by the Fatigues I have undergone, I must entreat the Indulgence of Congress, for the defects of this Letter, and have therefore sent Colonel Senf Chief Engineer and my Aid de Camp Major Magill to answer any Questions and clear up every Doubt, that can be suggested.*

Ten days later, Gates had regained his composure, and concluded that the defeat at Camden was not quite so disastrous as he had originally feared. On August 30, he sent George Washington an updated report from Hillsborough, which included a description of the steps he was taking to salvage the situation in the South.[13]

*My public Letter to Congress has surely been transmitted to yr Exclly—Since then, I have been able to collect authentic Returns of the killed wounded and missing of the Officers of the Maryland Line, Artillerists and those of the Legion under Colo Armand. They are inclosed. The Militia broke early in the Day, and Scattered in so many Directions upon their Retreat, that very few have fallen into the Hands of the Enemy.—By the Firmness and Bravery of the Continental Troops the victory is far from Bloodless on the part of the Foe;—they having upward of 500 men with officers in proportion killd and wounded. I do not think Ld Cornwallis will be able to reap any advantage of consequence from his Victory—as this State seems animated to re-instate and support the Army. Virginia I am confident, will not be less patriotic—and by the joint Exertions of the two States, there is good Reason to hope, that...all South Carolina might be again recovered. Ld Cornwallis remained*

> *with his Army at Camden, when I received the last accounts from thence;—I am cantoning ours at Salisbury, Guilford, Hillsborough and Cross Creek...This is absolutely necessary, as we have no Magazines of Provisions, and are only supplied from Hand to Mouth...What encouragement the numerous Disaffected in this State may give Lord Cornwallis to advance further into the Country; I cannot yet say.*[14] *Colonel Sumpter since his Surprise and Defeat upon the West Side of the Wateree, has reinstated and increased his Corps to upward of 1000 men.*[15] *I have directed him to continue to harass the Enemy upon that Side. Lord Cornwallis will therefore be cautious how he makes any considerable movement to the Eastward, while this Corps remains upon his Left Flank—and the Main Army is in a manner cantoned on his Front. Anxious for the Public Good I shall continue my unwearied Endeavors to stop the Progress of the Enemy—to reinstate our affairs—to recommence an Offensive War, and recover all our Losses in the Southern States. But if being unfortunate is solely a Reason sufficient for removing me from Command I shall most cheerfully submit to the Orders of Congress; and resign an office few Generals would be anxious to possess—and where the utmost skill and Fortitude is so subject to be baffled by the difficulties which must for a Time, surround, the Chief in Command here.*

Colonel John Christian Senf, a European volunteer serving with the American forces, was the engineer for the Southern army. Although Gates said little in his reports about the strategy that led him to advance toward Camden, Senf explained the reasons in detail because his survey of the ground was largely responsible for Gates's decision. Senf left the battlefield with Gates and later carried news of the defeat to the Continental Congress in Philadelphia.[16]

> *The 13th August, 1780, General Gates arriv'd with the Southern Army at Rugely's House, 13 miles this side Camden, on the Road from Charlotteburg*[17] *to Camden, where the Enemy had a Post, but retreated precipitately on the approach of Genl Gates. That afternoon, Night & next Morning Reconoitering partys were sent out, the Enemy at Camden and inferior to our Army. Upon intelligence of the Engineer the Genl detach'd in the Night of between the 14th and 15th inst. 400 men, with 2 field pieces, Conducted by Col. Senf, to join Brig Genl Sumpter of the South Carolina Militia (12 miles West from the Army), who was moving down the West Side of Wateree river...This junction was effected the 15th in the morning...Genl Sumpter march'd down the river (on which the Enemy evacuated several out posts on the river), Surprised a Guard on the West Side of Wateree Ferry, 3 miles from Camden, consisting of about 40 Men, under a Militia Col (Carey),*[18] *took them prisoners, with which he took also 40 waggons with Drivers, 4 Horses & Waggon, loaded with Rum, Flour, Corn, &c., 300 head of Cattle & some Sheep.*

*A few Hours after this a Detachment of 70 men of the 71st & 33d Regts came from Ninety Six to join the Enemy at Camden, were likewise taken Prisoners by Genl Sumpter, after which the Enemy made motion to cross the river below to attack him; he retreated up the River that Night for 10 miles, of which Col Senf return'd to report to Genl Gates.*

*The 15th Genl Gates, as the 700 Virg'a Militia, under B Genl Stevens made junction, consulted with all the General Officers on taking another Position for the Army, as the Ground where they were upon was by no means tenable. On reconoitering a Deep Creek,*[19] *7 miles in the front, was found impassable 7 miles to the Right, & about the same distance to the left, except only at the place where the Ford intersects the great road. It was Unanimously agreed upon to march that Night the Army to that Creek, by which means they would get a more secure Encampment, come nearer Genl Sumpter, occupy the road on the East side of Wateree river, and would be able to get nearer intelligence of the Enemy. As for to march back on that Road, and take an equal Strong or Stronger Position, was not certain, would have given the Enemy a weak opinion of our Strength & more encouragement to attack— The Communication with Genl Sumpter…would have been given up again, difficult of getting Intelligence of the Enemy, & our Horses in want of Forage. To march to the Right to fall into the road on the East side of Wateree river (if even the road would have admitted of it), but it would not without a great deal of work, & Pioneers*[20] *too were wanted, the Baggage of the Army would have been exposed; the Road where Supplys came from open to the Enemy & impossible to turn those Waggons directly into another road before the Enemy's Horse might have cut them off from the Army.*

*Certain Intelligence came the 15th to Genl Gates that Lord Cornwallis had arriv'd the Evening before at Camden, & a reinforcement had arriv'd that Day, but no certainty of the Strength could be obtain'd.*

*The 15th, the Evening, at 10 o'clock the Army march'd from Rugeley's to take Post in Front at the mentioned Creek…During the march Reconoitering Parties, sent out from the advanc'd Corps, came back, & nothing seen in the Road, soon after, (about half an Hour after two in the morning of the 16th August) Col. Armand's Van party got hail'd by an advanc'd party of the Enemy; an answer was made directly on our side on which the Enemy's Horse immediately charg'd furiously with a great deal of Huzzas.*[21] *Col Armand stood the charge, & Col Potterfield's light Infantry gave a crossing Fire upon the enemy's Horse, which made them retreat immediately, upon which the Enemy's Light Infantry advanced, and after a fire of about five minutes drove our Advanc'd Corps back upon our Advanc'd Guard and Main Body, and then likewise retreated; This affair caused a little Confusion in the Line, but was soon redress'd. The Army drew up in order of Battle, & having taken a Prisoner of the Enemy, who confirm'd that Lord Cornwallis Commanded the*

*Army himself consisting of not above 3000 men, and that he was come out with an Intention to attack General Gates in his Camp at Rugeley's, upon which Genl Gates call'd all the General Officers together to hear their opinion on that occasion, & it was their Unanimous Opinion that it was now too late to retreat, a Battle ought to be fought, & some of them were glad to have an opportunity of such, as they had no Idea of the Enemy's Superiority or of the following behaviour of the Militia.*

*General Gates form'd order of Battle, viz—*

*The Second Maryland Brigade about 400 men under Brig Gen Gist on the right of the road leading to Camden, two field pieces on his right & an almost unpassable Swamp & Gregs Quarter Creek on the right of field pieces, on the left of the Brigade in the main road two Field Pieces, the three Brigades of North Carolina Militia of 1200 Men under the Brigadiers Rutherford, Graigery & Butler,*[22] *two Field Pieces the Virginia Militia of 700 men under Brigadier Genl Stevens, the Light Infantry then about 300 men under Col Potterfield and Col Armand with the Horse about 60 in the rear of the Light Infantry to support the left. The first Maryland Brigade about 400 men under Brig Genl Smallwood in the rear of the Line across the road, as a Corps of Reserve.*

*Half an Hour before sun rise, the Enemy came in sight, drove in our advanc'd Posts, and as soon as they came in proper distance, our artillery began to play upon them. Their first Troops suppos'd Light Infantry, display'd, form'd and advanced on their left on the road with a field piece. Their Main Body display'd to their right, when in the time they displayed our Field pieces made a good fire upon their column. Before the Enemy had fully display'd their Line, Genl Gates gave orders to Genl Stevens of the Virginia Militia & Light Infantry to advance in good order & make the attack, gave likewise immediate orders to Genl Smallwood to advance with the Corps of reserve, to support the Left Wing and occupy the Ground of Genl Stevens. Genl. Gates rode up to Genl Gist, gave orders to advance slowly with the Brigade, to reserve their fire till proper distance, fire & charge Bayonets which has been according to orders Executed. They came close, Genl Gist's Brigade took a Field Piece from the Enemy and kept it some time…The North Carolina & Virginia Militia all broke & dispers'd in the utmost confusion, no sooner the Enemy's Horse discovered the confusion than they charg'd, they wheeled to their right & Left, took the 1st & 2d M. Brigade in their Flanks & rear, when in the mean time the Enemy advanced in their Front, to which of course our brave Troops have fallen a Sacrifice. General Gates, who was in the rear of the 2d Maryland Brigade, after having given the mentioned order look'd back to the road, saw the Militia run and the Enemy's Horse charge, rode to the militia & Endeavoured himself with the assistance of General Caswell and Aids to bring the Militia into order and fire, but all in vain, the Enemy's Horse then came so close upon the General & Col Armand oblig'd to wheel. The General then hop'd to bring them to order at some Distance, but neither this would do, the militia was struck with such a Panick & obeyed no more command. The Baggage, which had been ordered off to Retreat in the night, on the road to the Waxaws, was so retarded by obstruction of the Night, bad roads & tired Horses, as to fall likewise a Prey to the Enemy. The Enemy's Horse pursued as fast as possible Genl Gates & Col Armand, who had about 14 men, as the remainder of his Legion, Col Armand's Horse much fatigued. Genl Gates could not be escorted by him, to get free from the Enemy, he therefore made his Escape with two of his Aids de Camp & the Engineer. He arriv'd that Night at Charlotte but no view was left to assemble any Forces there, & if it was possible, there was no Ammunition, no Arms, no Provisions, and in the middle of a disaffected Country. The Genl therefore thought proper, with the advice of his officers, to get by the assistance of the Night…to Hillsborough, where there had been left some Detachments & Artillery, & that most chiefly the militia had directed their course that way, it was therefore more probable to reassemble some of the scattered Militia in that Quarter and Draw all the Detachments together 'till other Measures could be taken. General Gates arriv'd at Hillsborough the 19th August.*

Colonel Otho Holland Williams of Maryland was acting as deputy adjutant general of the army at the time of the battle. Unlike most of Gates's staff officers, Williams remained on the field after the militia fled. He sent this report from Hillsborough, North Carolina, to his friend Alexander Hamilton, who was serving on Washington's staff, on August 30, 1780.[23]

*About the 23d. Instant I wrote…a very hasty, particular account of the Defeat of Genl. Gates's Army at Suttons[24] near Campden the 16th Instant. We were truly unfortunate and compleatly routed. The infamous Cowardice of the Militia of Virginia and North Carolina gave the Enemy every advantage over our few Regular troops whose firm opposition and Gallant behaviour have gain'd them the applause as well of our successful Foes as of our runaway Friends…*

*Our retreat was the most mortifying that cod. have happen'd. Those who escaped the Dangers of the Field knew not where to find protection. The Wounded found no relief from the Inhabitants who were immediately in arms against us, and many of our Fugitive Officers and men were disarm'd by those faithless Vallains who had flatter'd us with promises of joining us against the Enemy.[25] The Tories are now assembling in different parts of the Country, and there is actually a sort of partizan War Waged between them and the Whigs of this Country.*

*The greatest part of our Baggage was plunder'd by those who first left the Field. The Enemy took a part and much of what escaped them has been pillaged by the Inhabitants on the Retreat. The Waggon Horses have been stolen and frequently taken from the drivers and some of those desperate Rascals have been daring enough to fire upon parties of our Regular Troops many miles from the place of Action.*

*General Gates used the utmost expedition in getting from the lost Field to this place. As this step is unaccountable to me you must expect to know the reason another time and from better authority. An unfortunate Genl. usually looses the Confidence of his Army, and this is much the case with us at present. However I suppose every thing necessary will be done in justification of the Steps that have been taken and then all will be understood. Besides my ignorance there is another reason for my silence on this subject. The General is extremely mortified at the disappointment his hopes have met with, and I think it ungenerous to oppress dejected spirits by a premature censure.*

*...The Officers of North Carolina talk confidently of Reembodying a great number of Militia. Genl. Stephens had collected about Eight hundred of the Va. Militia at this place since the action but, I'm sorry to add, at least half that number have deserted. The Maryland Division, including the Delaware Regt., will, I hope, muster six hundred when all are collected...*

*From the best accounts I can get Ld. Cornwallis had with him on the Day of Battle...about 3000 Men...we are resolv'd not to dispair but bear our fortunes like Veterans.*

On November 24, Williams provided an interesting detail of his experience at Camden in a letter to his sister.[26]

*My gay old Friend Liberty*[27] *is as bold as Bucephalus,*[28] *He behaved so gallantly in action that I was confident of my security from ever thing but Balls*[29]*—An Officer of the British Army was ungenerous enough to direct the fire of his Platoon particularly at him, but as I was lucky enough to see and hear him at the instant he gave the work and pointed with his Sword, I hastily chang'd my situation and escaped by crossing the line.*

Sometime after the battle, possibly late in 1780, Williams wrote a detailed account of the campaign. His criticism of Gates's leadership sparked a new debate between Gates's critics and defenders that has continued to the present day.[30]

On April 16, 1780, Washington ordered the Maryland and Delaware Continentals to march from Morristown, New Jersey, to aid the beleaguered defenders of Charleston. With De Kalb in command, the troops reached Petersburg, Virginia, in early June. By then, the army in Charleston had surrendered, but De Kalb continued his march until July 6, when food shortages forced the troops to halt at Wilcox's Iron Works on Deep River in North Carolina. De Kalb ordered General Richard Caswell to unite his North Carolina militia with the Continentals, but Caswell refused. Gates arrived to take command on July 25, much to De Kalb's relief, and two days later Gates marched southward. Lacking supplies, the troops ate green corn, beef and green peaches that they gathered along their route. Gates also ordered Caswell to join him, but the North Carolinian refused. The Continentals finally reached Caswell's camp on August 7 and the combined force advanced, forcing Lord Rawdon to abandon his lines at Lynch's Creek four days later.

*Lord Rawdon, who commanded the advanced corps of the British army, wisely collected his whole force at Camden, which, besides being flanked by the River Wateree, and Pinetree Creek, was considerably strengthened by a number of redoubts.*

*As his lordship's emissaries were in all parts of the country, he could not fail to be informed, that General Gates was in his neighborhood with a brigade of regular troops, and two brigades of militia, besides some small corps of artillery and cavalry—that Brigadier General Stevens was on the same route, with a brigade of Virginia militia—that Colonel Marion,*[31] *below, and Colonel Sumpter above Camden, were stimulating their countrymen to re-assume their arms; and that, in short, the whole country were ready to revolt from the allegiance which had been extorted from them but a few weeks before. He, therefore, permitted General Gates to march unmolested to Clermont,*[32] *(where the Americans encamped on the 13th,) and employed his men in strengthening his post for defence…*

*Brigadier General Stevens arrived with his Virginians, at Clermont, on the 14th…On the same day, (or the 15th,) an inhabitant of Camden came, as if by accident, into the American encampment, and was conducted to head quarters. He affected ignorance of the approach of the Americans—pretended very great friendship for his countrymen, the Marylanders, and promised the general to be out again in a few days with all the information the general wished to obtain. The information which he then gave was the truth, but not all the truth, which, events afterward revealed; yet, so plausible was his manner, that General Gates dismissed him, with many promises, if he would faithfully observe his engagements. Suspicions arose in the breasts of some of the officers about head quarters, that this man's errand was easily accomplished;—the credulity of the general was not arraigned—but, it was conceived that it would have been prudent to have detained the man for further acquaintance.*

*Colonel Sumpter of the South Carolina militia, had intelligence that an escort with clothing, ammunition and other stores, for the troops at Camden, was on the road from Charleston, by way of McCord's Ferry on the Congaree; and that it would necessarily pass the Wateree at a ferry about a mile from the town, under cover of a small redoubt on the opposite side of the river. This intelligence he communicated to the general, requesting a small re-enforcement of infantry, and two small pieces of artillery to join his volunteers, promising to intercept the convoy. The colonel's accurate knowledge of the geography of the country, and the qualities of the men who were his followers, favoured the execution of this enterprise. The general ordered a detachment of one hundred regular infantry, and a party of artillery, with two brass field-pieces, under Lieutenant Colonel Woolford,*[33] *to join Colonel Sumpter, and act under his command.*

*To attract the attention of the garrison in Camden, if they did not choose to retire, which seemed to be but too confidently expected; and to facilitate the execution of the little expedition under Sumpter, all other objects seemed to be suspended.*

*…No supply of provisions of any sort was collected, more than to serve from day to day. The obscure route the army had marched, actually kept their friends ignorant of their movements; and the arrival of General Gates at Clermont was, when known, a subject of more surprise to the patriots, than to the enemies of the country. It is probable…that if General Gates had taken a secure position with his army, and waited only a few days, abundance of provisions would have flowed into his camp; and that, by the addition of volunteers from the Carolinas, he would have acquired such a superiority over the British army, which did not much exceed four thousand men, that he would have found no difficulty in recovering the country as far as Charleston…*

*After writing this order,*[34] *the general communicated it to the deputy adjutant general, showing him, at the same time, a rough estimate of the forces under his command, making them upwards of seven thousand. That this calculation was exaggerated, the deputy adjutant general could not but suspect, from his own observation. He, therefore, availed himself of the general's orders, to call all the general officers in the army, to a council, to be held in Rugley's Barn—to call also upon the commanding officers of corps for a field return; in making which, they were to be as exact as possible; and, as he was not required to attend the council, he busied himself in collecting these returns and forming an abstract for the general's better information. This abstract was presented to the general just as the council broke up…He cast his eyes upon the numbers of rank and file present fit for duty, which was exactly three thousand and fifty-two. He said there were no less than thirteen general officers in council; and intimated something about the disproportion between the numbers of officers and privates. It was replied, "Sir, the number of the latter are certainly much below the estimate formed this morning; but," said the general, "these are enough for our purpose." What that was, was not communicated to the deputy adjutant general. The general only added—"there was no dissenting voice in the council where the orders have just been read"—and then gave them to be published to the army.*

*Although there had been no dissenting voice in the council, the orders were no sooner promulgated, than they became the subject of animadversion. Even those who had been dumb in council, said that there had been no consultation—that the orders were read to them, and all opinion seemed suppressed by the very positive and decisive terms in which they were expressed. Others could not imagine how it could be conceived, that an army, consisting of more than two-thirds militia, and which had never been once exercised in arms together, could form columns, and perform other manoeuvres in the night, and in the face of an enemy. But, of all the officers, Colonel Armand took the greatest exception. He seemed to think the positive orders respecting himself, implied a doubt of his courage—declared that cavalry had never before been put in the front of a line of battle in the dark*[35]*—and that the disposition, as it respected his corps, proceeded from resentment in the general, on account of a previous altercation between them about horses, which the general had ordered to be taken from the officers of the army, to expedite the movement of the artillery through the wilderness. A great deal was said upon the occasion; but, the time was short, and the officers and soldiers, generally, not knowing, or believing any more than the general, that any considerable body of the enemy were to be met with out of Camden, acquiesced with their usual cheerfulness, and were ready to march at the hour appointed.*

*As there were no spirits yet arrived in camp; and as, until lately, it was unusual for troops to make a forced march, or prepare to meet an enemy without some extraordinary allowance,*[36] *it was unluckily conceived that molasses, would, for once, be an acceptable substitute; accordingly the hospital stores were broached, and one gill*[37] *of molasses per man, and a full ration of corn meal and meat, were issued to the army previous to their march, which commenced…at about ten o'clock at night of the 15th…The troops of General Gates' army, had frequently felt the bad consequences of eating bad provision; but, at this time, a hasty meal of quick baked bread and fresh beef, with a desert of molasses, mixed with mush, or dumplings, operated so cathartically, as to disorder very many of the men, who were breaking the ranks all night, and were certainly much debilitated before the action commenced in the morning.*[38]

*…the direct march of the American army towards Camden, and the prospect of considerable re-enforcements of militia, had induced…Lord Rawdon, to collect there, all the forces under his directions. And it is certain, that the seeming confidence of the American general, had inspired him with apprehensions for his principal post. Lord Cornwallis, at Charlestown, was constantly advised of the posture of affairs in the interior of the country; and, confident that Lord Rawdon could not long resist the forces that might, and probably would, be opposed to him, in a very short time resolved to march himself, with a considerable re-enforcement, to Camden. He arrived there on the 14th, and had the discernment, at once, to perceive that delay would render that situation dangerous, even to his whole force; the disaffection from his late assumed, arbitrary, and vindictive power, having become general through all the country above General Gates' line of march, as well as eastward of Santee, and to the westward*

*of Wateree Rivers. He, therefore, took the resolution of attacking the new constituted American army in their open irregular encampment at Clermont. Both armies, ignorant of each other's intentions, moved about the same hour of the same night, and...met about half way between their respective encampments, at midnight.*

*The first revelation of this new and unexpected scene, was occasioned by a smart, mutual salutation of small arms between the advanced guards. Some of the cavalry of Armand's legion were wounded, retreated, and threw the whole corps into disorder; which, recoiling suddenly on the front of the column of infantry, disordered the first Maryland brigade, and occasioned a general consternation through the whole line of the army. The light infantry under Porterfield, however, executed their orders gallantly; and the enemy, no less astonished than ourselves, seemed to acquiesce in a sudden suspension of hostilities. Some prisoners were taken on both sides; from one of these, the deputy adjutant general of the American army, extorted information respecting the situation and numbers of the enemy. He informed, that Lord Cornwallis commanded in person about three thousand regular British troops, which were, in line of march, about five or six hundred yards in front. Order was soon restored in the corps of infantry in the American army, and the officers were employed in forming a front line of battle, when the deputy adjutant general communicated to General Gates the information which he had from the prisoner. The general's astonishment could not be concealed. He ordered the deputy adjutant general to call another council of war. All the general officers immediately assembled in the rear of the line; the unwelcome news was communicated to them. General Gates said, "Gentlemen, what is best to be done?" All were mute for a few moments—when the gallant Stevens exclaimed, "Gentlemen, is it not too late now to do any thing but fight?" No other advice was offered, and the general desired the gentlemen would repair to their respective commands.*

*The Baron De Kalb's opinion may be inferred from the following fact: When the deputy adjutant general went to call him to council, he first told him what had been discovered. "Well," said the baron, "and has the general given you orders to retreat the army?" The baron, however, did not oppose the suggestion of General Stevens; and every measure that ensued, was preparatory for action.*

*Lieutenant Colonel Porterfield, in whose bravery and judicious conduct great dependance was placed, received, in the first rencontre, a mortal wound...and was obliged to retire. His infantry bravely kept the ground in front; and the American army were formed...*

*Frequent skirmishes happened during the night, between the advanced parties—which served to discover the relative situations of the two armies—and as a prelude to what was to take place in the morning.*

*At dawn of day...the enemy appeared in front, advancing in column. Captain Singleton,*[39] *who commanded some pieces of artillery, observed to Colonel Williams, that he plainly perceived the ground of the British uniform at about two hundred yards in front. The deputy adjutant general immediately ordered Captain Singleton to open his battery; and then rode to the general, who was in the rear of the second line, and informed him of the cause of the firing which he heard. He also observed to the general, that the enemy seemed to be displaying their column by the right; the nature of the ground favored this conjecture, for yet nothing was clear.*

*The general seemed disposed to wait events—he gave no orders. The deputy adjutant general observed, that if the enemy, in the act of displaying, were briskly attacked by General Stevens' brigade, which was already in line of battle, the effect might be fortunate, and first impressions were important. "Sir," said the general, "that's right—let it be done." This was the last order that the deputy adjutant general received. He hastened to General Stevens, who instantly advanced with his brigade, apparently in fine spirits. The right wing of the enemy was soon discovered in line—it was too late to attack them displaying; nevertheless, the business of the day could no longer be deferred. The deputy adjutant general requested General Stevens to let him have forty or fifty privates, volunteers, who would run forward of the brigade, and commence the attack. They were led forward, within forty or fifty yards of the enemy, and ordered to take trees, and keep up as brisk a fire as possible. The desired effect of this expedient, to extort the enemy's fire at some distance, in order to the rendering it less terrible to the militia, was not gained. General Stevens, observing the enemy to rush on, put his men in mind of their bayonets; but, the impetuosity with which they advanced, firing and huzzaing, threw the whole body of the militia into such a panic, that they generally threw down their loaded arms and fled, in the utmost consternation. The unworthy example of the Virginians was almost instantly followed by the North Carolinians; only a small part of the brigade, commanded by Brigadier General Gregory, made a short pause. A part of Dixon's*[40] *regiment, of that brigade, next in the line to the second Maryland brigade, fired two or three rounds of cartridge…The regular troops, who had the keen edge of sensibility rubbed off by strict discipline and hard service, saw the confusion with but little emotion. They engaged seriously in the affair; and, notwithstanding some irregularity, which was created by the militia breaking, pell mell, through the second line, order was restored there—time enough to give the enemy a severe check, which abated the fury of their assault, and obliged them to assume a more deliberate manner of acting. The second Maryland brigade, including the battalion of Delawares, on the right, were engaged with the enemy's left, which they opposed with very great firmness. They even advanced upon them, and had taken a number of prisoners, when their companions of the first brigade (which formed the second line) being greatly outflanked, and charged by superior numbers, were obliged to give ground. At this critical moment, the regimental officers of the latter brigade, reluctant to leave the field without orders, inquired for their commanding officer, (Brigadier General*

*Smallwood) who, however, was not to be found; notwithstanding, Colonel Gunby, Major Anderson,[41] and a number of other brave officers, assisted by the deputy adjutant general, and Major Jones, one of Smallwood's aids, rallied the brigade, and renewed the contest. Again they were obliged to give way—and were again rallied—the second brigade were still warmly engaged—the distance between the two brigades did not exceed two hundred yards—their opposite flanks being nearly upon a line perpendicular to their front. At this eventful juncture, the deputy adjutant general, anxious that the communication between them should be preserved, and wishing that, in the almost certain event of a retreat, some order might be sustained by them, hastened from the first to the second brigade, which he found precisely in the same circumstances. He called upon his own regiment, (the 6th Maryland) not to fly, and was answered by the Lieutenant Colonel, Ford,[42] who said—"They have done all that can be expected of them—we are outnumbered and outflanked—see the enemy charge with bayonets." The enemy having collected their corps, and directing their whole force against these two devoted brigades, a tremendous fire of musketry was, for some time, kept up on both sides, with equal perseverance and obstinacy, until Lord Cornwallis, perceiving there was no cavalry opposed to him, pushed forward his dragoons—and his infantry charging, at the same moment, with fixed bayonets, put an end to the contest. His victory was complete. All the artillery, and a very great number of prisoners, fell into his hands—many fine fellows lay on the field—and the rout of the remainder was entire—not even a company retired in any order every one escaped as he could. If, in this affair, the militia fled too soon, the regulars may be thought almost as blamable for remaining too long on the field; especially, after all hope of victory must have been despaired of. Let the commandants of the brigades answer for themselves. Allow the same privilege to the officers of the corps, comprising those brigades, and they will say, that they never received orders to retreat, nor any order from any general officer, from the commencement of the action, until it became desperate. The brave Major General, the Baron De Kalb, fought on foot, with the second brigade, and fell, mortally wounded, into the hands of the enemy…a fate which probably was avoided by other generals, only by an opportune retreat.*

*The torrent of unarmed militia, bore away with it, Generals Gates, Caswell, and a number of others, who soon saw that all was lost. General Gates, at first, conceived a hope that he might rally, at Clermont, a sufficient number to cover the retreat of the regulars; but, the farther they fled the more they were dispersed; and the generals soon found themselves abandoned by all but their aids…*

*The militia, the general saw, were in air; and the regulars, he feared, were no more. The dreadful thunder of artillery and musketry had ceased, and none of his friends appeared. There was no existing corps with which the victorious detachment might unite; and the Americans had no post in the rear. He, therefore, sent orders to Sumpter to retire in the best manner he could; and proceeded himself with General*

*Caswell towards Charlotte, an open village on a plain, about sixty miles from the fatal scene of action. The Virginians, who knew nothing of the country they were in, involuntarily reversed the route they came, and fled, most of them, to Hillsborough. General Stevens pursued them, and halted there as many as were not sufficiently refreshed before his arrival, to pursue their way home. Their terms of service, however, being very short…General Stevens soon afterwards discharged them.*

*The North Carolina militia fled different ways, as their hopes led, or their fears drove them…Whatever these might have suffered from the disaffected, they probably were not worse off than those who retired the way they came; wherein, they met many of their insidious friends, armed, and advancing to join the American army; but, learning its fate from the refugees, they acted decidedly in concert with the victors; and, captivating some, plundering others, and maltreating all the fugitives they met, returned, exultingly, home. They even added taunts to their perfidy; one of a party, who robbed Brigadier General Butler of his sword, consoled him by saying, "you'll have no further use for it."*

*"The regular troops…were the last to quit the field. Every corps was broken and dispersed; even the boggs and brush, which in some measure served to screen them from their furious pursuers, separated them from one another. Major Anderson was the only officer who fortunately rallied, as he retreated, a few men of different companies; and whose prudence and firmness afforded protection to those who joined his party on the rout.*

*Colonel Gunby, Lieutenant Colonel Howard, Captain Kirkwood,*[43] *and Captain Dobson, with a few other officers, and fifty or sixty men, formed a junction on the rout, and proceeded together.*

*The general order for moving off the heavy baggage, &c. to Waxaws, was not put in execution, as directed to be done, on the preceding evening. The whole of it, consequently, fell into the hands of the enemy…Other waggons also had got out of danger from the enemy; but the cries of the women*[44] *and the wounded in the rear, and the consternation of the flying troops, so alarmed some of the waggoners, that they cut out their teams, and taking each a horse, left the rest for the next that should come. Others were obliged to give up their horses to assist in carrying off the wounded; and the whole road, for many miles, was strewed with signals of distress, confusion and dismay. What added, not a little to this calamitous scene, was the conduct of Armand's legion. They were principally foreigners, and some of them, probably, not unaccustomed to such scenes. Whether it was owing to the disgust of the colonel, at general orders, or the cowardice of his men, is not with the writer to determine; but, certain it is, the legion did not take any part in the action of the 16$^{th}$; they retired early, and in disorder, and were seen plundering the baggage of the army on their retreat. One of them cut Captain Lemar,*[45] *of the Maryland infantry, over the hand, for attempting to reclaim his own portmanteau,* *which the fellow was taking out of the waggon. Captain Lemar was unarmed, having broke his sword in action, and was obliged to submit, both to the loss and to the insult. The tent covers were thrown off the waggons, generally, and the baggage exposed, so that one might take what suited him to carry off. General Caswell's mess waggon afforded the best refreshment; very unexpectedly to the writer, he there found a pipe*[46] *of good Madeira, broached, and surrounded by a number of soldiers, whose appearance led him to inquire what engaged their attention. He acknowledges, that in this instance, he shared in the booty, and took a draught of wine, which was the only refreshment he had received that day.*

*But the catastrophe being over…it may be excusable to consider, whether the measures which led to the necessity of fighting a general battle were justifiable? and whether such an event might not have been avoided, at almost any time before the two armies were actually opposed?*

*If General Gates intended to risk a general action…he certainly made that risk under every possible disadvantage; and a contemplation of those circumstances, would seem to justify Colonel Armand's assertion, made in the afternoon of the day in which the battle was fought—"I will not, said he, say that we have been betrayed; but if it had been the purpose of the general to sacrifice his army, what could he have done more effectually to have answered that purpose?"*

*General Gates, however…had, in the opinion of most of his officers, and particularly of the writer, no more apprehension of meeting the enemy in force, than the least informed man of his army…*

*It was only necessary for General Gates to have been informed of the march of Lord Cornwallis from Charleston, to have avoided, almost as long as he pleased, a conflict between the two armies.*

*In the opinion of the writer, it was not too late, even after Lord Cornwallis reached Camden. If, instead of meeting him, involuntarily, General Gates had been informed of his intended movement, and quietly, in the afternoon of the 15th, have followed, with his whole army, the detachment under Woolford, over the Wateree, it would have been impossible for the armies to have met until the next day, and after the success of Sumpter's expedition. If his lordship should then have thought of forcing a passage over the Wateree, General Gates would have had the alternative of opposing him under that disadvantage, or of retiring to any position he might prefer, higher up the river. Lord Cornwallis could not have adventured the passage of the river, much above Gates' army, because the river being fordable in many places, his garrison and magazines at Camden would have been jeoparded; the forces he could afford to leave for its defence, would have been insufficient for half a day; and, if the post and its stores had been gained by the Americans, the British army, destitute of supplies, would have been obliged to retire towards Charleston. On the other hand, if his lordship should keep his post in his rear, he must consequently leave the communication open between the American army and their friends in the upper country; which would have rendered more practicable the avoiding of a general engagement. But, these are subsequent reflections on measures, the idea of which, perhaps never occurred, nor was suggested to the general. Involved, as he was, in the necessity of fighting, the disposition which was made for battle, after the alarm, was, perhaps, unexceptionable, and as well adapted to the situation, as if the ground had been reconnoitered and chosen by the ablest officer in the army of the United States…*

*The only apology that General Gates condescended to make to the army for the loss of the battle, was, "a man may pit a cock, but he can't make him fight."*[47]*—"The fate of battle is uncontrollable"—and such other common maxims as admit of no contradiction.*

*It is, however, morally certain, considering the disposition of citizens generally, and the respectable body of militia that had already joined the army, that time was, of all things, the most important to the success of General Gates' army.*

*Lord Cornwallis, conscious of this truth…seized the first moment to hasten the decision of an experiment, which was to gain or lose the country. For that season at least; perhaps for ever.*

*Generals Gates and Caswell arrived at Charlotte on the night of the action. The ensuing morning presented nothing to them but an open village, with but few inhabitants, and the remains of a temporary hospital…*

*General Caswell was requested to remain there, to encourage the militia of the country, who were to rendezvous there in three days…General Gates perceived no effectual succour short of Hillsborough, where the general assembly of North Carolina were about to convene; thither he repaired, with all possible expedition; and was followed the next day by General Caswell, who despaired of the meeting of the militia; probably because he thought that their first object, the army, was annihilated.*

*On the two days succeeding the fatal action, Brigadier General Gist…arrived with only two or three attendants, who had fallen into his route. Several field officers, and many officers of the line also, arrived similarly circumstanced; and, although not more than about a dozen men of different corps arrived in irregular squads, from time to time, not less than one hundred infantry were collected in the village within that time; besides Armand's cavalry, which was very little reduced; and a small corps of mounted militia…under the command of Major Davy,*[48] *an enterprizing and gallant young man, who had been raising volunteer cavalry…*

*Very few of the fugitive militia resorted to this place…*

*Brigadier General Smallwood…deliberately came in on the morning, (or about noon) of the 18th, escorted by one of his aids de camp, and two or three other gentlemen, and about as many soldiers, all mounted…*

*The small squads assembled by Major Anderson, and the other officers already mentioned, were on the direct route. The latter were not yet arrived, but were hourly expected; and afforded, in addition to those already collected, and those with Colonel Sumpter, a prospect of forming such a body as might still encourage the militia to form, at least the semblance of an army, which might keep up some appearance of opposition, until the resources of the union could be called forth by Congress, or by the states most immediately interested.*

*An incident, which occasioned great distress the next day, must be here related... the tribe of Catawba Indians, good friends to the Americans, quitted their villages on the Wateree, and followed the remnant of the army towards the town of Charlotte,*[49] *where many of them had already arrived; some of them, in their irregular way, fired a number of guns after night, on the 18th, which gave a very general alarm; and many of the people fled in the night, taking as many of the horses as they could find, or had occasion for.*

Upon learning of Sumter's defeat at Fishing Creek, the American officers decided to withdraw to Salisbury; "a great number of distressed whig families" and three hundred Catawbas accompanied the retreating troops.

*It is not known, whether, if the Americans had not evacuated Charlotte, Lord Cornwallis would not have made it an object to have dispossessed them; but, as it was, his lordship contented himself, with having defeated the southern army—driven it out of South Carolina—and cut up the only detachment respectable enough to afford a head to which the patriots of the country might assemble. His lordship certainly gave the world another instance in proof of the assertion, that it is not every general, upon whom fortune bestows her favours, who knows how to avail himself of all the advantages which are presented to him... The British army retired to Camden.*

*So unexpected an event gave the poor Americans time to breathe.*

Major Thomas Pinckney of the South Carolina Continentals had left Charleston before the town's surrender in an attempt to bring the state's militia to relieve the siege. He later became an aide to Gates and served at Camden, where he was wounded and captured. Pinckney wrote little about the battle until Williams's account appeared in print. Responding to what he considered unjustified criticism of Gates, Pinckney defended his former commander in a letter to William Johnson dated July 27, 1822.[50]

*In a few days Genl. Gates assumed the command, & having been introduced to him, at his first interview with the Baron, he requested that Officer to permit me to serve as one of his Aides-de-Camp. From that day I was constantly with him until the fatal 16th of August. In this capacity I saw all the orders before they were issued; was employed in composing his proclamation, & in some of his correspondence… which circumstances I mention to show the confidential footing on which I was placed by the General; whence I may have been acquainted with his views & intentions, although they were not disclosed even to Coll. Otho Williams, who acted as Adjutant General.*

*This was an Officer for whom I had a sincere regard, whose military talents I highly respected & for the fidelity of whose narrative, as far as he was informed, I can safely vouch. But there was one circumstance, of which he appears…not to have been appraised, which being of the most material import, I will first notice; which is that the movement in the night of the 15th of August was not made with the intention of attacking the enemy, but for the purpose of occupying a strong position so near him as to confine his operations, to cut off his supplies of Provisions, from the upper parts of the Wateree & Pedee Rivers, & to harrass him with detachments of light Troops, & to oblige him either to retreat or to come out & attack us upon our own ground, in a situation where the Militia which constituted our principal numerical force, might act to the best advantage.*

*But you may ask how it appears that such was the General's intention. I answer in the first place from my testimony, for I perfectly well remember asking him if it was then his intention of attacking the enemy, he answered No! assigning as his reason the number of Militia who formed the bulk of his Army. In stating this…I can appeal to the testimony of all those with whom I have conversed on the subject, during the last forty years, for the consistency of my relation…But other facts strongly corroborate this statement; & the internal evidence arising from the circumstances of the Parties is conclusive that such was Genl. Gates' intention. The first fact is that previous to the movement, I think it was on the 14th of August, Col. Senf & Majr. Porterfield, the former an Engineer—the other a judicious & distinguished officer…were sent forward to select a position in front, calculated for the purposes I have mentioned. They returned & reported that they had found a position 5 or 6 miles in advance, with a thick swamp on the right, a deep Creek in front & thick low ground also on the left; but this flank not being so well secured as the right, Col: Senf proposed to strengthen it with a Redoubt or two & an Abbatis.*[51] *As those Officers were dispatched from headquarters, & returned & reported to the General in person, it is possible that Col. Williams…may not have known the transactions, but I have the most perfect recollection of it. But a circumstance which the Colonel does relate further corroborates my statement; it is this, after the breaking up of the Council of War on the 15th, Col. Williams presented the returns of the Army, from which it appeared that the number was considerably below that at which it had been estimated by the General, who after remarking on the great disproportion of the Officers to the privates, added "however they are sufficient for our purpose." That purpose he did not explain to him, but it certainly could not have been to attack a fortified post, well garrisoned. They were however sufficient to have repulsed any force the Enemy had in the vicinity, if so posted as to have rendered the Militia force efficient. Another corroboration is that a very short time before he left Clermont...the General detached some Artillerists with a field piece & 100 Continentals, under Col. Woolford, with two or three hundred North Cara. Militia to reinforce Gen. Sumter, but it is very improbable that he would have deprived himself, at any rate of the regular part of the detachment, if he had meditated an immediate attack. It is obvious also that the general order of the 15th August is only an Order of March comprising such precautions in case of their meeting the enemy, as should be taken in every movement when near him. But if an attack at the conclusion of the March had been contemplated, much more extended details for the Order of assault would have been indispensable. If we now consider the situation & circumstances of the two armies, & allow to Gates only a moderate share of Military judgement, the internal evidence is strong that what I have mentioned was the plan proposed. From different sources of information...the British force was stated at from 1200 to 2000 men. Lord Rawdon having retired before the American Army made it probable that their force did not amount to the largest statement. They were posted in Camden which they had fortified with strong Redoubts & stockaded lines. The American regulars did not amount to 1300 men including Armand's Corps; the Militia were about 1700. In Armand's Corps the General from previous knowledge, had no confidence, & he was too well experienced in the services of Militia to think them proper troops to attack Lines & Redoubts. If he estimated therefore the enemy at their smallest number, it is impossible that he should have designed an Attack on them in such a Post, with his force thus composed. But the plan which I have stated to have been that of Genl. Gates is consistent with sound Military principles & the best in my opinion, which in his situation could have been adopted. For if the force he commanded had been once established in the post he had reconnoitered, the situation of the British Army would have been rendered precarious. Col. W.H. Harrington[52]... had been detached to the upper part of the Pedee, to animate & take command of the militia; to forward supplies of provisions to our Army; to prevent any from being sent to the British, on whose right flank he was to endeavor to establish himself. Orders of a similar import had been given to Genl. Marion, on his being detached to the lower parts of Pedee & Santee. Genl. Sumter had been reinforced from the Main Army & ordered to act on the west side of the River Wateree. Under these circumstances what course could the Enemy have pursued? He could not have remained longer in Camden for want of provisions. His first object probably would have been, to attempt to force our position, but judging from similar attempts in the last War,[53] as well as in that of the Revolution, it is fair to conclude that this measure would have proved disastrous to him. If doubtful of attacking us in front, he had endeavored by a detour to have come round upon our rear, he could not spare a sufficient force to garrison Camden, so as to prevent our Army from occupying that Post, while he was on his march…His next resource would have been to occupy the Wateree & fallen back through the forks of that river & the Congaree, to meet his reinforcements & supplies coming from Charleston: but this he would have found difficult & hazardous to attempt. Genl. Sumter reinforced from the Main Army, was on the west of the Wateree…& from an intimation from Genl. Gates could have…taken post on the west side of the Ferry…& probably augmented by the accession of all the Whigs in the vicinity to whom the situation of affairs could have been communicated. With such a force at his front & Gates' Army so close to his rear, the Enemy could scarcely have effected his passage of the river without serious loss. If he had attempted to pass by the road on the east side of the River Wateree, it must still have been a perilous service. Harrington with the militia of Upper Pedee & probably reinforced from the Main army, would have hung on to what would then have been his left flank. Genl. Marion would have thrown himself in his front below, cutting trees across the Road & destroying bridges to retard his progress, & intercepting his supplies from the low country. Genl. Sumter by a parallel march on the west side of the Wateree, might have cut off his supplies from that quarter, & prevented his crossing at any of the passages below, which are all difficult, while Gates pursuing with the main Army, at a proper distance, by detaching light Corps of his most active troops detailed for that purpose under such officers as Williams & Howard, might have effectively harrassed his rear. If at any time Cornwallis should have turned upon his pursuers, with the hope of bringing on a general action, our Army might easily have retired over the ground recently passed and which of course would have been accurately reconnoitered with this view; & the enemy might have been retarded or opposed in force whenever a position offered, affording a decided superiority. Or in the last resort, Camden might have been re-occupied, where the works erected by the British themselves, would have rendered it improbable that they would have hazarded an attack. I have entered into the above detail of what it appears to me would have been the natural result, if our Army had occupied the position contemplated by Genl. Gates, to convince you that without my testimony, it is highly probable that his intention was such as I have related. I think it also shows that it was not a rash or ill advised attempt but better than any other he could pursue. For Rugely's was a bad position, a small detour would have placed an enemy on either flank. To have fallen back from thence would have discouraged the good men of the Country, & have given confidence to the opposite party. To have crossed the Wateree as has been suggested, by the same route as the reinforcements were sent to Genl. Sumter, besides having a similar discouraging tendency, could not have been effected without much hazard, embarrassed as we were with artillery & baggage, & the ferry within about six miles of Camden. To that place, no doubt intelligence of our movement would have been speedily conveyed, &*

*Tarleton's Corps…would have been immediately detached to harrass & detain us until their main body could have been brought up to attack us while embarrassed in our passage. Besides this movement, if successful would have abandoned to the enemy every thing to the eastward of the Wateree; all the produce of that side of the river… would have furnished them with supplies of provisions, which otherwise would have come to the American Camp…The General had no inducement to retire by this route, from the proximity of the Enemy, by the hope of being strengthened by reinforcements of Regulars; none being soon expected…And with respect to an augmentation of force by the junction of Volunteers or Militia Corps, he would probably have received more of them while exhibiting a confidence in the troops he already commanded, than when appearing to retire or shun a contest with the enemy. Indeed the troops of this description already in Camp, were sufficiently numerous, if so situated as to be available…That with his force, the occupation of the position contemplated, which was reported to be 6 or 7 miles distant from the enemy, was not too close, is sanctioned by the opinion of Genl. Greene,*[54] *as manifested by his own conduct, when at a subsequent period he took post within a mile of the same town with a force numerically inferior to that which composed its Garrison…*

*But the misfortune of the American Army is attributed principally to the want of intelligence of the British force, owing to a neglect of measures calculated to obtain it. Now of the General's anxiety to procure intelligence, & his endeavor to employ proper agents, I can more safely testify, because I was one of those whom he directed to engage persons who might be confided in for that purpose. This being a dangerous service, & always remunerated, I asked the General what money should be offered, when he assured me he had not one dollar. Our own paper was totally worthless,*[55] *& the only resource left, to which I was obliged to resort, was to impress the horse of one man, to pay for the secret services of the country…No opportunity of interrogating the inhabitants of the Country was omitted…Genl. Gates was not negligent on the subject of intelligence;…& did all in that line that could be expected from an Officer without secret service money, a stranger in the Country, & who had been in command of the Army only 18 or 20 days. But in fact he was not materially deficient in information of the enemy's force. The only circumstance of importance of which he was ignorant was of the arrival of Cornwallis at Camden, on the evening of the 14th of August, & that he may have been for one day without knowledge of that occurance will not appear strange, when it is considered, that the British General approached rapidly, & I believe with only his personal escort…Nor if the arrival of Cornwallis had been known & the most accurate information of his force, as it proved to be, had been received, were his 1700 regulars including Tarleton's Legion, & 300 No. Cara. loyalists, a force so imposing as to have rendered it dangerous for the American general to have occupied a well-selected position within 6 or 7 miles of him. The regular infantry & artillery which Gates commanded were of the first* *class. The 600 Militia from Virginia were men of the finest appearance; they were commanded by Col. Stevens an old Continental Officer, & several of their sergeants had seen service in the regular army; the North Cara. Militia, if properly stationed, would from their numbers have formed an imposing force. If the American Army had marched from Rugely's two hours earlier, or Cornwallis had moved from Camden two hours later, the event of the contest would probably have been very different…*

*It is suggested that the army should have retreated after the skirmish in the night; & some expressions of Baron De Kalb seem to be relied on in support of that opinion. But a little attention to the detail of the business will render it evident that such an attempt would have been more hazardous than risking the engagement on the ground occupied; and that the opinion of Genl. Stevens (which not being opposed by De Kalb or any other member was the opinion, of the Council of War) was correct, namely that it was too late to do anything but fight. The hour at which the first firing took place is correctly stated to have been at half past two o'clock in the morning of the 16th August. At that period the Sun in this climate rises at 24 minutes past four, two hours only from the time of the rencounter. Any person who has observed in the day & in time of Peace, the time usually occupied in forming a body of 1600 or 1700 militia for an ordinary review, may easily imagine how much more it must occupy under the circumstances of any Army. What was the precise time, I do not recollect, but I well remember that soon after the troops were formed, the General moved along their front, saying a few words of encouragement to them; & that it was but a short time after he had proceeded along the front of Smallwood's Brigade composing the reserve, when our Artillery opened on the enemy. Consider also that the armies were drawn up within two or three hundred yards of each other, & judge then of the possibility of avoiding an action, & decide whether it was most prudent to engage in it with the Army already formed for action, or to have been forced with troops so composed to have assumed an order of battle from the line of march, with our army disheartened & the enemy encouraged by the very circumstance of our retreat. No objection is made to the order of battle or to the conduct of Genl. Gates, as long as he was present, but it is asked why no attention was paid to the safety of the Continental troops who were waiting for orders from the Commander-in-chief; but he it seems, had been borne away by the torrent of Militia & could not find an Aid to convey his orders. The circumstance of his being borne away by the torrent of Militia…was truly if involuntary, the greatest misfortune, or if it could have been avoided the greatest error of the General on that day. In what I witnessed while with him, I saw no indication of want of presence of mind. As soon as the firing in the night commenced, he hastened to the head of the Line, where he met Armand retreating, who urged the General to retire, as a smart firing was carried on where he was. The General answered that it was his duty to be where his orders might be necessary; & he remained there until the firing grew slack & the troops were beginning to be formed. I well remember Col. Williams riding up to him just at daybreak, & giving him information of the movement of the Enemy's troops on their right, but I may not have adverted to all that the Colonel said. I however observed no hesitation, but admired the promptness with which he ordered that Col. Stevens should be directed to make an immediate attack while the Enemy were maneuvering, & with which he then turned to me & said "Now Sir do you go to the Baron de Kalb, & desire him to make an attack on the Enemy's left to support that made by Genl. Stevens on the Right." I according pressed on to the 2d Maryland Brigade on the right of our line, & as soon as I had delivered my orders, & had seen that Wing fairly engaged I hastened back to find the General. But by this time the militia had broken away; a few of those of No. Carolina only were opposing in small squards in the rear of the left of the Artillerists, who were then taken in flank, but still made a brilliant defence. In a few minutes more the enemy commenced their attack on the front & left flank of Smallwood's brigade which formed the reserve. I joined this Brigade near which I had left the General, & made the inquiry I could for him, but without success. While here I received a wound & becoming faint, I found myself supported on my horse by Majr. McGill,*[56] *another of the General's Aids, who conveyed me to an Ammunition Wagon then endeavoring to escape, into which I was thrown. This accounts for the disposal of two of the Aids & the General had but three. How Capt. Richmond*[57] *who was the third was employed, I know not, nor do I know of what Orders Majr. McGill was the bearer, but he must undoubtedly have been on the field with instructions from the General.*

*Genl. Gates is also censured for pursuing the route from Deep River where he joined the Army, by Mask's Ferry on the Pedee to Lynch's Creek, on the road to Camden. It is however observable that this was nearly the precise route which Genl. Greene pursued the succeeding April, the country being in both cases destitute of provisions, owing to previous exhaustion, & the natural sterility of a great part of the Soil. When Genl. Gates joined the Baron de Kalb on the 25th July, the American Army had been in that neighborhood three weeks & had exhausted all the provisions within their reach. I therefore admired Genl. Gates' prompt decision, when on being informed of the condition of the Army in this respect, then we may as well march on & starve, as starve lying here. The only doubt was concerning the most eligible course, & this was a choice of difficulties. In whatever direction the Army might move, the country exhausted by the residence of the Army must be passed over; the barrens between the upper branches of the Cape Fear & the Catawba must be traversed, of course it was inevitable that they should be distressed for food for several days march…As far therefore as that point on the march whereto the Army suffered most, no blame can attach for the selection. The only question then is whether from Mask's ferry the Army should have deviated westward, or have taken the course it pursued towards Camden, & this question was decided by a consideration which could scarcely fail to preponderate. Col. Williams discloses the circumstance, & I can fully testify to the accuracy of his account of the improper conduct of Genl. Caswell who commanded a body of about 1200 No. Caro. Militia. This Officer having advanced beyond Mask's ferry, had been urged by Baron de Kalb, & repeatedly by Genl. Gates to form a junction with the regular Army, instead of complying with those injunctions, he continued to advance towards Lynch's Creek, where the Enemy was in some force. The only means then of securing this accession to the Army, & probably of preserving them from defeat & destruction, was to form a junction as rapidly as possible. Could Genl. Gates under these circumstances have retired to refresh his Army in summer quarters at Charlotte or Salisbury, leaving this body of Militia, the only hope of immediate support from the State in which he was acting, to be sacrificed by the imprudence or misconduct of their commanding Officer? Sound policy forbade it. Ought he from a remote situation, to have been an inactive spectator of the triumph of the British, & the discomfiture of a body of our Countrymen, dedicated to the same service with the Army of the U. States? Patriotism & Humanity revolted at the Idea. He determined to hasten to their succour, & no doubt can exist that but for the approach of the regular Army, the enemy would have made a dash at this Corps…*

*The only remaining censure on the conduct of Genl. Gates…is that he did not attack the enemy's Post on Little Lynch's Creek in order to force a direct passage to Camden. But as I have shown that he did not contemplate an immediate attack on Camden, even after he had formed a junction with this Militia Corps, he could scarcely have had an intention previous to his receiving this reinforcement. Being desirous however to destroy the detachment of the Enemy, Col. Williams relates that he directed their position to be accurately reconnoitered; but finding them to be very advantageously posted on a deep Creek, not passable for several miles, but over a single causeway & bridge, which they occupied, it is obvious that he must have sustained considerable loss in the Assault; he then effected his only remaining object, which was to drive them into Camden by a simple flank march. This maneuvre is considered to have been judicious & strickly consonant to military principles.*

*…I have endeavored to do justice to an Officer, to whom as far as the services of a Commander of an Army avail, the United States are indebted for one of the most important & brilliant victories of the Revolutionary War. In so doing I have endeavored to prove that when he assumed the command of the Southern Army he was not to blame in immediately moving forward. That the Route he selected was in the first instance a choice of nearly equal difficulties, & finally such as, from circumstances not within his control, it became his duty to continue. That his conduct was strictly correct in refraining from the attack of the British Post on Little Lynch's creek. That his movement from Rugely's was not a rash or injudicious measure, but that the Plan he thereby contemplated to execute, was the most advisable he could then adopt…& a plan that but for the unfortunate rencounter at night, offered the*

> *fairest prospects of success. That after that rencounter an immediate action became inevitable. That the order of battle & the directions given by him while present were judicious. That he did not neglect to obtain intelligence...That however deficient in some of the means of obtaining it, he had sufficient information on the enemy's force. That this force was not such as ought to have imposed on him the necessity of foregoing material advantages in order to avoid an action upon advantageous terms; and that his ignorance for 24 hours of the arrival of Cornwallis, must have been owing to some accidental circumstance.*

Another of Gates's aides, Major Charles Magill of Virginia, wrote a letter to his father from the "Field of Battle Within Eight Miles of Camden" describing the engagement. Although it is undated, the letter must have been written shortly after the battle.[58]

> *In the Evening of the 15th Inst, a Council of Genl officers were unanimously of opinion that our Army should move within five miles of Camden, to an advantageous post with a swamp in our front, fordable only at the Road, and no other within seven miles on each side—At ten o'clock the Army moved in the following order—*
>
> *Colo Armand's Corps, about seventy Horse in front, Colo Porterfield with 50 men belonging to our Regt, and 150 Militia upon Armand's right flank, about two Hundred yards off the road—Majr Anderson with a party of No Carolina militia upon Armand's left Flank, in the same order—Colo Armand's orders were, should the Enemy's Horse attack him, to stand their charge, and Porterfield with the other Light Infantry to flank them—Genl Smallwood's Brigade in front, Genl Gist's followed, the No Carolina Division under Genl Caswell next, and in the rear the Virginia Brigade commanded by Genl Stevens—After marching in this order nigh five miles, about half after two in the morning the British Horse made a most violent onset Huzzaing all the time, but were bravely repulsed by Porterfield with considerable loss—The Enemy's Light infantry next came up, the Virginia militia or the Greatest part that were with Porterfield took to their heels, and left the men belonging to our Regt to stand the Attack of the whole light troops; which to their Honour they did for about five minutes, in which a warm and incessant fire was kept up—Colo Porterfield then ordered a retreat, and in turning his horse about had his leg shattered by a musket ball, which struck him upon the shin Bone—After some time the firing ceased, our line was formed, and Half an Hour before sun rise the Enemy advanced...Immediately on the Enemy's driving in our Party in Front, Genl Stevens was ordered to advance & Attack their right, and Gist with his Brigade to attack their left, the orders were immediately complyed with, but upon the first fire the whole line of militia broke and ran; the firing upon our right had begun; I was there with Genl Gates, who perceiving the militia run, rode about twenty yards in*

*the rear of the line, to rally them, which he found impossible to do there; about half a mile further, Genl Gates and Caswell made another fruitless attempt, and a third was made at a still greater distance with no better success—Genl Smallwood, on Stevens advancing to the attack advanced to support him, and...occupy'd the ground where the Right of Stevens, and the left of the No Carolina militia were drawn up; this made a chasm between the two Brigades, through which the Enemy's Horse came and charged our rear; the men to their Immortal Honour made a brave defence, but were at last obliged to give ground, and are allmost all killed or taken; Gist's Brigade behaved like heroes, so did Smallwood's, but they being more to our left afforded us no opportunity of saving them; upon Genl Gates Riding to stop the militia, Gist's Brigade charged Bayonets and at first made the Enemy give way, but they were reinforced—We owe all misfortune to the militia; had they not run like dastardly cowards, our Army was sufficient to cope with them, drawn up as we were upon a rising and advantageous ground.*

Another of Gates's aides, Lieutenant Christopher Richmond of the First Maryland Regiment, sent an account of the battle to Maryland Governor Thomas Sim Lee on August 30.[59]

*You will have heard of our Defeat near Camden,—towards which we had approached with great Rapidity, notwithstanding the violent Heat of the Weather, the Want of Provisions, and other Obstacles. On the 15th Inst. in the Night we marched against the Enemy, with the greatest Hopes, nay a moral Certainty of Success—but alas! our fair Hopes, Wishes and Confidence, were withered & blasted, by the uncommon, and most unheard of Cowardice, of the Militia which was with us; and composed at least two Thirds of our Army. The Maryland & Delaware Regimts. behaved like Men—how many of them are saved I cannot at present tell—but believe, between Six & Seven hundred of the Whole that were in, and out of Action.*

Charles-Francois, Le Chevalier Du Buysson des Hays, a French volunteer assisting the Americans, served as De Kalb's aide during the campaign and was captured at Camden. In a letter written at Charlotte on August 26, he conveyed the Baron's last message to his subordinates, Generals Smallwood and Gist.[60]

*Having received several wounds in the action of the sixteenth instant, I was made prisoner with...the Baron de Kalb, with whom I served as aide-de-camp and friend, and had an opportunity of attending that great and good officer, during the short time he languished with eleven wounds, which proved mortal on the third day.*

*It is with pleasure I obey the Baron's last commands, in presenting his most affectionate compliments to all the officers and men of his division; he expressed the greatest satisfaction in the testimony given by the British army of the bravery of his troops, and he was charmed with the firm opposition they made to superior force when abandoned by the rest of the army. The gallant behaviour of the Delaware regiment and the companies of artillery attached to the brigade, afforded him infinite pleasure, and the exemplary conduct of the whole division gave him an endearing sense of the merit of the troops he had the honor to command.*

On September 2, Du Buysson described De Kalb's conduct during the battle in a letter to an unknown recipient.[61]

*The Baron DeKalb, taken by the British and mortally wounded, desired me to repair immediately to Philadelphia, to give, in his name, to Congress, a full account of his transactions relative to his command of the Maryland and Delaware line…to clear his memory of every false or malignant insinuation, which might have been made by some invidious persons, but as my wounds do not permit me to travel as fast as I could desire, I thought it convenient to acquaint you, Sir, of my repairing to Congress with all the baron's papers and accounts, that no measure be taken towards this affair before my arrival…*

*The Baron DeKalb…withstood with the greatest bravery, coolness and intrepidity, with the brave Marylanders alone, the furious charge of the whole British army; but superior bravery was obliged at length to yield to superior numbers, and the baron, having had his horse killed under him, fell into the hands of the enemy, pierced with eight wounds of bayonets and three musket balls. I stood by the baron during the action and shared his fate, being taken by his side, wounded in both arms and hands. Lord Cornwallis and Rawdon treated us with the greatest civility. The baron, dying of his wounds two days after the action, was buried with all the honors of war, and his funeral attended by all the officers of the British army. The doctor having reported to Lord Cornwallis the impossibility of curing my wounds in that part of the continent, he admitted me to my parole, to go to Philadelphia for effecting an exchange.*[62]

General William Smallwood managed to extricate himself from the battlefield and made his way to Salisbury. On August 22, he sent Gates a report of his activities since the battle.[63]

*I retreated with the shattered remains of the Maryland Division by the way of Wacksaw thence to Charlotte where I intended to have made a stand but upon hearing of Sumpters Defeat and dispersion and that the enemy were advancing to that Post I thought it more eligible to order the Sick, wounded and such Baggage as was saved forward to this place following slowly with the handful of cavalry and Infantry which I had collected on the Retreat.*

General Mordecai Gist of Maryland commanded the brigade that included the Delaware Regiment. From Hillsborough on September 12, he wrote to Delaware Governor Caesar Rodney describing the conduct of that state's troops during the battle and the situation of the prisoners.[64]

> *A number of your Officers having unfortunately fallen in the hands of the Enemy in the Action of the 16th ultimo, remain prisoners of War; and having lost all their baggage are in the greatest want of Cloaths and money to support them.*[65]
>
> *I have the pleasure to inform you that the Officers and men of this Regiment, with the whole of the Regular Troops behav'd with the firmness and Intrepidity which would have ensured us a Compleat Victory, had not the scandalous conduct of the Militia, left us to oppose the Torrent of superior numbers…*
>
> *The loss of Men will render it necessary to reduce the Brigade and incorporate the whole into one Regiment, of which your Troops will form two Companies.*

The commander of the Fourth Maryland Regiment, Colonel Josias Hall, wrote an account of the battle on August 28. He noted that the troops' morale had already begun to recover from the defeat.[66]

> *You have before this I suppose heard of our defeat or rather rout for there was no retreat for us. We never attempted to stand till we got to Charlotte about 70 miles from place of action, we lost the whole of our artillery stores Baggage & The Mangl*[e]*d Divisions acquired a great deal of honor even from the enemy. True it was purchased at a great expense—we lost one half the men we conveyed into action, the quarter part of those killed in the field. This is the 4th general defeat I have been in but I never saw men behave so cool and determined after the whole left wing had given way. The ad*[utjant] *Brig. pushed the enemy some distance & continued the action over time* [words missing] *with the horse & foot in the van alternately facing one way & the other. Lt. Rawdon's Corps had fairly given up the contest until Cornwallis discovered our whole left wing had given way & ordered him up again. They could not turn our right at last. The first Brid*[ade] *was about 100 Yards on our left & in our van with both flanks exposed…& broke before us tho they behaved as well as men could. Of the militia who composed 4/5 of the whole had behaved tolerably well contrary to my expectations. We should have obtained a complete victory…This affair tho unfortunate to individuals & to none more so than to Gates is trifling in the general scale. Our fate must be decided at N. York or perhaps rather at Sea. The people have recovered their spirits & have more militia in the field than before the action determined to regain their Credit.*

An anonymous Continental officer wrote an account of the battle on August 22 in which he accused Southerners of pressuring Gates into a hasty advance. The letter somehow came into the hands of newspaper publishers and was printed in some Northern papers.[67]

> *It is natural for mankind, who have lost their country and property, to be too anx'ous in their pursuits to regain them, and while they partially grasp at the shadow, lose the substance. Men of this complexion, constantly surrounding the commander in chief, lessening his difficulties, and number of the enemy, and pointing out the certainty of success, excite measures which in the event become fatal. We marched from Hillsborough about the first of July, without an ounce of provision being laid in at any one point, often fasting for several days together, and subsisting frequently upon green apples and peaches; sometimes by detaching parties, we thought ourselves feasted, when they by violence seized a little fresh beef, cut, threshed out, and ground a little wheat; yet, under all these difficulties we had to press forward.*
>
> *Just before, and on the arrival of General Gates, both he and the Baron seemed disposed to give the army a little respite; but General Caswell, with the North-Carolina militia, having moved over the Pedee, obliged us to make a six days hard march, before we could form a junction with him; this effected, our march was rapidly continued for six days longer, when we arrived at Claremont, within thirteen miles of Camden, on the 13th. instant.*
>
> *Our supplies began here to come in more amply, and had we waited a few days, our forces must have been considerably augmented, which would have enabled us to have harassed the enemy, and in a great measure cut off their resources; this must have effected our purpose in the event, without risking a general engagement, the last step in my opinion to be taken where so much was* [words missing] *down on the evening of the 15th to attack the enemy, and General Sumpter was to proceed down to the ferry opposite to Camden, to create a diversion in that quarter, to facilitate our making an impression on Camden. Here the British had collected their whole force, and gaining intelligence of our view, moved out at nine o'clock in the evening to meet us, and forming an ambuscade on the road, surprized us about one o'clock in the morning on our march. Our advanced and flanking parties endeavoured to resist the attack, but were broke, and threw the continental brigades into disorder; but they rallying immediately, advanced, engaged and forced the enemy to give way in turn; this gave respite to the troops to form, and so we remained in anxious expectation, till near day-break, nothing material occuring but partial firings from the advanced and reconnoitering parties of each army, when the General ordered the first Maryland brigade to form a corps de reserve, about 200 yards in rear of the center of the line; this was immediately effected, and the troops rested upon their arms till a little after day break, when the action commenced.*

*The attack was made by Lord Cornwallis...on the center and left wing of our front line, which was altogether composed of militia, who upon the first fire of the enemy, gave way, and were pursued by the British, which threw the corps de reserve into disorder; but they rallying immediately under a very hot fire, charged the British so warmly, that they entirely broke their center; by this time the fire commenced very hot on the right, where the second Maryland brigade behaved with great gallantry and firmness; but the enemy's line of regular troops being far more extensive on the right than ours on the left, after the militia had given way, exposed the left flank and rear of the first brigade, which, notwithstanding manfully maintained their ground, till the left wing was ordered to retreat to a point in view about 80 yards in the rear, to the extremity of the flanking party, where it instantly formed, renewed, and continued the attack with great vigour; but being again hard pressed in front, flank, and rear, retreated a second time, formed, and disputed the ground with great obstinacy, till borne down by numbers, they were obliged generally to retreat; at this time the second brigade, which before had not been so hard pressed, was also borne down by superior numbers, after behaving with the greatest firmness and bravery. The retreat now became general, and the militia, by this time six or eight miles in the rear, some of whom together with our camp women, waggoners, and some scattering light horse, plundered all our baggage.*

*General Smallwood endeavoured to cover the retreat, and is collecting the remains of our scattered troops, for which purpose he has established posts at Salisbury and Charlotte.*

Four days after the battle, General Edward Stevens of the Virginia militia provided his state's governor, Thomas Jefferson, with his own version of what had occurred at Camden.[68]

*Our Army moved from Rugeleys on the Night of the 15th Inst. about Ten OClock with an intention to take post on a Creek about 6 Miles from Camdon, where the Enemy had collected all their force. They under the Command of Lord Cornwallas moved out of Camdon about 9 OClock and our advanced party's of Cavelry and Infantry fell in with each other about five Miles from Rugesleys between 10 and 12 OClock. This occasioned a halt of Both Armeys, as our meeting at this time was unexpected to both Parties; for from some Prisoners that was taken I am informed they moved out with an intention to attack us in our Encampment at Rugesleys and if what they say with respect to their numbers be true, General Gates has been greatly deceived. We formed and remained on the ground till about day Break when we advanced a few Hundred Yards and fell in with each other. I was flushed with all the hopes Possible of Success as our left where I was had gained such an Advantage over the Enemy in outflanking their Right; but alas on the first Fire or two they*

> *Charged and the Militia gave way, and it was out of the power of Man to rally them…This gave the Enemy an Opportunity of pushing their whole force against the Maryland line, who was not able to stand them long, and in a very little time the whole was in the utmost Confusion, and the greatest Panick prevailed that ever I had an Opportunity of seeing before; a more compleat Defeat could not possible have taken place…in short picture it as bad as you possible can and it will not be as bad as it really is. We had to retreat through a Country of upward of a 100 Miles which may be truly said to be Inhabited by our Enemies and before any large party of ours could be Collected the Inhabitants rose in numbers, took and disarmed the cheif of our men. I am now where scarce a Friend is to be found. We are still in such a dispersed situation, that I cant pretend to say, what may be the loss of our men but with respect to the Militia, themselves, it matters not, for from their Rascally Behaviour they deserve no pity. Their Cowardly Behaviour has indeed given a Mortal Wound to my Feelings. I expect that near one half of the Militia will never halt till they get Home. And from what I have already seen I think I may venture to say that out of those who may be Collected, there will not be more than one fourth of them that will have their Arms, many of them…have thrown away their Arms with an expectation of getting Home by it. I am doubtfull it will be a very difficult matter to Collect any number of the Militia of this State together again, tho' if any thing else could be done it had better, for Militia I plainly see wont do. If Virginia dont exert herself, I fear this State will be in the same Predicament as the South which I think is for a time firmly fixed to the British Government, and through Choise of a very great part of the Back Inhabitants.*

Among the many wounded soldiers left behind when the American army retreated was Thomas Pinckney. Two days after the battle, he reported his condition to Gates and expressed his gratitude for the good treatment he had received from the British.[69]

> *I avail myself of the opportunity of a Flag of Truce to request the Favor of you to send me my Servant, horse and Cloaths, if they are in your Possession. My Wound was dressed at Head Quarters, on the Day of the Action, where I received every Mark of kindness and Attention. I am likewise under great obligation to the officers in General & the Gentlemen of the Faculty for their Civility and Care of me.*
>
> *…tho' the bone is entirely shattered, I have hopes of retaining my Leg.*

# 2

# British Commanders' Accounts

EARL CORNWALLIS was attending to administrative duties in Charleston when worrisome news of Gates's advance prompted him to go to Camden, as he informed Sir Henry Clinton in a letter written on August 10.[70]

> *I yesterday received an express[71] from Camden, informing me that Gates, with Caswall and Rutherford, was advancing and making every appearance of attacking Lord Rawdon; he had assembled on the west branch of Linches Creek at Robertson's, the 23rd, 33rd, 71st, and Volunteers of Ireland. Our troops are in general sickly, the 71st so much so, that the two battalions have not more than 274 men under arms…I am just going to join the army, and hope to get there before anything of consequence happens.*

When the battle was over, Cornwallis prepared two reports to Lord George Germain. The first letter, written on August 20, described the events leading up to the battle.[72]

> *Everything wearing the face of tranquillity and submission, I set out on the 21st of June for Charleston leaving the command of the troops on the frontiers to Lord Rawdon…*
>
> *About this time I heard that two thousand of the Maryland and Delaware continental troops were entering North Carolina under Maj.-General Baron de Kalb and that he meant to take his quarters at Hilsborough. There was then in that country a corps of three hundred Virginia light infantry under Colonel Porterfield, some militia at Salisbury and Charlottetown under Generals Rutherford and Sumpter, and a large body of militia at Cross Creek under General Caswall. As all these corps were at a great distance from us, and as I knew it to be impossible to march any considerable body of men across the province of North Carolina before the harvest, I did not expect that our posts on the frontier would be much disturbed for two months and by that time I hoped to be able to undertake offensive operations…*

*Baron de Kalb moved early in July to Deep River where he was joined first by General Caswall from Cross Creek*[73] *and about the 25th by General Gates who took the command of the army. But as he was still above an hundred miles from Major McArthur,*[74] *which was the nearest post to him, Lord Rawdon did not think it necessary to make any material alteration in the disposition of the troops. From this time until the 20th of July many skirmishes happened on the frontiers of Ninety-Six and towards Waxhaw but none of any material consequence. The enemy had, however, in the meantime filled this province with their emissaries and in all the eastern part of it were planning a general revolt which our lenity had left but too much in their power. The Cheraw Hill was a post of great consequence and had the appearance of being healthy, but it proved so much the contrary and sickness came on so rapidly that in nine days at least two-thirds of the 71st regiment were taken ill of fevers and agues and rendered unfit for service. About this time the enemy were known to be in motion but the rigour of the government (many of our principal friends in N. Carolina being confined in dungeons loaded with irons and several having been put to death) had so intimidated those, on whose goodwill and ability we had the greatest reason to depend, that Lord Rawdon could obtain no certain accounts of them.*

*The salvation of the 71st regiment as well as every other consideration determined his lordship to withdraw the post at Cheraw Hill. This the active incendiaries of the enemy represented as an act of fear and so encouraged the disaffected and terrified the wavering that the whole country between Pedee and Black River openly avowed the principles of rebellion, and collecting in parties commenced acts of hostility…*

*Lord Rawdon waited for General Gates at Robertson's with the 23rd, 33rd, 71st, and Volunteers of Ireland, who came up but did not think proper to attack him. In the meantime his lordship performed the arduous task of removing the sick of the 71st regiment to Camden. General Gates showing no disposition to attack the corps at Robertson's, Lord Rawdon, wisely apprehending that his intention might be either to reinforce Sumpter and make a more vigorous attack on the posts at Rocky Mount or Hanging Rock, or by getting round his right destroy his stores and take his sick at Camden, retired from Robertson's to that place where he was joined by the corps which had been before moved from Hanging Rock to Rugeley's Mill and directed Lieut.-Colonel Turnbull*[75] *to quit Rocky Mount and either come down the west side of the Wateree to Camden or fall back on the militia posts commanded by Major Ferguson on Broad River.*[76]

Cornwallis's second report to Germain explained his strategy and gave a detailed account of the battle. Written on August 21, the letter caused a great deal of public rejoicing in Great Britain after it appeared in a special edition of the *London Gazette* on October 9.[77]

*It is with great pleasure that I communicate to your lordship an account of a complete victory obtained on the 16th instant, by His Majesty's troops under my command, over the rebel southern army, commanded by General Gates…*

*On the 9th instant two expresses arrived with an account that General Gates was advancing towards Lynche's creek with his whole army, supposed to amount to six thousand men, exclusive of a detachment of one thousand men under General Sumpter, who, after having in vain attempted to force the posts at Rocky mount and Hanging rock, was believed to be at that time trying to get round the left of our position, to cut off our communication with the Congarees and Charles town; that the disaffected country between the Pedee and Black river had actually revolted;*[78] *and that Lord Rawdon was contracting his posts, and preparing to assemble his force at Camden.*

*In consequence of this information…I set out on the evening of the 10th, and arrived at Camden on the night between the 13th and 14th, and there found Lord Rawdon with all our force, except Lieutenant-colonel Turnbull's small detachment, which fell back from Rocky mount to Major Ferguson's posts of the militia…on Little river.*

*I had now my option to make, either to retire or attempt the enemy; for the position at Camden was a bad one to be attacked in, and by General Sumpter's advancing down the Wateree, my supplies must have failed me in a few days.*

*I saw no difficulty in making good my retreat to Charles town with the troops that were able to march; but in taking that resolution, I must have not only left near eight hundred sick and a great quantity of stores at this place, but I clearly saw the loss of the whole province, except Charles town, and all of Georgia, except Savannah, as immediate consequences, besides forfeiting all pretensions to future confidence from our friends in this part of America.*

*On the other hand, there was no doubt of the rebel army being well appointed, and of its number being upwards of five thousand men, exclusive of General Sumpter's detachment, and a corps of Virginia militia, of twelve or fifteen hundred men, either actually joined, or expected to join the main body every hour; and my own corps, which never was numerous, was now reduced, by sickness and other casualties, to about fourteen hundred fighting men, of regulars and provincials, with four or five hundred militia and the North-Carolina refugees.*[79]

*However, the greatest part of the troops that I had being perfectly good, and having left Charles town sufficiently garrisoned and provided for a siege, and seeing so little to lose by a defeat, and much to gain by a victory, I resolved to take the first good opportunity to attack the rebel army.*

*Accordingly, I took great pains to procure good information of their movements and position; and I learned that they had encamped, after marching from Hanging rock, at Colonel Rugeley's, about twelve miles from hence, on the afternoon of the 14th.*

*After consulting some intelligent people, well acquainted with the ground, I determined to march at ten o'clock on the night of the 15th, and to attack at daybreak, pointing my principal force against their continentals, who, from good intelligence, I knew to be badly posted, close to Colonel Rugeley's house. Late in the evening I received information, that the Virginians had joined that day; however, that having been expected, I did not alter my plan, but marched at the hour appointed, leaving the defence of Camden to some provincials, militia, and convalescents, and a detachment of the 63d regiment, which by being mounted on horses which they had pressed on the road, it was hoped would arrive in the course of the night.*

*I had proceeded nine miles, when about half an hour past two in the morning my advanced guard fell in with the enemy. By the weight of the fire I was convinced they were in considerable force; and was soon assured by some deserters and prisoners, that it was the whole rebel army on its march to attack us at Camden. I immediately halted and formed, and the enemy doing the same, the firing soon ceased. Confiding in the disciplined courage of His Majesty's troops, and well apprised by several intelligent inhabitants, that the ground on which both armies stood, being narrowed by swamps on the right and left, was extremely favourable for my numbers, I did not chuse to hazard the great stake for which I was going to fight, to the uncertainty and confusion to which an action in the dark is so particularly liable; but having taken measures that the enemy should not have it in their power to avoid an engagement on that ground, I resolved to defer the attack till day: At the dawn I made my last disposition, and formed the troops in the following order: The division on the right, consisting of a small corps of light infantry, the 23d and 33d regiments, under the command of Lieutenant-colonel Webster; the division of the left, consisting of the volunteers of Ireland, infantry of the legion, and part of Lieutenant-colonel Hamilton's North-Carolina regiment, under the command of Lord Rawdon, with two six and two three-pounders, which were commanded by Lieutenant McLeod.*[80] *The 71st regiment, with two six-pounders, was formed as a reserve, one battalion in the rear of the division of the right, the other of that of the left, and the cavalry of the legion in the rear, and the country being woody, close to the 71st regiment, with orders to seize any opportunity that might offer to break the enemy's line, and to be ready to protect our own, in case any corps should meet with a check.*

*This disposition was just made when I perceived that the enemy, having likewise persisted in their resolution to fight, were formed in two lines opposite and near to us; and observing a movement in their left, which I supposed to be with an intention to make some alteration in their order, I directed Lieutenant-colonel Webster to begin the attack, which was done with great vigour, and in a few minutes the action was general along the whole front. It was at this time a dead calm, with a little haziness in the air, which preventing the smoke from rising, occasioned so thick a darkness, that it was difficult to see the effect of a very heavy and well-supported fire on both sides. Our line continued to advance in good order, and with the cool intrepidity of experienced British soldiers, keeping up a constant fire, or making use of bayonets, as opportunities offered, and, after an obstinate resistance during three quarters of an hour, threw the enemy into total confusion, and forced them to give way in all quarters. At this instant I ordered the cavalry to complete the rout, which was performed with their usual promptitude and gallantry; and after doing great execution on the field of battle, they continued the pursuit to Hanging rock, twenty-two miles from the place where the action happened, during which, many of the enemy were slain, and a number of prisoners, near one hundred and fifty waggons, (in one of which was a brass cannon, the carriage of which had been damaged in the skirmish of the night) a considerable quantity of military stores, and all the baggage and camp equipage of the rebel army, fell into our hands.*

*The loss of the enemy was very considerable; a number of colours, and seven pieces of brass cannon, (being all their artillery that were in the action) with all their ammunition waggons, were taken; between eight and nine hundred were killed, among that number Brigadier-general Gregory,*[81] *and about one thousand prisoners, many of whom were wounded, of which number were Major-general Baron de Kalbe, since dead, and Brigadier-general Rutherford.*

*I have the honour to inclose a return of the killed and wounded on our side. The loss of so many brave men is much to be lamented; but the number is moderate in proportion to so great an advantage.*

*The behaviour of His Majesty's troops in general was beyond all praise; it did honour to themselves and to their country. I was particularly indebted to Colonel Lord Rawdon, and to Lieutenant-colonel Webster, for the distinguished courage and ability with which they conducted their respective divisions; and the capacity and vigour of Lieutenant-colonel Tarleton, at the head of the cavalry, deserve my highest commendations. Lieutenant McLeod exerted himself greatly in the conduct of our artillery. My aid-de-camp, Captain Ross, and Lieutenant Haldane,*[82] *of the engineers, who acted in that capacity, rendered me most essential service; and the public officers, major of brigade England, who acted as deputy adjutant general, and the majors of brigade Manley and Doyle,*[83] *shewed the most active and zealous attention to their duty. Governor Martin became again a military man, and behaved with the spirit of a young volunteer.*[84]

*The fatigue of the troops rendered them incapable of farther exertion on the day of action...The rebel forces being at present dispersed, the internal commotions and insurrections in the province will now subside. But I shall give directions to inflict exemplary punishment on some of the most guilty, in hopes to deter others in future from sporting with allegiance and oaths, and with the lenity and generosity of the British government.*

*On the morning of the 17th I dispatched proper people into North Carolina, with directions to our friends there to take arms and assemble immediately, and to seize the most violent people, and all military stores and magazines belonging to the*

> *rebels, and to intercept all stragglers from the routed army; and I have promised to march without loss of time to their support. Some necessary supplies for the army are now on their way from Charles town, and I hope that their arrival will enable me to move in a few days.*
>
> *My aid-de-camp, Captain Ross, will have the honour of delivering this dispatch to your lordship, and will be able to give you the fullest account of the state of the army and the country.*

Cornwallis did not write a report to his superior, Henry Clinton, until August 23, and his account of the battle was very brief.[85]

> *I left Charlestown on the Evening of the 10th. & arrived here in the night of the 13th. having Suffered the most anxious Suspense on the road, where I met frequently the most alarming reports, & had the greatest reason to apprehend, that if our Affairs did not speedily take a more favorable turn, the greatest part of the inhabitants between Camden, & Charles Town, would appear in Arms against us…*
>
> *I must beg leave to recommend in the strongest manner to you the brave Troops who fought with me on that day. Their behaviour was indeed above all praise, & deserves every encouragement.*

Lord Rawdon had the task of opposing Gates's advance until Cornwallis arrived at Camden. He informed Cornwallis of his efforts in a letter dated August 11.[86]

> *I have endeavored to delay Gates as much as possible in his progress without risquing any thing; & I have in some degree succeeded; No opportunity offered of attacking him, consistent with the safety of our Magazines, tho' I thought my force fully equal to the attempt. Gates's Army is called Five thousand; but I do not believe they exceed Three thousand, five hundred. Whensoever he threatened to pass round my flank & get between me & Camden, I was always obliged to fall back; At last, I have collected every thing, but Turnbull's Regiment, at this place. Gates may attack me tomorrow morning: If he does, I think he will find us in better spirits than he expects; If he does not, it will become every day more difficult; & he will be seriously distressed by want of Provisions.*
>
> *I understand that Gates is two miles on this side of Rugeley's Mills; but am not positive, Part of his troops are there. I can procure but miserable intelligence.*

After the battle, Rawdon elaborated on the strategy he had used against Gates before the battle, as well as the situation since, in a September 19 letter to his mother, the Countess of Moira.[87]

*Had I thought the tinsel of unweighed applause an object superior to the consciousness of having acted right, I should have given Mr. Gates battle while the command remained with me. It was in my power; I had fair prospect of success; the reputation to be attained was great; and if I was beaten there would have been credit in making a bold attempt, for the failure of which the disparity of force would have been a sufficient apology. But I felt that the step would be false; for, by maintaining the conduct which I pursued, I was certain of forcing the enemy either to retire across the Pedee, to attack me upon terms almost hopeless for them, or to take the ruinous part which they actually did embrace.*

*De Kalb, who was a good officer, saw so clearly the consequences of reducing their attacks to one point, and thereby enabling me to unite my detachments, that he strenuously advised Gates to pass Lynches Creek and fight me, at all events: this was related to me by De Kalb's aid-de-camp,*[88]*…who was made prisoner. Gates rejected the advice, threw himself across the country into the other road above Hanging Rock Creek, and gave us three days to prepare to meet him, in a country likewise very favorable for us.*

*Since that action the sickness of the troops, added to want of provisions and almost every kind of stores has detained us inactive. We are now in march toward Hillsborough, where Gates has collected a small body of militia. At present there is no prospect of serious opposition, but I cannot believe that the Congress will not make an effort to stop the advance of our successes.*

In 1801, Rawdon, then known as the Earl of Moira, was asked for an account of the operations leading up to the battle. Rawdon's reply, written on January 19, 1801, provides insight into his own strategy prior to the battle as well as to the extent British officers jealously guarded their military reputations by seeking proper credit for their services.[89]

*Your wish for a detail of the circumstances which preceded the defeat of Gates at Camden shall be gratified as far as my recollection will serve…I must…express my hope that there is no intention of impeaching the just credit which has always been given to Lord Cornwallis for that battle, altho' I am not to disguise that, when I saw his public letter, I did not think myself equitable treated in his recital of the event. I was simply classed with Colonel Webster as having done my duty in the action with proper exertion at the head of the wing which I commanded: whereas I think it will appear to you that I stood upon very different ground, both as to particulars of earlier date which led to that battle & as to special services in the very decision…*

*Having been left in the command of the back country when Ld. Cornwallis went to Charlestown, I had (by my spies) kept a vigilant eye over the force which was collecting in North Carolina for the invasion of our newly acquired territory. Tho' Ld. Cornwallis had not thought it probable that the attack would be made upon South Carolina till the violent heat of the summer should be passed, I had suspected that Gates might calculate on our inability to stand the climate (especially as it was known that we were very sickly) & might then make a speedier effort. I had on that account minutely examined the country & formed my eventual plans. Camden had from the first day appeared to me an objectionable station for the army. It was a false position relative to the country, & in itself indefensible beyond any ground that I ever saw. On learning that a body of the enemy's militia had advanced to the Pedee, I considered it a sure indication that Gates would move immediately. I therefore detached Webster, a good & gallant officer, to the east branch of Lynche's Creek, & I reinforced a post which I had at Hanging Rock. As soon as I had made the necessary arrangements at Camden, I followed Webster…My object in taking this forward position was to retard the progress of Gates' till Ld. Cornwallis should collect force from other parts of the Province, or to reduce the enemy to hazard an action where my peculiar advantages of situation would compensate for my disparity in numbers. I had 1100 men with me, all regulars or provincials; the detachment at Hanging Rock consisted of 400 provincials & 800 militia. The latter was a requisite post, because Sumpter menaced that road to Camden with a corps of militia. Gates came opposite to me. Aware of the danger of attempting to force the pass & of the difficulties that would be entailed by seeking another route, he apparently waited the issue of an enterprize that was meditated against Hanging Rock. One evening, news was brought to me that Sumpter had surprised & carried that post…It appeared a clear consequence that Sumpter, whose men were all mounted, would lose no time in pushing for Camden, by which, in addition to the loss of our magazines, I should have had him on my rear whilst Gates pressed my front. I addressed the Officers around me, who seemed struck with the obvious magnitude of the evil. I told them, in the hearing of the soldiers, that we were in a scrape from which nothing but courage could extricate us, & that we must march instantly to crush Sumpter before he could further co-operate with Gates. We marched in less than half an hour; and crossed the west branch of Lynche's Creek, directing our course to Granny's Quarter. In the morning, I received the information that the fate of the day had been most unexpectedly turned at Hanging Rock: Sumpter, after beating everything else out of the field, had assaulted the Legion infantry in a peculiarly steep part of that strong position, and his militia had not merely been repulsed but were so broken & dismayed by a vigorous charge with the bayonet that they had abandoned the whole ridge. That position was, therefore, still ours. I immediately hastened to occupy the bridge across the western branch of Lynche's Creek. Having sent my cavalry across it, they speedily saw the enemy's dragoons, by which I found that Gates had followed me. In the afternoon, I learned that he was encamped on the other side of the Creek. The communication from my new position to Hanging Rock was much longer than it had been from my former one; & the detachment, weakened & (except the Legion infantry) depressed, was a doubtful barrier against the future attempts of Sumpter. I therefore ordered those troops to fall back & take post behind Granny's Quarter Creek; because, altho' there was no strength of ground there as there was at Hanging Rock, I could in that situation give them ready support. You will see in this the same principle of protracting the advance of Gates untill our cavalry from Charlestown & our Light Infantry from Ninety-six should arrive. Had I repassed the western branch of Lynche's Creek to encounter Gates, I must have met him in a pine-barren even more advantageous for his superiority of numbers than a plain could have been. He had nearly four times as many men as I had with me. Had I concentrated my force at Camden, I must have stood an action before the arrival of the reinforcements, in a position that would give every imaginable advantage to the assailant, with the certainty that the mischief of a check was irretrievable, as there would be no space for rallying & the first success of the enemy put them in possession of our stores. Tarleton, with a childish pretension to Generalship, censures me for not having thus collected my troops at Camden, & arraigns Gates for incapacity in not comprehending that the getting round me & destroying my magazines must be fatal. Tarleton…ought to have known that which it is evident by his procedure Gates did know, namely, that there was no turning my right flank without going fifty miles down Lynche's Creek, there was no turning my left by a shorter process than heading the Creek & getting into the other road above Hanging Rock. Lynche's Creek runs thro' swamps of perhaps a mile in breadth on each side; impenetrable, except where a causeway has been made at the passing-places on the great road. The thick woods of those swamps prevented us from seeing each other's encampments across the Creek. In my second position, Gates had a post at the outlet of this causeway on his side, but he appeared never to have discovered a pass which came out about two miles from his camp, communicating with a ford on the Creek, from which there was a path into the causeway in my front. By this track I used to send out & receive my spies. The circumstance afforded a great temptation for an attempt to surprise the enemy's camp, and when you recollect that I was then young, not backward in enterprize, & confident in my troops, you may be of opinion there was some honesty in the forbearance. I could have assigned reasons such as everyone must have been obliged to take upon trust from me to prove the expediency of the hazard; but it would, in truth, have been an unfit stake of the public interest. I might have been discovered so that Gates might have had time to form his army, & in that case I should have to fight under signal disadvantage. On the other hand, I was well apprized that Gates's army was suffering severe distress from being detained in that desart. But there was one consideration which would alone have been decisive with me: I mean that Ld. Cornwallis was then on his way to join us; and had I atchieved a victory it must have been tarnished by the consciousness that I had availed myself of my temporary command to snatch a palm which ought to have been reserved for my General. To seduce Gates, however, into ruinous error was licit. I retired a mile from the outlet of my causeway in order to tempt him to pass the Creek; when I might have attacked him where branches of the swamp would have hindered him from profiting by his numbers: but he was too wise to make the attempt. At length, he could no longer delay a decision. If, by a march of fifty miles he crossed Lynche's Creek below me, he would still have to make his way towards Camden thro' a succession of defiles in the swamps where the Black River has its source, with almost a certainty that I should meet him there. He therefore determined to march to Hanging Rock; at which point he would be thirty-five miles from Camden, whereas in his present position he was but fifteen. My view of gaining time, of course, had succeeded. As soon as I had assured myself that this was not a feint, I broke up the bridge & causeways: and I retired to Camden, whither I summoned the troops from Granny's Quarter Creek. The motive for this was a conviction that matters must now be decided between that Creek & Camden. The banks of the Creek were not defensible; and the pine barren between it & Hanging Rock was the sort of extensive waste which we were always to shun. Ld. Cornwallis arrived, as did also the reinforcements. Having informed himself from me of the preceding movements, he asked me what had been my further purpose. I told him that, as nothing appeared to me so ineligible as receiving the enemy at Camden, I had intended to wait till my spies should apprize me of Gates's being approached within an easy march, when I meant to move forward & attack him. Ld. Cornwallis entered at once into the reasoning, adopted my plan, & reposed himself for its prosecution on the measures I had taken to secure information. In the meantime, he made all the arrangements which he judged expedient. It was I who brought to him the intelligence that Gates had arrived at Kingsley's*[90] *Plantation. With a pencil I sketched for him the ground, with which I was well acquainted, indicating the position of the enemy, as I understood it by the relation of the spies, & pointing out a path from the main road by which we might possible get undiscovered on the enemy's flank. On these data the attempt against the enemy was determined. We marched at night. At two in the morning the leading battalion, in the rear of which I was, was charged by cavalry. Their pieces being loaded, our infantry shrunk to the right & left into the bushes, thrusting at the cavalry with their bayonets. The cavalry retreated precipitately & we thought it had been only a strong patrole. When the confusion was over we resumed our march: but we soon had a heavy fire poured into us, apparently from two battalions. A Brigade of ours immediately formed, advanced in line, & soon exchanged fire with the enemy. The latter were broken & fell back. When we came to where their dead lay, I got off my horse to feel by the uniforms if they were the Continental Infantry which I suspected them to be by the nature of their fire. I was immediately satisfied on the point. I told Ld. Cornwallis of it, saying that it certainly was the enemy's army which we had met, and I then told his Lordship that he could not have better ground to fight upon, as it was a sort of neck between two swamps which would prevent the enemy from getting round his flanks. On this assurance, it being quite dark, he determined to rest till morning & then to attack the enemy. In the battle which ensued, I behaved neither better or worse than my neighbors: therefore Lord Cornwallis's mention of me in common with Webster was the fair compliment paid as a matter of course to officers of rank after a successful action; and, as far as referred to the hour of battle alone, was all that any justice could require towards me. But the preliminary events had not been unimportant, nor had the management been such…as had no claim upon Lord Cornwallis's special acknowledgement…Lord Cornwallis had the real merit of cool decision, judicious arrangement, & steady firmness in the conduct of the action. Tho' the thickness of the fog in the morning left him to rely as much upon my representation of the nature of the ground as he had been obliged to do during the night, his claim to all the credit of the victory cannot thence be weakened: for it is a part of the skill of the General to avail himself of the lights that he may gather from any inferior officer; & the latter cannot have a pretension to share in the fame…I should be disingenuous did I not avow that the final result furnished as much of that confidence which one draws from one's own successful experience as if the conclusion had been solely mine. The plan pursued without wavering, tho' with infinite anxiety, for so many days, had completely answered the end proposed & had brought the matter to an issue on more favorable terms than any lesser degree of perseverance could have fashioned; an issue which, as it had been the distinct object of my preceding movements & was prosecuted exactly according to the line which I had laid down, I have ventured to believe would not have had any different termination had the function of ordering the attack fallen to my share.*

*Now…in return for having given me the labor of travelling over an obsolete tale which can no longer be interesting to anyone upon ordinary grounds, let me claim from you that you shall not suffer a copy to be taken of the account.*

Lieutenant Colonel Banastre Tarleton and his legion, who had already distinguished themselves during the siege of Charleston and at the Battle of Waxhaws, acquired more laurels at Camden, further enhancing their reputation as a hard-hitting, highly skilled combat unit. Tarleton recounted the campaign in his memoirs, in which he referred to himself in the third person.[91]

*On the 13th, General Gates moved the American army to Rugeley's mills: The Maryland brigades, the Delawar regiment, the cannon, the cavalry, the baggage, and the militia, were posted on the north side of Granney-quarter's creek; and Colonel Porterfield and Major Armstrong's corps of light infantry were advanced over the creek, on the road leading to Camden. On the same day the four companies of light infantry arrived from Ninety Six, and in the night Earl Cornwallis…joined the British army. The arrival of the noble earl and of the light infantry were fortunate events: A reinforcement of seven hundred Virginia militia…which reached Rugeley's on the morning of the 14th, prompted the American commander in chief to make an addition of one hundred continentals, three hundred militia, and two pieces of cannon, to the corps under Colonel Sumpter, who was immediately directed to interrupt the communications between Charles town, Ninety Six, and Camden. Colonel Sumpter appeared on the morning of the 15th on the western bank of the Wateree, and captured some waggons with rum and stores below Camden, several waggons loaded with sick and tired light-infantry soldiers on the road from Ninety Six, and the escorts of loyal militia and regulars attending each convoy.*

*Lord Cornwallis, upon his arrival with the army, adopted the most likely measures to obtain intelligence of the enemy's force and position; he likewise directed his attention to strengthen the British regiments and provincial corps, by mustering the ablest convalescents; and he was not unmindful of his cavalry. Upon application from Lieutenant-colonel Tarleton, he ordered all the horses of the army…to be assembled: The best were selected for the service of the cavalry, and, upon the proprietors receiving payment, they were delivered up to the British legion. These active preparations diffused animation and vigour throughout the army.*

*On the 15th the principal part of the King's troops had orders to be in readiness to march: In the afternoon Earl Cornwallis desired Lieutenant-colonel Tarleton to gain circumstantial intelligence, by intercepting a patrole, or carrying off some prisoners, from an American picket: About ten miles from Camden, on the road to Rugeley's mills, the advanced guard of the legion, in the evening, secured three American soldiers: The prisoners reported, that they came from Lynche's creek, where they had been left in a convalescent state, and that they were directed to join the American army, on the high road, that night, as General Gates had given orders for his troops to move from Rugeley's mills to attack the British camp next morning near Camden. The information received from these men induced Tarleton to countermarch before he was discovered by any patrole from the enemy's outpost: The three prisoners were mounted behind dragoons, and conveyed with speed to the British army: When examined by Earl Cornwallis, their story appeared credible, and confirmed all the other intelligence of the day. Orders were immediately circulated for the regiments and corps, designed for a forward move, to stand to their arms. The town, the magazine, the hospital, and the prisoners, were committed to the care of Major M'Arthur with a small body of provincials and militia, and the weakest convalescents of the army: A part of the 63d regiment, who had been supplied with horses at Charles town, were expected to join this detachment in the night…for the security of Camden.*

*At ten o'clock the King's troops moved from their ground, and formed their order of march on the main road to Rugeley's mills: Lieutenant-colonel Webster commanded the front division of the army: He composed his advanced guard of twenty legion cavalry, and as many mounted infantry, supported by four companies of light infantry, and followed by the 23d and 33d regiments of foot. The center of the line of march was formed of Lord Rawdon's division, which consisted of the volunteers of Ireland, the legion infantry, Hamilton's corps, and Colonel Bryan's refugees: The two battalions of the 71st regiment, which composed the reserve, followed the second division. Four pieces of cannon marched with the divisions, and two with the reserve: A few waggons preceded the dragoons of the legion, who composed the rear guard.*

*About twelve o'clock the line of march was somewhat broken, in passing Saunders' creek, five miles from Camden. A short halt remedied this inconvenience, and the royal army proceeded in a compact state with most profound silence. A little after two the advanced guard of the British charged the head of the American column: The weight of the enemy's fire made the detachment of the legion give way after their officer was wounded, and occasioned the light infantry, the 23d and 33d regiments, to form across the road. Musketry continued on both sides near a quarter of an hour, when the two armies, finding themselves opposed to each other, as if actuated by the same present feelings and future intentions, ceased firing. On examining the guides, and the people of the country, Earl Cornwallis discovered that the ground the British army now occupied was remarkably favourable to abide the event of a general action against the superior numbers of the enemy: The fortunate situation of two swamps, which narrowed the position, so that the English army could not be outflanked, instantly determined the British general to halt the troops upon this ground, and order them to lie down to wait the approach of day: These commands were executed as soon as a few small pickets were placed in the front: A by-way, beyond the morass upon the left, which led to Camden, gave Earl Cornwallis for a short time some uneasiness, lest the enemy should pass his flank; but the vigilance of a small party in that quarter, and the recollection of the hazard incurred by such an attempt, soon dissipated his jealousy. Except a few occasional shots from the advanced sentries of each army, a silent expectation ushered in the morning.*

*At dawn the two commanders proceeded to make their respective arrangements for action…The legion cavalry remained in column, on account of the thickness of the woods, to the right of the main road, close to the first battalion of the 71st, with orders to act offensively against the enemy, or in defence of the British troops, as opportunity offered, or necessity required. The British, the provincials, and the militia of the royal army, officers and soldiers inclusive, amounted to something above two thousand men…*

*When the day broke, General Gates, not approving of the situation of Caswall's and Stevens' brigades, was proceeding to alter their position: The circumstance being observed by the British, was reported to Earl Cornwallis, who instantly, in person, commanded Webster's division to advance, and dispatched the same order, by an aid-de-camp, to Lord Rawdon on the left. The action became immediately general along the front, and was contested on the left and in the center with great firmness and bravery. General Gist preserved perfect order in his brigade, and, with his small arms and artillery, continued a heavy and well-directed fire upon the 33d regiment and the whole of the left division. The morning being hazy, the smoke hung over, and involved both armies in such a cloud, that it was difficult to see or estimate the destruction on either side. Notwithstanding the resistance, it was evident the British moved forwards: The light infantry and the 23d regiment being opposed only by militia, who were somewhat deranged by General Gates's intended alteration, first broke the enemy's front line, which advantage they judiciously followed, not by pursuing the fugitives, but by wheeling on the left flank of the continentals, who were abandoned by their militia. The contest was yet supported by the Maryland brigades and the Delawar regiment, when a part of the British cavalry, under Major Hanger,*[92] *was ordered to charge their flank, whilst Lieutenant-colonel Tarleton, with the remainder of his regiment, completed their confusion. Baron de Kalbe, on the right of the Americans, being still ignorant of the flight of their left wing and center, owing to the thickness of the air, made a vigorous charge with a regiment of continental infantry through the left division of the British, and when wounded and taken, would scarcely believe that General Gates was defeated.*

*After this last effort of the continentals, rout and slaughter ensued in every quarter. Brigadier-general Gist moved off with about one hundred continentals in a body, by wading through the swamp on the right of the American position, where the British cavalry could not follow; this was the only party that retreated in a compact state from the field of battle. The continentals, the state troops, and the militia, abandoned their arms, their colours, and their cannon, to seek protection in flight, or to obtain it from the clemency of the conquerors. As soon as the rout of the Americans became general, the legion dragoons advanced with great rapidity towards Rugeley's mills: On the road, General Rutherford, with many other officers and men, were made prisoners. The charge and pursuit having greatly dispersed the British, a halt was ordered on the south side of the creek, in order to collect a sufficient body to dislodge Colonel Armand and his corps, who, together with several officers, were employed in rallying the militia at that pass, and in sending off the American baggage. The quick junction of the scattered cavalry counteracted the designs of the enemy: Colonel Armand's dragoons and the militia displayed a good countenance, but were soon borne down by the rapid charge of the legion: The chase again commenced, and did not terminate till the Americans were dispersed, and fatigue overpowered the exertions of the British. In a pursuit of twenty-two miles, many prisoners of all ranks, twenty ammunition waggons, one hundred and fifty carriages, containing the baggage, stores, and camp equipage of the American army, fell into the hands of the victors.*

*In the action near Camden, the killed, wounded, and missing of the King's troops, amounted to three hundred and twenty-four, officers included. The destruction fell principally upon the center, owing to the well-directed fire of the continentals, and the execution done by the American artillery. The Americans lost seventy officers, two thousand men, (killed, wounded, and prisoners)…and all their…stores, ammunition, and baggage…*

*On reviewing the striking circumstances preceding and during the battle, the conduct of Earl Cornwallis cannot be placed in a clearer light than by contrasting it with that of his opponent. The faults committed by the American commander, during his short campaign at the head of the southern army, were neither unimportant in themselves, nor inconsiderable in number. The first misconception imputable to General Gates, was the not breaking in upon the British communications as soon as he arrived near Lynche's creek. The move up the creek, and from thence to Camden, was practicable and easy before the King's troops were concentered at that place; or he might, without the smallest difficulty, have occupied a strong position on Saunders' creek, five miles from Camden, before Earl Cornwallis joined the royal forces. His second error was moving an army, consisting of young corps and undisciplined militia, in the night: A manoeuvre always to be avoided with troops of that description, in the neighbourhood of an enterprising enemy; and only to be hazarded, when regiments are perfectly officered, and well trained. His third mistake was in the disposition of his army before the action: If the militia had been formed into one line, in front of the continentals, they would have galled the British in the wood, when approaching to attack the main body: Or, if the militia had been kept totally separate from the continentals, and too much confidence had not been placed in them, perhaps that confusion in part of the Maryland line, owing to the early flight of Caswall's brigade, had never happened. His last and greatest fault, was attempting to make an alteration in the disposition the instant the two armies were going to engage; which circumstance could not escape the notice of a vigilant enemy, who by a skilful and sudden attack threw the American left wing into a state of confusion, from which it never recovered. The favourable opportunities which presented themselves to Earl Cornwallis during the march and the action, were seized with judgement, and prosecuted with vigour; a glorious victory crowned the designs of the general, and the exertions of the troops.*

*Immediately after the action every possible assistance was given to the wounded of both parties: The loyal militia were ordered to explore the adjacent woods, and to collect the disabled: Waggons were afterwards assembled, in which they were placed with care, in order to follow the principal part of the British army, which fell back to its position at Camden. Lord Cornwallis, with the light and legion infantry, and the 23d regiment, moved forwards to Rugeley's mills, where he was joined in the afternoon by the legion cavalry, on their return from Hanging rock.*

North Carolina's former royal governor, Josiah Martin, was with the British army at Camden. He had gone to South Carolina expecting to be appointed governor of that province, but General Clinton decided to leave the colony under military rule. Cornwallis hoped that once the British invaded North Carolina, Martin's knowledge of the province and former ties to its inhabitants would help him to mobilize the Loyalists there. Martin described the battle and its importance to the British in an August 18 letter to Germain.[93]

*My Lord, it is with inexpressible satisfaction that I have the honour to offer to your lordship my sincerest congratulations on a victory gained over the rebel army by His Majesty's forces under the command of Earl Cornwallis on the 16th instant, of which I had the honour and happiness to be a spectator and which I am warranted to say was in all its circumstances as glorious, complete, and critical as has been obtained by the arms of Britain for ages. In one word, my lord, it could receive no additional splendour. Everything was achieved that was to be acquired by the general's magnanimity and conduct and the most intrepid bravery and vigour of troops: the enemy's army, of much more than three times our strength, being entirely routed after a very sharp action of three-quarters of an hour with the loss of fifteen hundred men killed, wounded and prisoners…*

*The state of our affairs in this country in the hour of this memorable action was as delicate and full of embarrassment and difficulty as can be imagined. From the time the rebel army assembled at Hillsborough early in June every device had been practised upon the adherents of the usurpation in this province to prepare them for a new revolt, and it appears they were found very generally prone to the enemy's purposes as they could wish; for by the latter end of July or sooner they were joining the rebel armies or arming against us more or less in all quarters of it, being unhappily too well fitted to receive impression from the rebel casuistry on the score of political obligations to us (I am sorry to say it) by the premature absolution of them, from the paroles they had given to Lord Cornwallis in his march through the country, by the proclamation of Sir H. Clinton of the 3rd of June which in their estimation emancipated and discharged them from the only engagement by which they were bound to His Majesty.*[94] *The dangerous operation and effect of this measure, conceived in that disposition of mistaken lenity which had theretofore been found so utterly abortive, if not prejudicial to our affairs, was so obvious that it was clearly seen by every man of the commonest reflection in this army and was accordingly lamented and I may truly add generally reprobated. It cannot be doubted at the same time that Sir Henry Clinton was influenced in this act by motives of generosity to which this people had no corresponding feelings. They felt, on the contrary, the spirit of rebellion enfranchised by this fresh instance of liberality that ought to have been a new bond of their attachment, and it accordingly diffused itself over the whole country. Two considerable bodies of militia under Generals Sumpter and Rutherfurd very soon menaced the cordon we had formed in our front from Savannah to Pedee River and which Sumpter afterwards attacked at the two points of Rocky Mount and Hanging Rock, failing in both attempts through the judicious and timely precautions of Lord Rawdon who commanded the army in the absence of Lord Cornwallis at Charleston, and with ability of which I cannot speak in too high terms of admiration.*

*While these corps were thus employed to amuse us, the main body of the enemy's army, masked by the North Carolina militia under Caswell,*[95] *crossed the Pedee about the 1st or 2nd instant, by their approach spreading such terror and dismay among the well affected as intimidated all the ordinary as well as extraordinary spies employed by Lord Rawdon to a degree so great that every channel of intelligence failed him, a circumstance I could have scarcely believed if I had not been witness to the fact, considering the number of our friends in North Carolina interested to hold us advised of the enemy's motions and Lord Rawdon's unremitting pains and assiduity in procuring information from all quarters through the whole course of his command, during the greatest part of which I lived with him honoured with his entire confidence and acquainted with all his measures.*

*The 71st regiment which had occupied the post at the Cheraw Hill for some time, becoming there very sickly, had been drawn back to the east branch of Lynches Creek by Lord Rawdon and very lately joined by the 33rd regiment. From this time intelligence was received there from day to day of the advance of a body of the enemy's militia under Caswell by very slow movements. The 7th instant, on receipt of some advice of the enemy's approach that was not entirely satisfactory, I accompanied Lord Rawdon to the post on Lynches Creek, where learning that Caswell with his militia corps was within thirteen miles of us his lordship determined to attack him that night or early in the morning. In a short space of time, while the necessary arrangements were making for this purpose, a man arrived from North Carolina who had been two days before in the enemy's camp and now gave us the first information of the movement of the main body of their army towards us under the command of General Gates and that he was then only 26 miles in our front, Caswell's corps of militia being advanced as we had heard before. Having obtained this certain intelligence of the enemy's motions and of their being in great force, it became necessary now to collect our little army…to cover our magazines at Camden and the communication by the Santee to Charleston as far as might be possible. In this design Lord Rawdon immediately put the army in march to fall back 12 miles and to take post behind the west branch of Lynches Creek, the Volunteers of Ireland who lay upon the communication to Camden on the east side of it having moved forward the same morning and joined the 33rd and 71st regiments. Orders were at the same time dispatched to the troops in post at Hanging Rock to fall back about 16 miles nearer to the village of Camden and to take a strong position parallel to us at Rugely's Mills on the road leading thence to Charlotte and Salisbury. The Welch Fusiliers[96] and cavalry from Camden, in consequence of orders, joined us early in the morning of the 8th on our new ground with three pieces of artillery. On the 9th, soon after daybreak, a party of the enemy's cavalry charged a small picquet of ours advanced beyond the creek and obliged it to retire, a cornet commanding it being made prisoner. On reconnoitring the ground in our rear this day Lord Rawdon found a much better position might be taken at the distance of 3 miles nearer Camden, and it was hoped by our movement to it the enemy might be tempted to cross the west branch of Lynches Creek to occupy the ground we then lay upon, in which case they would afford us opportunity to attack them with advantage. This move,* *however, did not induce Mr Gates to follow us. He took up his ground on the east side of the creek. On the $10^{th}$ in the morning he showed a very few of his cavalry and militia in our front who, after exchanging some shot with the sentries of our picquet, retired. We remained in the position we took in the evening of the $9^{th}$ behind the Beaver Dam Creek until 4 o'clock in the afternoon of the $12^{th}$, expecting from day to day the attack of the enemy, whose main body lay within 3 miles of us and their advanced picquets of mounted militia close to ours without an act of hostility. The troops at Rugely's Mills had been directed in the evening of the $11^{th}$ to fall back within 4 miles of Camden or to that place if the commanding officer there should think it necessary, Lord Rawdon having formed the design of falling back this day with the main body to ground about six miles distant from Camden. The moment before the army was to begin to march, the cavalry under the command of Lieut.-Colonel Tarleton, being ordered to scour the ground in our front, fell in with 2 deserters from the enemy coming into us who[se] intelligence was that their army had marched very early that morning to their right to the distance of 13 miles. This information naturally begot apprehensions in Lord Rawdon for Camden, and the army was accordingly instantly put in motion. His lordship, whom I had the honour to attend, hastened with all the cavalry towards that place in hopes to anticipate the enemy and to succour it if he should have turned to his left and taken that route. We arrived here between 7 and 8 o'clock in the evening and the infantry and artillery joined us about 12 at night, making everything secure for the present at this point, where we found the troops from Hanging Rock, the enemy according to our intelligence being at Rugely's Mill 12 miles distant from Camden. On the $13^{th}$ our accounts of the enemy during the day were various but it was ascertained that he was not the preceding day at Rugely's. Lord Rawdon with his usual promptitude and decision determined, as soon as Mr Gates should take any position within his reach in one day's march, to attack him, as a measure not only of military expediency and propriety but of indispensable necessity as Mr Gates, being left for any time at leisure to take his measures, from the number of his army and the disposition of the country in his favour, would find it easy to cut off our communications that must be fatal to us at a time we depended upon it for our daily subsistence, it having been yet impossible to form any magazine of provisions here.*

*Lord Rawdon having now greatly surmounted a scene as pregnant with difficulty and embarrassment as can be imagined (in which he had been involved during the greater part of his command and in the conduct of a very extended defensive plan with a very small army exceedingly reduced and daily diminishing by sickness) had at this period with unwearied diligence and attention, and firmness and address above all praise, wound up everything most opportunely and happily to the great point of decision. He had Lord Cornwallis's arrival in anxious expectation every moment, decided at the same time on the part he was to take in all events, possessing himself entirely, and inspiring every man with that confidence which he derived from the steady countenance of the troops.*

*On the 14th about 4 o'clock in the morning, Lord Cornwallis after a most expeditious and painful journey joined us here to the great joy of Lord Rawdon and the whole army. His lordship, whose mind and whose attention comprehends every object, was fully master of the crisis of our affairs and instantly discerned that an immediate meeting with the enemy could alone retrieve them. He made his preparations for it accordingly, the corps of light infantry from Ninety-Six joining him this morning in a very weak state.*

*Between 9 and 10 o'clock in the evening of the 15th his lordship moved from hence with his little gallant army towards the enemy who by his intelligence was now certainly at Rugely's Mills. About 2 o'clock in the morning of the 16th, our army being on the march in column, the advanced guard was fired upon and fell back on the 33rd regiment, which steadily supported it and returned the enemy's fire. The column halted, the army was formed with all expedition, the firing ceased. Two deserters from the enemy now informed Lord Cornwallis that their whole army had marched at 10 o'clock the night before with design to attack him at Camden, and was now formed in two lines in his front and very near him, being more than six thousand strong, after having detached a considerable corps under Sumpter with 2 pieces of cannon to cross the Wateree and pass down its west bank to cooperate with the main body in the meditated attack on Camden, and in the meantime to straiten it by interrupting our communications with the country. In this position the army lay till daybreak, at which time the enemy fired a gun that we could discern to be in the road nearly opposite the centre of our line and at the distance of about 400 yards. A thick fog impending and the dawn not yet fair, the enemy was discovered advancing in a heavy column and very near to the right of our line, on which Lord Cornwallis ordered with the utmost promptitude the necessary change of disposition and that the enemy should be instantly attacked in the point, which was executed in the moment with equal vigour and alacrity on the part of the troops who performed everything that can be expected of men and of soldiers.*

*As a spectator of the action merely, I am not entitled or qualified to give a detail of it. If I was, it would be unnecessary as your lordship will have it perfect from Lord Cornwallis. His presence, activity, and vigour everywhere during the whole course of it that animated the troops to invincible exertions, make him master of each circumstance attending it; and I shall therefore beg leave to refer your lordship for particulars to the better information of the noble general who greatly won this glorious day, which beyond doubt or comparison is in all its circumstances infinitely the most brilliant of the war. It is consequential to the nation, my lord, in proportion to the importance of America to Great Britain, for her cause and interest on this continent, depending as I conceive absolutely on the issue of this action, may be fairly said to be rescued, saved, and redeemed, and restored to promising condition by the magnanimity and conduct of Lord Cornwallis, which in one critical hour have dissipated a prospect more gloomy than I have yet seen through the whole course of the American war.*

# 3

# American Soldiers' Accounts

Lieutenant C.P. Bennett of the Delaware Continentals recorded his memories of the battle on January 1, 1843.[97]

> *By forced marches we arrived on Deep River, in North Carolina, where the Baron DeKalb was superseded…by Major-General Gates, who immediately on taking command, although the army at that time were not in a situation, from the extreme difficulty in obtaining supplies necessary for the present pursuit, ordered us to proceed on our route by forced marches…until our arrival at a striking distance of Camden, South Carolina, where the British army was concentrated. We encamped at Rugely's Mill, twelve miles from the British post. We remained in this situation but a day or two, to recruit and refresh the army after a long and fatiguing march, when orders were issued to parade at retreat beat,[98] and wait for further orders. It was understood and believed General Gates meant that evening to move in a direction for Camden, and attack the enemy by surprise in their quarters. Late in the evening our whole force moved in that direction…The advance of the two armies met on the high road, exchanged firing, and both parties fell back on their main bodies. During the night General Gates selected his ground and formed the line of battle, and waited for the coming day to meet the enemy in battle array. During the night, it was presumed, the British, with the aid of the disaffected of that country, being perfectly acquainted with the ground, took advantage to reconnoitre our position and the situation of our forces. At early dawn the enemy made a furious attack on our weakest position, where the militia were posted, being on the left of the front line. After the first fire they gave way and left the field, although they were commanded by officers of the Virginia line, who made every exertion to rally them, but all in vain; they left the field helter-skelter…The Continental troops…were left to sustain the heat of the battle, when and where they acquitted themselves like soldiers devoted to their country. Eventually they were put to the rout, after sustaining serious losses both of officers and men, killed,*

*wounded, and prisoners. Baron DeKalb, highly esteemed by the whole army, both from his gentlemanly deportment as well as the accomplished soldier, with many other valuable officers and men, shared the same fate.*

*Little Delaware felt that she had sustained her full proportion both in officers and men; two field and seven commissioned officers*[99] *were taken prisoners, and the regiment was reduced to two companies by killed, wounded, and prisoners. Our whole remaining forces were put into a complete rout, and were pursued for fifty miles from the field of action, when the enemy drew off…We continued the retreat to Hillsborough, North Carolina, two hundred miles from the battle-ground. On our route we collected together the scattered remains of our defeated army…By the time we arrived there we found ourselves in a most deplorable situation, without arms, ammunition, baggage, and little sustenance, and for some time our situation was unenviable.*

Captain Robert Kirkwood also served in the Delaware Continentals and entered a brief description of the battle in his journal on August 16, 1780.[100]

*About one in the morning met with the British Army at Black Swamp and Drove in their Advance Guards we then Halted and formed the line of battle…and Lay on our arms untill Break of Day when the British advanced and attacked our Left Flank where the Militia Lay, who gave way which gave the enemy's horse an opportunity to gain our Rear, their Infantry at the same time gaining our Flank, and their Line advancing in our front which Caused the Action to become very Desparate; which continued for the space of half an hour. In this Action Lt. Col. Vaughan, Major Patten,*[101] *six officers and Seventy Rank and file of our Regt. were taken Prisoners, with all the Cannon and Baggage of the Army—I can give no account of our Marches on the Retreat untill we came to Sallisbury which we arrived at on the 21st.*

William Seymour, a sergeant in the Delaware Regiment, also recorded his experience at Camden in his journal.[102]

*We encamped at Rugeley's mill on the 13th of August, which the Enemy had abandoned on our approach, and retreated into Campden. Here came and joined us a vast number of Militia, in number about 3000 men, from Virginia, North and South Carolina, which seemed to us to be a good omen of success, but proved to be our utter ruin in the end, for, placing too much confidence in them, they at length deceived us and left us in the lurch…*

*We lay on this ground till the 15th, at night, when the General thought proper to advance and attack the enemy at Campden…We marched off the ground at 8 o'clock at night, the baggage following close in the rear, so confident was the General,*

> *and indeed it was every one's opinion, that we should drive the enemy, we being far superior to them in numbers, we having three thousand militia and about thirteen hundred standing troops, and they not exceeding thirteen hundred here. You must observe that instead of rum we had a gill of molasses per man served out to us, which instead of enlivening our spirits, served to purge us as well as if we had taken jallap,*[103] *for the men, all the way as we went along, were every moment obliged to fall out of the Ranks to evacuate. The enemy having notice of our approach made a movement to meet us, and having met at Sutton's Tavern, about seven miles from Campden and six from Rugeley's mill, our advance guard and light infantry and that of the enemy meeting together, upon which ensued a very hot fire, in which the infantry and advance picquet suffered very much. Here we were drawn up in order of battle…The first fire commenced about two o'clock in the morning. We lay in this posture till daybreak, when the enemy…advanced and attacked us. We advanced at the same time, and began the attack from both cannon and small arms with great alacrity and uncommon bravery, making great havock among them, insomuch that the enemy gave way till, observing that our militia were in great confusion, they having retreated off, the chief part of them without so much as firing a single shot, and great numbers of them threw down their arms and run in to the enemy. This gave them an opportunity of coming round us…They were quite round us before discovered, upon which we were obliged to retreat and left the enemy entire masters of the field, the enemy's horse making great slaughter among our men as they retreated. As for Col. Armand's horse, they thought upon nothing else but plundering our waggons as they retreated off. This action continued about three-quarters of an hour, in which the brave General de Kalb was killed, with many more brave officers and soldiers…Here was a most shocking scene to behold, our poor scattered troops everywhere dispersed through the country, and the Tories, every day picking them up, taking everything from them which was of any value.*

After the war, Guilford Dudley of North Carolina wrote a lengthy memoir in which he described the night encounter between the two armies and the retreat after the battle in great detail.[104]

> *Finding S. Carolina overrun by the enemy…and the State of North Carolina menaced with instant invasion, I could no longer remain an idle (though much interested) spectator of these alarming events, but immediately turned out myself; and in a very few days collected a very fine company of 75 or 80 men…we unanimously determined to solicit Col. Samuel Lockhart, a continental officer then at home, to take the command, which he instantly consented to do…and putting himself at our head instantly marched with the view of joining Gen. Gates's army…this company was placed at the head of the light infantry corps of Gen. Gates's army, first placed*

*under the direction of Major Armstrong, a continental officer, and then under that of Col. Porterfield of the Virginia line, which corps, strange as it may seem, for more than a fortnight, while moving slowly on to Camden, was never within supporting distance, being often 6 or 8 miles in front, without being but once molested by the enemy, although we kept close upon his heels, moving as he moved…At length the light corps reached Rugeley's Mill…on the great Waxhaw road, the enemy moving slowly before us, and withdrawing post from this place retired into Camden. In the meantime Gates was advancing on another road more to our right and reached Rugeley's shortly after us, where he established his head-quarters for about four days, (until the Virginia militia under Stevens arrived,) pushing the light infantry corps, consisting at that time of only about 250 foot, four miles in his front, out of supporting distance again, should Tarleton recoil and strike at us, as he had it in his power to do with effect for four successive days.*

*At length the fatal night of the 15th August, 1780, arrived, when Gates, precisely at 10 o'clock, agreeably to general orders just issued, put his army in motion—the light troops moving simultaneously, joined…by 200 exhausted raw Virginia militia, and Col. Armand's corps of dragoons, consisting of about 60 privates, marching in order of battle after the following disposition: the foot divided into two bodies, moved by files through the open piney woods plain, 25 yards out of the great Waxhaw road; the right flank headed by Col. Porterfield…whilst Capt. Drew*[105] *with his Virginia regulars, (about 55, and mostly raw levies,) composed the leading company of that flank. The left flank of infantry, under the care of Major Armstrong, moved in like order, having the Halifax volunteers, headed by Capt. Lockhart, for his leading company. Col. Armand, with his dragoons in column, occupied the road which was here a dead level and very spacious. It became my duty by direction, to post myself on the right side of Colonel Porterfield, as he had on several occasions before, made use of me…to carry his orders…we slowly advanced, to give time to the main army to approximate us in the most profound silence; it being expressly stated in Gen. Gates's last orders, that any person speaking above his breath, should be instantly put to death on the spot where the violation occurred. Lord Cornwallis…by a singular coincidence, put his army in motion at the same hour in the night that Gates moved, to strike him in his camp at Clermont the next morning at break of day, while Gates's object was to move down upon Camden that night. The consequence of this simultaneous movement of both armies was, that we met about half way near Sutton's plantation between 12 and 1 o'clock in the night. The moon was at full and shone beautifully…Consequently, we could see to fight in the open piney wood plains…as well in the night as in the day. Tarleton, with his dragoons, (said to be 350,) with a suitable number of infantry, composed the British van. Armand's videt,*[106] *who rode about 300 yards in our front, descried the enemy advancing upon him, and at that instant emptied his pistol, and came clattering in with all the speed his horse could make. The discharge of the pistol was most distinctly heard through all the American corps. A pause ensued, when Col. Armand…discovered the British dragoons, put spurs to his horse, and at full speed dashed from the road to the front of our right flank of infantry; and leaning over his saddle, in an audible whisper said to Col. Porterfield, "there is the enemy, Sir—must I charge him." Porterfield, who was a serious man, of few words, and slow of speech, gravely replied in the tone of Armand, "by all means, Sir"…Armand, instantly wheeling his horse, rushed on to the head of his column… when Tarleton, sounding a charge, came on at the top of his speed, every officer and soldier with the yell of an Indian savage—at every leap their horses took, crying out, "charge, charge, charge," so that their own voices and the echoes resounded in every direction through the pine forest. Armand stood his ground and received the enemy's charge: the front sections of each party emptying their pistols before the dreadful clashing of sabres, which instantly succeeded. Col. Porterfield, now breaking silence, as soon as he heard the enemy's clamor, and saw their swift approach towards the front of Armand's column, with his usual composure and deliberate manner, ordered his right flank of infantry to "advance," which order was hastily executed in a step approaching to a trot, keeping our due distance from the road, and in a line parallel to it, when pretty well covering Tarleton's left flank, though we were far from seeing to its rear, by reason of the great length of his column. Porterfield ordered "halt, face to the road and fire." This order was executed with the velocity of a flash of lightning, spreading from right to left, and again the piney forest resounded with the thunder of our musketry; whilst the astonished British dragoons, looking only straight before them along the road, counting no doubt with certainty upon extirpating Armand's handful of cavalry, and not dreaming that they were flanked on the right and on the left by our infantry, within point-blank shot, drew up, wheeled their horses, and retreating with the utmost precipitation, were out of our reach before we could possibly ram down another cartridge. This firing, however, announced to the two commanding generals their certain proximity, unexpected as it was, and they both took their measures with promptitude accordingly…The shock and clangor of the charge of cavalry just mentioned, in the sight of raw, fatigued, and undisciplined militia, (except Drew's leading company on the right flank, and the Halifax volunteers, under Lockhart, on the left,) who had never before seen an enemy in arms…instantly fled and retreated to our main body, and Armand's dragoons did the same—a few of the leading sections in front, who fought near the person of their Colonel, excepted. Near the whole of his column, without waiting to ascertain the success of the front sections engaged with the enemy…shamefully abandoning their Colonel, and the few that fought about him, wheeled and retreated in inextricable confusion, carrying dismay and disorder into the ranks of the Maryland troops, composing the front division of*

*Gates's army, advanced, it seems, to within a mile of the ground where the light troops were engaged—such, I mean, as maintained their posts, who were indeed but few out of 450 who composed our front. Armand bravely maintained the onset at first against vastly superior numbers, was forced to save himself by flight with the loss of his horseman's cap, and followed his dispersed troops to the main body. What gave me infinite pain, at this critical juncture, was to see the left of Drew's company of regulars, with his subalterns, on whose firmness and prowess I had made sanguine calculations, fall back in much disorder upon the first meeting of the cavalry, and before we had fired a single musket. Watching the motions of our own troops, as well as those of the enemy…and seeing the shameful defection of this portion of our infantry…I turned my horse, and galloping down the line along the rear of those who stood firmly, and rushing among the confused men who had fallen back, with the authority of an officer who had a right to command, in a loud tone of voice, called to them to "halt, rally and form the line," without appearing to recognize any individual, or calling upon any name, although I knew them all, having served day and night with them from the time Col. Porterfield took the command of the light corps, until that moment. My command was instantly obeyed, and thus order was promptly restored…I hastened back and resumed my post by the side of the Colonel. Whilst these things were transacting on the right flank of infantry, the left, under Major Armstrong, were equally panic struck, by the charge of Tarleton's dragoons, and all fled, except the Halifax volunteers, under Captain Lockhart, who, taking their part with decision, poured in a heavy fire upon the British Colonel's right flank of cavalry, which must have done great execution, although we were never able to ascertain the enemy's loss, as we were shortly after compelled to yield the ground upon which we fought without entering the road at all. No sooner had Tarleton received one destructive fire on his right and on his left, and retreated out of our reach, than the British infantry, who were close at hand, advanced in column to the number, it was said, of about 500, but which, probably, did not exceed 350. Porterfield, holding up his fire until he saw his enemy between our two flanks of infantry, commenced his fire at close distance, which was answered by our left flank, under Capt. Lockhart, with equal spirit and deliberation. The enemy seemed for an instant to pause, but conscious of their superiority in numbers as well as discipline, facing to their right and left, returned upon us a heavy fire, which enveloped us from our right to left, in consequence of the recession of so large a number of troops in the commencement of the action, leaving us only 100 or less on both flanks to contend with the unbroken, undismayed column of the enemy; but soon the remains of our left flank, under Capt. Lockhart, receded also, and hastily falling back in an oblique direction from the road, formed on the extreme of the left wing of our army, now forming…The conflict on our right, where Porterfield in person commanded, became, therefore, more unequal and destructive;*

*yet Porterfield maintained his ground with great firmness and gallantry for about five rounds, with this handful of men, not more than 50 at this time. The enemy, without leaving the road and advancing upon us as he might have done, pushed his column along until he passed our left, when giving us a cross-fire from both his flanks, as well as from his centre directly in our front, he threatened instant extermination to our brave little band.*

*At length both sides being simultaneously prepared, poured in upon each other the heaviest fire that had been yet exchanged during the conflict. At this fire, Porterfield… received a horrid wound in his left leg, a little before the knee, which shattered it to pieces, when falling forward upon the pommel of his saddle, he directed Captain Drew, who was close by his side, to order a retreat, which was done in a very deliberate tone of voice by the Captain, and instantly our little band retreated obliquely from the road, which was wholly secluded from us by the enemy…Glancing my eye from left to right as the enemy poured his fire, I fixed it upon Porterfield at the instant he received the ball and….I dashed up to the Colonel, while Drew having given the order for retreat, was on his left side, in the act of wheeling his horse from the enemy, with the intent to carry him off. Locking my left arm in the Colonel's right to support him in the saddle on that side, and having completely turned his horse, we received another hot fire from the enemy directed solely upon us at the distance of thirty yards or less. Upon this the Colonel's horse…having no doubt been grazed by a ball which he sensibly felt, reared, plunged forward and dropt his rider on the spot, who had a severe fall in his maimed condition, and had liked to have dragged me off my horse with our arms locked, and the horse going off with his accoutrements at the top of his speed, followed the track of the retreating soldiers. At the very instant Porterfield's horse reared and plunged forward, Captain Drew fell prostrate on his face…I entertained no doubt but he was killed. The Captain, however, receiving no injury, and being an active, nimble little man, was presently on his feet, and…was in a moment out of sight. Thus left entirely alone with the Colonel, who was flat upon the ground with his head towards the enemy and his shattered leg doubled under him, entreating me not to leave him, I sprang from my horse and seizing him with an Indian hug around the waist, by a sudden effort jerked him up upon his well leg. Then again the Colonel, in the most pathetic manner, apparently dreading instant death, brave as he was, or captivity, entreated me, as he had done before, not to forsake him; the blood, in the meantime gushing out of his wound in a torrent as big as a large straw or goose-quill, which presently overflowed the top of his large, loose boot and dyed the ground all around him. Pale as a piece of bleached linen, and ready to faint with the loss of blood and the anguish of his wound, he made another appeal to my feelings in the manner above described, from an apprehension, as I then believed, that I would not have firmness enough to stand by him under the trying circumstances I had then to encounter, knowing also that this was the first of my battles…when I replied the second time, as I had in the first instance, with much earnestness and energy, "that I would carry him off or perish with him." Upon this assurance, twice repeated, the Colonel became tranquillized and seemed patiently to wait his doom, which he expected would be nothing less than instant death or captivity…While we stood thus in front of the enemy…we received another fire from a platoon of the enemy just in our front, whilst the rest of their line seemed to have slackened theirs, and in no wise annoyed us. Still clasping Colonel Porterfield in my arms and supporting him upon his well leg, his back to the enemy, my face and right shoulder above his left, looking intently at the enemy to see if a file or section would leave the road and advance upon us with charged bayonets, I made three violent essays to throw him upon my horse, which was tall, and thus endeavor to carry him off. My efforts were perfectly fruitless. I was then young and light, and Colonel Porterfield was a man of the largest size, perhaps 6 feet and an inch or two in height, round limbed and fleshy, but not corpulent, although he weighed perhaps 210 pounds and was about 30 or 32 years of age…In this dilemma I ceased to make any further efforts to throw him upon my horse and resolved calmly to wait the result whatever it might be, nor did Porterfield attempt to give me any direction in this emergency…but appeared to be entirely resigned to whatever fate might await him in his exhausted and fainting condition. Still holding up the Colonel upon his well leg…casting a wishful and exploring eye on every side and in the rear, to see if no friendly assistance could be obtained, however improbable, (for all was silence; not a living soul to be seen but the enemy in the road, occasionally giving us a scattering but ineffectual fire.) I was at last so fortunate as to fix my eyes upon two men at the distance of about 150 yards in my rear, running back with great speed, half bent and with trailed arms, towards where they supposed the main body, under Gates, was by this time halted. Although I could not at the moment divine where these men came from, I…recognized them for American troops by their garb, their manner and by their clumsy wooden canteens slung over their shoulders upon their blankets and knapsacks, all which I could plainly discover by the brilliant light of the moon…Believing this providential discovery would be the last resource I should be favored with to save Porterfield and myself, I was determined to avail myself of it if possible at every risk, and therefore…with great eagerness I called out to them, "come here, come here"…they instantly turned their heads in the direction where Porterfield and myself stood, though without slackening their pace, and kept on with rather increased speed…Seeing them no ways disposed to come at my call to our assistance, and knowing that we should be lost without it, I resolved to make one desperate effort to draw them to us before they should get out of my sight or hearing. I therefore in a very loud tone of voice and with much energy, regardless of the immediate proximity of the enemy, cried out, "by G-d, come and help me away with Colonel Porterfield." This name…operated on the feelings of these two honest young soldiers like magic, and they instantly wheeled and came running to us with all their speed, no longer half bent to conceal themselves among the wire-grass, but with erect countenance and a determined air. No sooner had they reached us…than they seized Porterfield by both his arms and around his body to sustain him in the position they found him in upon coming up. Then I sprang into my saddle and ordered them to lift him up carefully over the stern of my horse and place him close to the hind tree of my saddle, (the Colonel instantly clinging to me with both arms around my waist,) and then directing them to resume their muskets with one hand and each with the other to sustain him in his seat across the loins of the horse, taking care to steady his shattered leg so as to keep it from swinging about under the flanks of the horse, and to prevent his falling off behind. All these instructions were obeyed with an alacrity and cheerfulness that instantly won my affections and confidence; and thus fixed, with the reins of the bridle in my own hand, I moved slowly off in a direction perpendicular to the road, not daring to oblique to my right or march parallel to the road to gain our main body, lest I should be intercepted by the enemy, who had pushed the front sections or files of their light infantry along up the Waxhaw road, for some distance beyond the spot where we had fought, and gave us all in a group as we were, a scattering, parting fire, with no more effect than if it had been made with little boy's pop-guns…*

*…thus fixed, with the Colonel clinging around my waist, we marched very slowly off to save him all the pain we possibly could in his melancholy situation. We had, however, scarcely progressed more than 30 or 40 yards before he fainted with loss of blood and the anguish of his wound, and was very nearly falling off backwards over the stern of my horse, but was sustained in his seat by my two faithful companions. We were then compelled to halt, although still in sight of the enemy, to give the Colonel time to breathe a little, I ordering the soldiers to dash some water they fortunately had in their awkward wooden canteens in his face… we moved quietly off again, but had scarcely proceeded more than 40 yards further when he fainted the second time, but was soon revived by the use of the same means as were first applied. He then, in the most pathetic and moving accents, entreated me to lay him down and let him abide his fate, whatever it might prove; but this I refused, and exhorted him with all the energy and force of reasoning that I was master of, to bear his miserable situation a little longer and he should be safe, telling him that the enemy was yet still in view, although he did not pursue at that moment; yet in all probability, nay, to a certainty, his discomfited cavalry would, in a few minutes, return and scour the whole plain in our front, rear and all around us, when we should all be inevitably lost. Yielding to these arguments, the Colonel became passive, and then directing my companions to hold him fast in his present seat, (finding there was great danger of his falling off as he became more exhausted,) I sprang from my saddle upon the ground and joining with them, directed them to assist me to lift the Colonel over the hind-tree into the seat of the saddle that I had just left, and then springing up myself behind him and clasping my arms around his*

*waist, I directed one of the men to take the reins of the bridle and guide the horse himself, as I could no longer do it in my changed position...and thus we moved on the third time as before. But unfortunately, although the Colonel's new position was more safe and easy than before, yet, nevertheless, growing more weak and exhausted every moment, he presently fainted the third and then the fourth time, while I pressed him around the body with both my arms and sustained him in his seat without his saying another word...But in both these last cases he revived by the free use of the contents of the wooden canteens, which contained nothing but warm, dead water, only drinkable from necessity. Most fortunately, at the last instance of his fainting, we were emerging into a little thicket of small persimmon bushes, about waist high... And directing the soldier who had the bridle-rein in his hand and was guiding the horse to halt, I slipped off from behind Porterfield and requested him to tear off a bandage from one side of his blanket its whole length, whilst I should, pulling out my pocket knife for the purpose, cut a bundle of twigs 10 or 12 inches in length and hastily trim them to apply all around the Colonel's leg before the bandage was wrapped over them. This request was also instantly complied with, and the bundle of pliant twigs being expeditiously prepared with the assistance of this soldier, whilst the other held Porterfield fast in the saddle, I very soon bound up his leg in many folds of the strip of blanket as tight as I could draw it, which almost entirely stanched the blood, and then resuming my seat behind him we soon moved on again for the last time, steering our course as before, due West as near as possible. This surgical-like operation was of infinite advantage to Porterfield, who no more fainted or complained. And thus we moved on without any further interruption or delay, perhaps a mile and a half from the road where we fought, when we were stopped by one of those large, flat, impassable morasses, that so frequently occur in the pine plains of South Carolina, extending an unknown distance from North to South and nearly parallel to the road we had recently left. Here, of necessity, we were obliged to halt, and fortunately striking the margin of the morass, where grew a large laurel sapling with its dark green and glossy leaves just in the edge of the marsh, with a wide spreading bushy top which cast a deep shade upon the ground eastward, I determined to lay the exhausted Colonel down, and stretching him at full length in the shade of the laurel with his leg and thigh bolstered up with my great-coat which was fastened to the pommel of my saddle, and taking time to tie my horse to a limb of the same laurel with his fore feet in the water and mud to conceal him as much as possible in the dark shade of the sapling, as well as Porterfield and myself, resolving to remain alone by Porterfield's side, I sent off my two faithful companions...The order I gave them was, upon finding the army, to bring up two or three surgeons and as many men as would afford a relief or two to bear off the Colonel on a litter. No sooner did I deliver this request, than these two willing, generous soldiers...departed almost in a run to execute the order just received, upon the speedy execution of which depended the life of the Colonel as well as my own. Porterfield was lying in the shade of the laurel on the edge of the morass with his feet towards Camden. I laid my unsheathed sabre and pistols on the ground by his side and within a few feet of my horse. It now being two hours before day-break, I laid myself down along-side of the Colonel, feeling weary after fatiguing marches in the hot season.*

*July, but especially for the last seventeen or eighteen days after the volunteers were placed in the light infantry corps, where, in the midst of starvation, we spent sleepless nights, and consumed the long days of July and August in fatiguing marches over scorching bald sand hills and burning piney wood plains, often without a drop of water to slake our thirst or cool our parched lips and tongues; never remaining in one position ten minutes at a time, often only five, but were continually shifting our ground from one undulation of the plain, and from one copse of black-jack shrubs to another, to be safe from surprise, or the charge of British dragoons, always to be expected and easily effected by their overwhelming superiority, while we had literally none; Armand's dragoons never acting with us, and the few militia light-horse from the upper country of North Carolina sticking close to Major General Caswell's division, which, as well as the continental troops, was always out of supporting distance. Thus prostrate on the earth…a painful silence ensued, which however, was sometimes interrupted first, by our own light-horse in full gallop sweeping along the plain within thirty or forty yards of the spot where we lay close to the ground in the shade of the laurel, and then bearing to their left further off the morass into the plain 'till we lost sight of them and then the British dragoons, who were all in motion, coming in the other direction and scampering over the plain, sometimes at a considerable distance…patrolling in every direction. On these occasions, Porterfield, in a feeble voice, would make some remarks as well as myself, but finding from the direction they took as I reported it to him, (for he never raised his head,) that they would not be upon us, he sank again into a state of silence and apathy. At last a large patrol of British dragoons came from the South in the direction of Camden, and in a brisk gallop came on pressing close in upon the margin of the swamp, coming apparently, directly upon us, when, as before, I was aroused first by the trampling of their horses and then by a full view of them, after raising myself up upon my left elbow, at the distance of thirty or forty yards, when seizing my pistols, I hastily cocked one and was about to stand upright, but Porterfield, who now expected we should be discovered and consequently lost, feebly stretched out his right arm and laying his hand on mine, entreated that I would not fire, alleging that if I did they would cut us to pieces without mercy; for being in a desperate situation, and feeling no inclination to fall into their hand and trust to the clemency of British dragoons, I had resolved to sell my life as dear as possible, and after emptying both my pistols, to resume my sabre and defend myself to the last extremity as long as possible, announcing, however, at the same time, the name of Porterfield and asking quarter for him, and then with my arms in hand, leaving my horse behind, plunge into the morass and scramble over as well as I could, knowing that further pursuit was impracticable…but fortunately, the same kind Providence who had so wonderfully protected and shielded us during the various past scenes of the night after Porterfield was wounded, did not forsake us now; for almost in the same instant that I descried them, they bore away to their right and I presently lost sight of them among the lofty pine trees of the forest. This was the last patrol that made its appearance on either side, and as soon as we felt safe from further search, we sank down in our sleepless repose. In fifteen or twenty minutes after this last occurrence, as the Colonel and myself were lying in profound silence and the day beginning to break, we heard most distinctly the report of a cannon, fired in the direction of Camden, which echoed through the plains at the distance of six miles, when asking the Colonel the meaning of it, he informed me in a feeble voice, that it was their morning gun…This was not only a morning gun fired to awaken the garrison, but was also designed, as I believed to serve as a signal for Lord Cornwallis to put his army in motion and prepare for the battle just at hand, both armies having formed in the night and lain on their arms within two hundred and fifty yards of each other. Just at this crisis, at break of day, my two faithful companions returned, bringing with them three or four surgeons…together with Capt. Drew, Lieut. Vaughn, Ensign V___, and eight privates of Drew's company, and several more, who, hearing of Porterfield's situation and the place where he lay, followed after them. The surgeons immediately fell to work upon the Colonel, but did nothing more than to take off my bandage and twig splinters and put on their own boards and bandages, whilst the rest of us were busily engaged in cutting down small pine saplings of which to form a litter to carry him off. These things were speedily accomplished, the Colonel was carefully placed on the litter, which was…placed on the shoulders of four men, when the procession began to move off in solemn silence. The dawn of day then appearing, I stepped back a few paces and putting up my arms and mounting my horse, accompanied them thirty or forty yards in the direction they were going, when suddenly the stillness of the dawn was startled by one of our parks of artillery, which at once served as a signal for battle and as a guide to direct me to the spot where our army was formed, of which I was before, as well as Colonel Porterfield, entirely ignorant…Upon this firing, the meaning of which I was at no loss to understand, I wheeled my horse and riding back a few paces to the side of the litter, took an affectionate farewell of Colonel Porterfield, telling him at the same time, that I hoped to join him again in the course of an hour or two, which was in sincerity my expectation, so sanguine were my hopes of immediate victory, notwithstanding the disasters of the past night. Vain hope! I never more set my eyes on Porterfield, for here we parted—I steering my course to the army by the roar of our cannon, and the rest of the company, with the surgeons, falling back northwardly and shaping their course in a direction where they hoped to find some plantation at which to leave the Colonel with the necessary attendants, until the battle should be over.*

*Putting spurs to my worn-down horse, I hastened on alone towards where the firing of our cannon commenced, which was kept up with great spirit while Lord Cornwallis was advancing upon Gates, whose army being already formed, awaited the onset. The enemy coming up within musket shot, the most tremendous firing I have ever heard, ensued, accompanied by the continued roar of cannon. Urging my horse on, I presently reached the right wing of our army, composed of the regular troops of Maryland and Delaware, when, passing on in the rear of these lines through a shower of balls that whizzed incessantly around me, I eagerly bent my course down the line without meeting any one except a few wounded that were falling back to make their escape from the dire conflict, in search of my own company or some of Armand's dragoons, with whom to fall in. And passing Dixon's regiment of North Carolina militia, posted on the left of our regular troops, who maintained their ground with great firmness and gallantry, at one time driving the enemy opposed to them in front out of line, I presently, with horror and surprise, saw the whole of our left wing falling back in confusion and dismay, throwing away their arms and all accoutrements, in order to run the swifter; our park in the road, under the direction of Captain Singleton of the Virginia artillery, silenced and in possession of the enemy, the Captain wounded in the breast and the mattrosses[107] either killed, wounded or dispersed. In vain I looked for my own company, for it had been posted in the night, after the repulse of our light infantry, on the extreme point of our left wing beyond the Virginia militia, under Brigadier Stevens. Seeing all was lost in this quarter, and recognizing at a little distance several gentlemen belonging to Major General Caswell's suite, with whom I was personally acquainted. I hastened up to them while they were engaged in the vain attempt to stop the torrent of flying militia, and eagerly enquired for General Gates, whom I supposed to be somewhere on the ground; the answer was, "he's gone." "Gone where?" I rejoined. "He has fled and by this time is past Rugeley's mill." "And where is General Caswell?" "He is gone, too," was the reply; for Gates had posted himself about the centre of the army near the reserve under General Smallwood. Seeing how matters were going on our left, the hero of Saratoga being panic-struck, rode up hastily to Major General Caswell, who was near him, and in much agitation observed to him, "Sir, this is no place for us," and without waiting for a reply, wheeled his horse and putting spurs to him, dashed up the Waxhaws road at full speed and was instantly lost sight of. Caswell, however, remained on the ground for several minutes longer, but at last followed the inglorious example of his commander and fled, while Dixon's regiment, a part of his division, was yet bravely sustaining the unequal conflict.*

*About the time Gates left the ground, Smallwood's reserve, which was posted about the road, was brought up, and taking post on Dixon's left, which before was wholly uncovered, after the recession of so large a body of the militia, the contest was renewed with redoubled vigor, the continentals on the right of Dixon led on by the brave De Kalb, having under him Brigadiers Gist and Smallwood, never yielding an inch of ground, but on the contrary, often driving the enemy out of line, and at one time had Lord Rawdon, who commanded Cornwallis' left wing a prisoner. But Lord Cornwallis, who had posted himself about the centre of his army, vigilantly watching every movement of his enemy, and finding that three fourths of Gates's army had abandoned the field, ordered Lieutenant Colonel Webster, who commanded his right wing…to wheel and strike at Smallwood's uncovered flank and Dixon's regiment, still standing firm and concentrating his army, knowing the great advantage he then possessed over his enemy, made a decisive charge upon our remaining troops and drove first Smallwood's reserve and Dixon's regiment out of line, and the noble De Kalb, covered with wounds and glory, falling about this time, the remnant of our right wing, about 300, also gave way and betook themselves to the woods and swamps, led by Major Anderson, of the Maryland line, a brave and valuable officer, whose grade was of the highest then left on the field of battle. In the mean time…I had joined myself to Caswell's numerous suite…uniting our efforts to rally the militia, I hastened up to some squadrons of Armand's dragoons, whom I observed in detached parties without their Colonel or any other commissioned officer that I could distinguish, scattered over the plain in front of our flying troops, and dashing in among them, entreated their assistance to stop the fugitives, even if they had to cut them down with their sabres. Yielding for a few moments their reluctant services, we had actually stopped an hundred and fifty or more, and made them face about in line, before I discovered that there was not a single musket in the hand of either of them…Not only the road but the whole plain to the East, as far as our line had extended, was covered with the flying troops, some of whom were bearing towards the road, while others kept straight forward through the pine plain and over the sand hills, to gain the Cheraw road on their right. By this time Tarleton…was ordered to pursue with his dragoons. Here, indeed, was a fine field already opened for the hero to satiate his revenge and thirst for blood, for he had nothing more to do than to sound the charge, spread out his squadrons in single file from left to right, and rush upon the defenceless, unarmed militia, and hack them down with the sabre without the smallest risque to his own troops, and he accordingly availed himself of the glorious opportunity, nothing more being necessary than to overtake the fugitives, which was easily done with their fresh and pampered horses, and to bleed freely. It would have been stubborn temerity to have remained any longer on or about the field of action; and Armand's scattered squadrons without a leader having also left us, the gentlemen of Gen. Caswell's family before mentioned, together with myself, after remaining behind too long for own safety, took the road with our wearied and almost broken down horses, in order to gain Rugeley's mill, about six miles in our front, and although the chances of our all getting safe there were much against us, especially if we clung to the road, we willingly ran all the risques in the hope, nay, in the almost certain expectation of finding Generals Gates and Caswell there, collecting the scattered troops—regulars as well as militia—and that a stand would be made. Vain hope! Vain expectation! Although I possessed the best horse in the army, yet mine was at that time in the worst condition of any in the company, and accordingly, they all left me to take care of themselves, whilst I, at the very outset, was two or three times in the most imminent danger of falling into the hands of the enemy, and nothing saved me then but the crowds of soldiers a little in my rear, who literally choked up the road and its margins, who were, of necessity, to be disposed of before the enemy could come at me…but Tarleton's cavalry having cleared the road of these unfortunate men by hacking, killing or dispersing them to the right and left…I was pushing on by dint of the free use of the spur; but finding I should invariably be overtaken if I kept the road…and fortunately coming to an extended grove of no great width of black jack, stretching along the right side of the road, amidst white and scorching sand, I reined my horse over on that side and falling behind the grove, which was impervious to horse and almost to man, described almost the segment of a circle before I attempted to strike the road again, knowing that the unhappy group before me consisting, perhaps of 150 to 200, would be soon overtaken by the enemy, and that the carnage which would ensue would necessarily delay him until I could get the start of them all again by some two or three hundred yards. This manoever succeeded very well; for as soon as I had regained the road in their front, my ears were saluted with the savage yells and shouts of the enemy and the lamentable heart-rending cries and screams of their unfortunate victims. They spared none at this stage of their butchery that they could possibly reach, nor lost a moment in capturing and giving quarter to any individual. Here, then self-defence, imperious law of nature, compelled me to struggle to get on, and regardless of the straggling soldiers which lined the road in my front, who had out-run their companions, some singly, others in squad of two or three without arms, and all aiming for Rugeley's mill. These I readily passed and meeting with no other obstruction I soon reached the top of the long hill on the South side of the mill…As all was silent around me and in my rear, I presumed to hope that the enemy had slackened his pursuit…when the straggling soldiers I had just passed, being now condensed and fast approaching the summit of the hill, I suddenly heard a repetition of the same yells and shouts, cries and screams before described…and applying the spur again to my horse's side descended the hill with all the speed the poor but willing animal could perform. In descending the hill, I intermixed with a number of soldiers, rapidly flying without a gun, except in one solitary instance, which I will mention presently; and when about half way down met with Colonel Thomas Blount, the Adjutant General and my particular acquaintance. Locking horses with him just as we descried the British dragoons descending from the summit of the hill gaining fast on us, we made a violent push to gain the bridge over the large and deep canal which formed the race of the mill situated on our right and crossing the road to the West ran through Rugeley's large plantation, (Clermont,) and emptied itself into the Wateree. Now it became doubtful whether we should not be overtaken before we reached the bridge, and consequently our retreat cut off, having a large mill-pond on the right and a high staked and ridered fence on the left. Very providentially, however, as we were in the act of passing a little, active, resolute man, by the name of Durham, from Warren county, N.C., just alluded to, who had preserved all his arms and accoutrements, about one troop of dragoons pressing upon us and within killing distance, we hastily requested him to wheel and give the fellows a fire. He instantly obeyed, and facing about with great spirit gave them a blazing fire in the lump with a cartridge composed of a large ball and seven buck shot, which certainly, if it did not kill, most likely wounded some horses and dragoons, for they instantly hauled up, filed to their left out of the road and formed in line under the high fence on that side and began to sound the bugle to collect, as we supposed, their scattered squadrons…And thus Blount and myself on horse-back and perhaps more than a hundred on foot, gained the bridge without further interruption and safely passed over…*

*After we crossed the bridge, looking forward eighty or an hundred yards, we discovered half a dozen baggage wagons close by the side of the road, with horses unhitched, notwithstanding the confusion all around, and several of Armand's dragoons plundering them of their valuable contents, for they bore the baggage of many of the Maryland officers, who came from the North well provided with clothing, camp-stores, and even specie,*[108] *(though a scarce commodity.) Their trunks were broken up and rifled; their Holland gin cases ripped open and the case-bottles profusely handed about and eagerly seized and emptied by the thirsty soldiers, whilst casting our eyes over Rugeley's large gate by the road side, along the avenue leading up to his house, we discovered the rest of the baggage wagons, perhaps two hundred in all, just filing off and coming out to save themselves by retreat, when the enemy was actually upon them; likewise the grass-guards, who had the care of all the beeves belonging to the army, (fresh beef, and that a scanty allowance, our only food,) just then driving their cattle from the large pastures of Clermont to the road, although it must have been then near 8 o'clock in the morning; so wretchedly were matters conducted in that unfortunate campaign. But here I must do General Gates the justice to say, that the loss of our baggage and wagons was not solely attributable to him, for I well remember in his last orders he expressly directed that the baggage should be forthwith marched off to the Waxhaw Settlement, under the direction of the proper officer, most probably the Quarter-Master General…Hastily passing these few wagons by the road-side, indignantly viewing this scene of rapine and plunder by our own soldiers, and recollecting the halted troop of Tarleton's dragoons a little in our rear…I hastened on to save myself, but soon lost my friend and companion in distress, Colonel Blount, whose horse was better able at this critical juncture to carry his rider off than mine…*

*Passing the few wagons by the road side…I pushed on with the stragglers and soon overhauled several others that were ahead with camp-women, upon the top of the baggage, of which useful commodity it was said the Maryland line contained four hundred. The waggoners, having taken the alarm from the flying troops, drove on at full speed, and now and then coming in contact with a stump overset, when away went the camp-women, dashed twelve or fifteen feet, and some of them with new-born infants in their arms, a sight lamentable to view. The baggage was also strewed about. The alarm increasing rapidly, from this flight of so many fugitives overtaking them, reporting that the enemy was close behind, the wagoners made no attempt to restore the order of things, but hastily cutting out, or throwing off the gear from their saddle horses, betook themselves to flight, leaving most of their horses for the next man that passed to do likewise, 'till the whole were borne off. Before I was out of sight of the wagons near Rugeley's gate, looking round to see how near the enemy was approaching, I saw these last in rapid motion; the wagoners in them throwing off the cover, and then strewing the baggage marquees, tents, trunks, boxes and every thing else in the road, in order to lighten their carriage, and in full speed drove on, until a new alarm added to the panic already operating upon their minds, compelled them also to halt, cut out their saddle horses, and away in their best speed, leaving the rest for the next footman that passed, and thus, the horses…were soon all carried away…I was constantly overtaking other wagons…they, too, were throwing the contents of their wagons all along the road, and thus it continued for many miles up the Waxhaws road, and it was literally strewed with baggage, so that a man might almost walk upon it without touching the ground. Happily, at last passing all these, with numbers on foot in my front, and continually overtaken by officers of every grade, some militia, but mostly continental, many of whom were wounded were the latest in leaving the field of battle, we all hastened on as circumstances would allow towards the Hanging Rock, eighteen miles from the field of battle…we were in the act of passing over a large flat surface of stone…when hearing behind us the sound of a horse's feet, coming over the flat surface of the rock at a-speed above any thing we could raise, I turned my eyes around to see who or what it might be, when I recognized Colonel Senf, a Saxon officer and chief engineer to the army, whom I had seen but once before, with his drawn sword flourishing in the air from right to left… and rebuking or chiding the troops as he passed, evidently doing his utmost to get away himself. He presently came along side of me, and flourishing his drawn sword at me in a menacing manner, sternly demanded, "what are you doing here!" and "why are you not behind with your troops!" I was far from being in the pleasantest humor. Mortified and chagrined to the last degree, I made him no reply as he passed me, but gave him a side-long look full in the face, which at once spoke my feelings and my contempt of his menacing manner, when the Colonel, too much engaged about his own preservation to parley or renew his threats, passed on in the same manner: he came up, digging his spurs into his exhausted horse's sides, and was presently out of sight of us all. Yet Colonel Senf was a brave man and an experienced engineer, and at any other time, and upon a more pleasing occasion, I should have exhibited towards him marks of the most cordial respect…He, no doubt, from my dress and equipage, took me for one of Armand's troopers…*

*I hastened on in company with a Maryland officer, who joined me hereabouts, and whose tired, broken down horse was incapable of outstripping mine, we agreed to keep together, and being left behind by all of our associates in distress, we moved slowly up the Waxhaw road, though frequently overtaken by others, who also passed us, when, after a tedious retreat for some few miles, both of us wholly unacquainted with that part of the country, we at last reached a small, unfrequented road on our right, called the Rocky River Road…We then agreed to dismount and drive our worn down horses on before us; the great crowds of discomfited troops of every description who had preceded us, as well as those about us then, and such as came up immediately after, while we were in view, keeping up the great road to the Waxhaw Settlement. Moving slowly on upon this unbeaten track, to favor our exhausted horses as much as possible, we presently arrived at a small bridle-way, which turned off to the left, that indicated we were near some plantation, where we might possibly procure some sort of refreshment for ourselves, if only water and peaches, and some grass for our starved horses. Taking this path by mutual consent, we soon arrived…at a neat but deserted plantation, with an elegant crop of corn growing on it, (already made,) with grass knee high in abundance; and…an excellent peach-orchard close at hand in full bearing, and the fruit in perfection. Driving our horses in through the yard-gate, and stopping them at the threshold of the house-door, which was shut up, no living creature to be seen, except a few poultry about the yard, we instantly had our horses in the fields…and it was delightful to see them mowing down the luxuriant grass; then putting some peaches into our pockets, we retired to the step of the dwelling house door and began our delicious repast…keeping a watchful look down the lane towards Camden…for we did not think ourselves entirely safe here from enemy, although 25 or 30 miles from the field of battle. But this precarious enjoyment, the evil genius of the day indulged us in only for a few moments; for glancing my eyes down the lane to the brush-wood that choked up its entrance at the distance of 250 yards…I descried a cluster of men on either side of the path peeping through the bushes at the mouth of the lane, which effectually screened themselves and their horses from our view, except their hats and hands down to the shoulders, peering at us with prying looks and timid caution…and pointing out to my companion he exclaimed, "the enemy, the enemy." Knowing that if it proved so, we should be lost with all belonging to us for there was no possibility of making a timely retreat, so completely were we hemmed in by fences on every side except along the lane, the mouth of which was already occupied by the supposed enemy…I resolved to make a merit of necessity, and snatching up my sword and pistols, which lay by me, dashed out of the yard gate with the determination forthwith to advance upon them, in order at once in remove all suspense as to the character of the persons so peering at us through the bushes, whilst my companion ran…to gather up our horses. Advancing along the lane with hasty strides towards our supposed enemy, closely watching their motions…my determination was, in case they showed themselves and charged upon me, to empty both pistols and then springing over the lane fence to evade them if possible among the high corn and grass…I at last got so near to them as to be recognized by Colonel Henry Dixon, who, with his large cocked hat, which was all I could see of him, rushed out, and in a broad laugh hailed me, asking, "is that you?" for the Colonel and myself had been long acquainted, though in the course of this campaign we had seen each other but seldom…I cordially invited the Colonel, with his company, to partake of our peaches; to unsaddle their horses, and for a few moments let them bite the luxuriant grass. Taking time to gather a handful or two of peaches and reentering the yard, Colonel Dixon suddenly paused and exclaimed, "gentlemen, we have no time to tarry here, saddle horses and let's be off." Prostrating a couple of fences, we dashed into the high corn, steering for the woods on the back of the plantation and keeping our course in that direction, through high brush and timbered land, presently reached a neat little cottage, the owner of which, a young married man, with one child, happened to be at home. Colonel Dixon, who wanted a guide, hailed him, and upon his coming up, asked him if he "had heard the news!"*

*"No-Sir, what news!"*

*"Gates is totally defeated."*

*The man looked wild; for he, as well as ourselves, was surrounded by tories, very few of whom, however, were at home, but were with the enemy, or lying out, in consequence of Gates's large army being in front and giving present security to the whigs, though only a short-lived one, the owner of the plantation we had just left being a tory. Colonel Dixon next informed the young man that we wanted a guide, and asked if he would undertake that office, to which he promptly assented, saying, "if that be the case," (alluding to the defeat of our army,) "I can no longer remain here," when, hastily stepping a few paces to the stable where he happened to have a horse up, quickly withdrew him, and hardly taking time to bid his wife and child adieu, was ready to conduct us whithersoever directed. After a moment's consultation about the course we should pursue, as most likely to afford security in our retreat, it was agreed to file off to our right and regain, as quick as possible, the aforesaid Rocky River Road, lying about a mile in our front. Striking this road upon the top of a small eminence, Dixon and our guide leading the way, the Colonel…discovered a small patrol of five or six British dragoons, whom he pointed out to the rest of us, riding forward in apparent ease and security, without at all discovering us in the rear. Upon this, Dixon proposed that we should instantly charge upon them, as they were but few and we were eleven armed men, though there was not a gun of any description in our company. This proposition was eagerly closed with, and we were saddled, upon the point of rushing upon our enemy, when some of the company providentially cast their eyes to the rear and at the distance of 250 or 300 yards discovered another party of dragoons, consisting of about a troop, slowly advancing upon us as if they too had not discovered us, for the road was here narrow and the woods very brushy. Thus placed between two fires, Col. Dixon desired that we should take to the woods and save ourselves, and leading the way himself with the guide, dashed to the left and we soon lost sight of the enemy, who, in all probability, did not pursue at all. But here again my unlucky genius recurred…and all my companions in disaster, the Maryland officer included, soon outstripped my horse, now totally exhausted, except two Virginia militia from Henry county, Va., who came up with Colonel Dixon to the plantation first mentioned. These were mounted upon two sorry tackies which they had picked up in their flight, and were as incapable of keeping up with the rest of the company as mine. And being frightened to the last degree, and without military arms of any kind, confessing themselves utterly lost in the woods…entreated that they might be permitted to accompany me. This was a favor my courtesy would not permit me to refuse, and all dismounting we drove our tired horses through the woods before us, not daring to aim towards the Rocky River Road any more, but steered a course forming an angle with it of 50 or 60 degrees, without any path or small neighborhood road to travel on, crossing the very few of those that occurred and avoiding every plantation we saw, the inhabitants of this country being not a few and generally disaffected. At length, after a tedious day's march on foot, through woods and around plantations…we struck a road 20 or 30 minutes after sunset, unknown to us, but supposed to be a branch of the one leading through the Waxhaw Settlement…Here we immediately came to a fine large farm with good buildings, and as soon as my two Henry county men saw a prospect of obtaining some comfortable cheer at this place, they entreated me to go in and ask for some milk and bread, alleging that they were nearly famished, not having tasted food for almost 30 hours. I could not refuse so reasonable a request, although, I neither felt hunger nor thirst myself, and therefore entered the dwelling house without delay, where I found a motherly looking lady employed in spinning flax, and asking for her husband was told that he had left home in the morning and had not yet returned. I then asked her if she had heard any news that day: to which she answered in the negative. Of course I informed her that General Gates was totally defeated and his army utterly destroyed, and the troops dispersed in every direction. Looking at me wistfully for a few seconds in utter astonishment and dismay, unconsciously dropping her flax thread and suspending the movements of her foot upon the treadle of the wheel, she exclaimed in much agony, "then we shall be burned up to-night and my husband killed." Giving this good lady time to calm the agitation of her mind, I made my request to her in favor of my two companions for something to eat. She arose, observing that she had nothing ready but some cold bread, milk and butter, the very articles that those men had so much desired: when stepping to a dairy she brought forth a large pan of milk, a pound or two of butter on a plate and plenty of cold bread, and spreading them before these two stout voracious men, inviting me to partake also, which I declined, they fell to work…and liked to have swept off the whole of the plentiful lading on the table. In the meantime I was conversing with the good lady about the disasters of the day and preceding night, and asked her if she thought we would be safe there, or in some out-house for the night, adding that our horses were even worse off than ourselves and that I wanted to procure some forage for them. To this she replied, "Oh no sir, you will not be safe any where upon this plantation, the tories will be all over it this night and perhaps burn up every house we possess." But with much forethought and apparent concern for us and our horses, she added, pointing to a large double barn near us, "In that house there is plenty of sheaf-oats, take as much as you can all carry, pass on through the lane some little distance and turn to your left through thick woods some 40 or 50 rods[109] and you will be safe for the night"…*

*Having reached our night quarters, we tied our horses securely to some bushes… and laid ourselves down to rest on the naked ground, without a great coat, blanket, or any other covering…When I arrived at the little village of Charlotte, I found it filled with soldiers and officers of every grade, both continental and militia, among the latter, Major General Caswell: among the former, at that time, was Colonel Otho Holland Williams, the Adjutant General, perhaps as valuable an officer as belonged to our discomfited army, who seemed to be at their head, for as yet Generals Smallwood and Gist had not arrived and the brave Baron de Kalb was killed. Among others I found a number of gentlemen, my own particular friends and acquaintances…These, with one accord as soon as they heard of my arrival, (for they were dispersed about town,) came to my quarters to shake hands and congratulate me on my good fortune.*

A native of South Carolina, William Gipson served with the North Carolina militia in the battle of Camden. Gipson recalled his experience there when he applied for a veteran's pension in 1832. His account helps to explain why the militia performed so poorly.[110]

*The two armies came near each other at Sutton's about twelve or one o'clock in the night…The pickets fired several rounds before day. I well remember everything that occurred the next morning:…I was among the nearest to the enemy…we had orders to wait for the word to commence firing; that the militia were in front and in a feeble condition at that time. They were fatigued. The weather was warm excessively. They had been fed a short time previously on molasses entirely. I can state on oath that I believe my gun was the first gun fired, notwithstanding the orders, for we were close to the enemy, who appeared to maneuver in contempt of us, and I fired without thinking except that I might prevent the man opposite from killing me. The discharge and loud roar soon became general from one end of the lines to the other. Amongst other things, I confess I was amongst the first that fled. The cause of that I cannot tell, except that everyone I saw was about to do the same. It was instantaneous. There was no effort to rally, no encouragement to fight. Officers and men joined in the flight. I threw away my gun, and, reflecting I might be punished for being found without arms, I picked up a drum, which gave forth such sounds when touched by the twigs I cast it away. When we had gone, we heard the roar of guns still, but we knew not why. Had we known, we might have returned. It was that portion of the army commanded by de Kalb fighting still…General Dickson*[111] *was wounded in the neck and a great many killed and wounded even on the first firing.*

Several Virginia militiamen also explained their flight in a petition to their state's legislature dated November 9, 1780.[112]

*Your petitioners were the first militiamen of this state who were ever ordered into service at such a distance as South Carolina. That on our arrival at Hillsborough we staid but a few days to rest before we marched to the south, from which time (except a few days halt that we made at Deep River) we were marched almost night and day and kept on half allowance of flour for eight or ten days before the battle. That from these circumstances, and being wholly unacquainted with military discipline, which we had not had time to learn; greatly exhausted by fatigue at that hot season, which we has not been inured to; dispirited for want of Rest and Diet; and Panic-Struck by the Noise and Terror of a Battle which was entirely New to most of us; We (amongst others, officers and privates) were so unhappy as to abandon the Field of Battle.*

Michael Awalt of the North Carolina militia had little to say about Camden in his 1832 pension application, but remembered a dispute that took place between his superiors before the battle began.[113]

*He…was in the battle called Gates' Defeat. He overheard Generals Gates and Smallwood arguing about the battle plans.*

Captain William Armstrong of North Carolina was one of the few militiamen who stood and fought while his comrades fled. He described an unusual change in the militia's organization made just prior to the battle.[114]

> *The rendezvous of the troops was near Charlotte, and his company was placed in the Regiment commanded by Colonel Alexander*[115] *and Gen. Rutherford commanded the Brigade, and Wm Rankin was Lieutenant of that company. From Charlotte we marched down the Yadkin river and there across Black river to Rugley's Mill (a tory) and there encamped for the night, but about 12 at night, the line of march was again formed and we proceeded towards Camden—that same night the advanced guard had skirmishing with the enemy guards. That we joined the main army during the night and at dawn of day, the battle of Camden commenced. That Rutherford's brigade and perhaps others were divided into platoons before the battle began and the Captains had command of their platoons instead of their companies; and that this applicant commanded a platoon on that memorable day, instead of his company. He states that he fought during the whole of the battle and knows he done his duty. The battle lasted but a short time, yet long enough to defeat Gen. Gates, who according to general opinion, acted dastardly on that occasion.*

Another North Carolina militiaman, Dan Alexander, was on his way to reinforce the army when the battle took place. In his 1836 pension application, he recalled seeing Gates after the general had left the field.[116]

> *In getting as far as Gaston which is near the South Carolina line we met the American Army retreating. Gen Gates and Maj. Davie had some conversation, we advanced some distance when in meeting some French officer*[117] *flying we also joined in the retreat. Gen Gates had on a pale blue coat with epauletts and velvet breeches, riding a bay horse. We retreated as far as Charlotte very much fatigued and worn down.*

4

# British Soldiers' Accounts

Several lower-ranking British officers wrote to friends in New York of their experiences at Camden. The recipients often made the letters available to printer James Rivington, who published them in his newspaper. Since these officers were not well known, their names were not given. This "Extract of a letter from an officer of Lord Rawdon's regiment" was dated August 19.[118]

> *I never saw a regiment behave with more courage than ours shewed on the 16th; but it is with greater satisfaction that I add my testimony of the remarkable discipline and order preserved by them throughout that very severe action. We have lost about 90 men killed and wounded. Poor Whitley is mortally wounded, Gillespie dangerously in the throat, and Thompson through the body, but likely to do well.*[119] *The behaviour of the officers universally was admirable. Flyn*[120] *carried the standard, and did it full justice. The enemy left above 800 dead on the spot, and about 1200 were made prisoners, including wounded…and we have reason to believe, that out of eight continental battalions, not above fifty men escaped. General De Kalb, who was made prisoner, is dead; General Gregory, of North-Carolina, was killed, and General Rutherford is prisoner, with a good mark in his cheek from a Legionary sabre. In short, it is an army annihilated.*

The following "Extract of a letter from an Officer of the Volunteers of Ireland" was written on August 25.[121]

> *I cannot help mentioning our glorious commanding officer Lord Rawdon, his conduct, coolness, and intrepidity do him immortal honour, he charged the rebels at the head of his regiment, and drove them, they rallied, and recharged us, the right of their column is supposed to have consisted of eight hundred men, they pushed for our standard which was in the center, and I must say without vanity was most nobly defended, their presumption they paid dear for, our men seeing the efforts at their*

*national badge fought like lions, overturned every thing that opposed them, and put the rebels to a total route, in which they were most dreadfully cut up.*

A North Carolina Loyalist probably wrote this "Extract of a letter from an officer, dated at Camp, Camden, August 21, 1780," since the writer mentioned several of that state's Rebel militiamen by name.[122]

*You'll no doubt...be surprized to hear of a large Rebel army having again assembled under the command of Gates and De Kalb in order to Burgoynade us they...made us withdraw our out posts, and attacked us at a place called Hanging Rock, but were repulsed. Mr. Gates being much elated at our retreat from Cheraw Hill, followed us close up to Lynch's creek, where we offered him battle, but he declined it, in order to be more in force, and to make Mr. Gates more confident and secure, we fell back with all our troops to this place the 11th instant at night, and waited with impatience for his advance and the arrival of Lord Cornwallis, until the 14th, when my Lord arrived; every thing was prepared for an attack on Mr. Gates's camp and the plan laid. On the 15th, at nine at night, the army marched from this place in order to attack Mr. Gates...in all some what under two thousand men, leaving a detachment from each regiment in garrison. We had only four field pieces; marching about seven miles we fell in with their advanced party, when a very heavy fire ensued, and we drove them. We then formed the line of battle and lay on our arms until day light, when we formed the column again, and marched on about a mile, then formed the line of battle, which was scarce done until the attack began, which continued for some time very severe, but they were repulsed on all sides with great loss, leaving their cannon, &c. We killed, wounded, and took about 2000 men....Never was there a more compleat victory, nor did British valour and courage ever shine more brilliant than on this occasion. Every officer and soldier was determined to conquer or die.*

*...Mr. Gates and Caswell with several other Generals, made their escapes; a General Gregory was killed, and a number of Colonels, Majors, &c. A great many of the Halifax folks[123] were here, but most of them made out to run off except Geddy, Samuel Lockhart, and Meacoms...Thus, my Dear Sir, in the course of five days, have we, with TWO THOUSAND men, killed, wounded, taken, and dispersed an army of at least 3000 men, with all their cannon, stores, baggage, waggons, &c. &c. Our loss in both actions don't exceed 250 killed and wounded. We had only four officers killed and wounded, among the latter your humble servant in the arm, with a grape shot; it's in a fair way of getting well, and I hope soon to be able to do duty.*

An officer in the light infantry was the author of this undated "Extract of a letter from an officer present in the two victories over Gates and Sumpter."[124]

*I had not the least conception of being able to furnish you with an account of such unparalelled success, as has attended us within these few days.—We arrived here Aug. 14th with our little battalion, in five days from Ninety-Six, one hundred miles across the country; the consternation we found our little army in here, distressed us much. General Gates with a force of 7000 men, sprung from the earth, like a multitude of toads from heavy rains, had driven in our outposts, and had taken post within fifteen miles of Camden. Lord Cornwallis fortunately arrived from town the same evening; immediately collected his scattered troops, and formed a plan of attack. From the curst unhealthiness of this climate, and the very extensive posts we were obliged to keep, for the preservation of the province, our army was reduced to about 1700 fighting men, including provincials, who equal any troops existing when properly officered, and who in my opinion will greatly contribute to settle the hash at last. From the many circular letters Mr. Gates had spread thro' the province,*[125] *and his apparent success, with the very numerous appearance of his army, the people had formed a plan of revolting to a man, upon his surrounding us at Camden: This he most assuredly would have accomplished in less than twenty four hours had he been let alone, for in less than forty eight hours, the militia in great numbers would have been in arms against us, had seized our magazines, cut off our convoys which were upon the road, and totally blasted our future hopes.—In this very critical situation our provision amounted to one days indian meal,*[126] *and two days fresh beef; and to add to our pleasing prospect, we had the mortification to see the rebels in possession of the ferry on the opposite side, with two field pieces; 100 continentals, and 700 militia, under Brigadier General Sumpter, which in a great measure cut off our retreat or communication with the town; in this state, our little army undauntedly marched the 15th at nine o'clock at night; at one, about six miles from town we fell in with the van of the rebel army, which it seems had moved forward at the same hour, the van of both formed immediately within thirty yards, and attacked, but our fire being so much superior, and so well directed, obliged them to move off with a quick step, leaving about thirty dead on the field.—The army immediately formed, and remained in that position until near day-break, when we formed our line of march, and proceeded for near three quarters of a mile; we discovered the main body of their army endeavouring to gain our right and left flanks, which from their numbers they were very equal to. We formed again within 80 yards of them, and at this short distance we were manoeuvring fourteen minutes without exchanging a shot, and repeated attempts were made on both sides to out-general each other; this I think surpassed everything that I ever yet beheld; the two armies struggling to out-do each other in military operation. I assure you it was a little farcical to see us drawn up against 7000 men, who appeared formidable; I had not an idea of surviving an instant after their first volley; but our little body regardless of their numbers, and with their usual bravery and undauntedness, gave a screech, that made the woods and vallies re-echo, and dashed with their bayonnets into the center of them, as lions and tygers do at their prey. The miscreants not accustomed to this method of fighting, fled before us; we wheeled to the left, and gained the rear of the rebels right, which was engaging our left with great advantage, on account of the superiority of cannon and numbers, but at our near approach, they broke and fled in the utmost confusion.—Our horse, formed in the rear, instantly dashed out, and dealt havock and destruction amongst them; pursued them twenty miles…and the road was strewed with waggons, arms, baggage, and stores of every kind.*

Sergeant Roger Lamb of the Twenty-third Regiment, the Royal Welsh Fusiliers, described his experiences at Camden in his postwar memoirs. In an ironic twist, Lamb had been taken prisoner by Gates's troops at Saratoga, escaped and made his way back to British lines. At Camden he found himself facing Gates once again and he drew particular satisfaction from his part in the defeat of his old nemesis.[127]

*As the American army approached to South Carolina, our army, which then consisted of seventeen hundred infantry, and two hundred cavalry was concentrated at Camden. The army with which Gates advanced, was by the arrival of the militia, increased nearly to six thousand men. On the night of the 15th we marched from Camden, intending to attack the Americans in camp at Rugeley's Mills. In the same night Gates put his army in motion, with an intention of surprising our camp, or posting himself on an eligible position near Camden. Our army was ordered to march at ten o'clock P.M. The American army was ordered to march at the same hour. The advance guard of both armies met about two o'clock in the morning. Some of the American cavalry, being wounded in the first fire fell back on others, who recoiled so suddenly, that the first Maryland regiment was broken, and the whole line of their army thrown into confusion. The enemy soon rallied and both they and we kept our ground, and a few shots only from the advanced centries of each army were fired during the night. A colonel Patterfield,[128] on whose abilities general Gates particularly depended, was wounded in the early part of this skirmish[.] As soon as day light appeared, we saw at a few yards distance our enemy drawn up in very good order in three lines…*

*It happened that the ground on which both armies stood, was narrowed by swamps on the right and left, so that the Americans could not avail themselves of their superior numbers in out flanking us. We immediately began the attack with great vigor, and in a few minutes the action became general along the whole line; there was a dead calm with a little haziness in the air, which prevented the smoke from rising; this occasioned such thick darkness, that it was difficult to see the effect of the fire on either sides. Our army either kept up a constant fire, or made use of their bayonets as opportunity offered. After an obstinate resistance for some time*

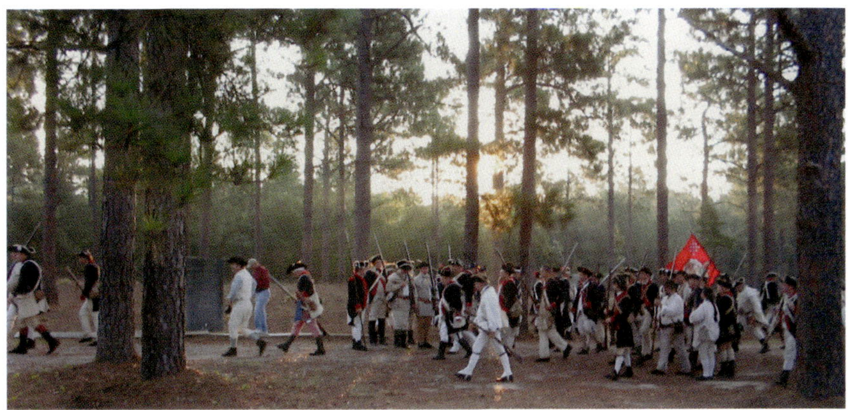

1. American troops form line of battle. *Courtesy of Partisan Pictures and Historic Camden Revolutionary War Park.*

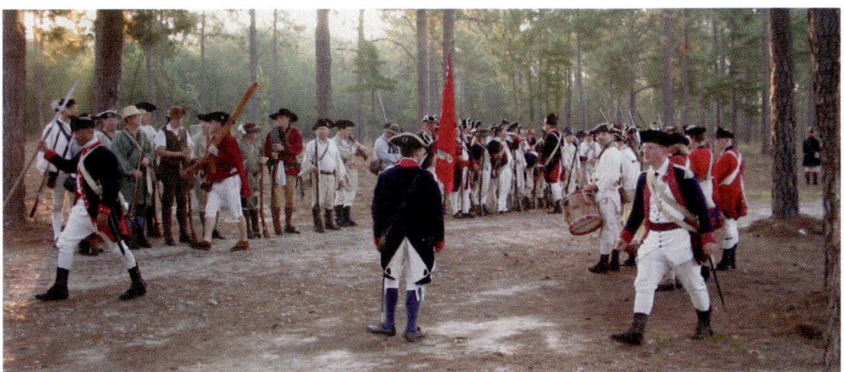

2. Another view of the Americans preparing to meet the enemy. *Courtesy of Partisan Pictures and Historic Camden Revolutionary War Park.*

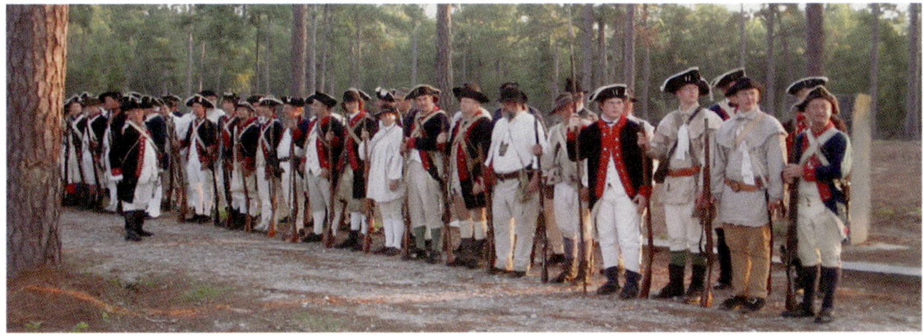

3. The Americans in line of battle. *Courtesy of Partisan Pictures and Historic Camden Revolutionary War Park.*

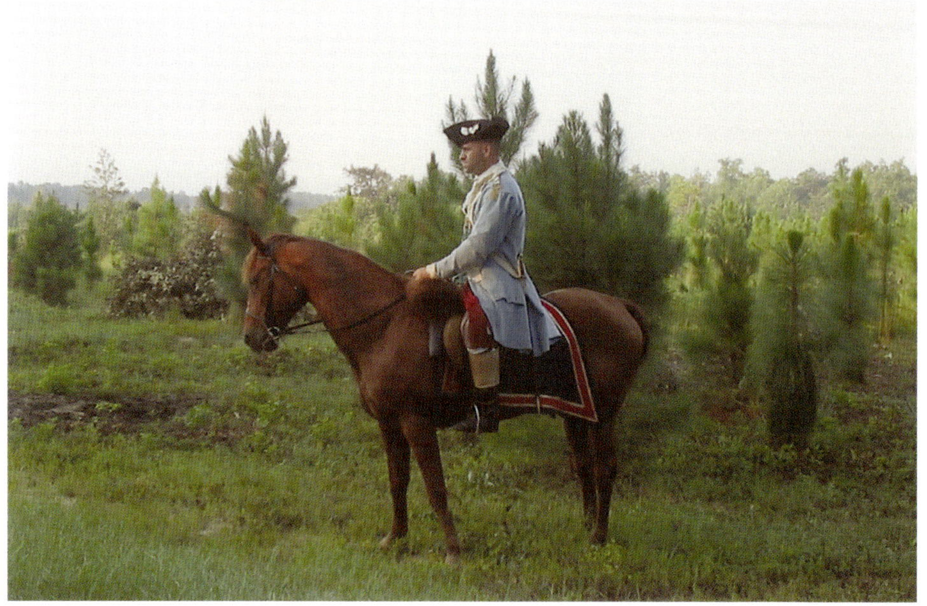

4. An American officer overseeing his men. *Courtesy of Partisan Pictures and Historic Camden Revolutionary War Park.*

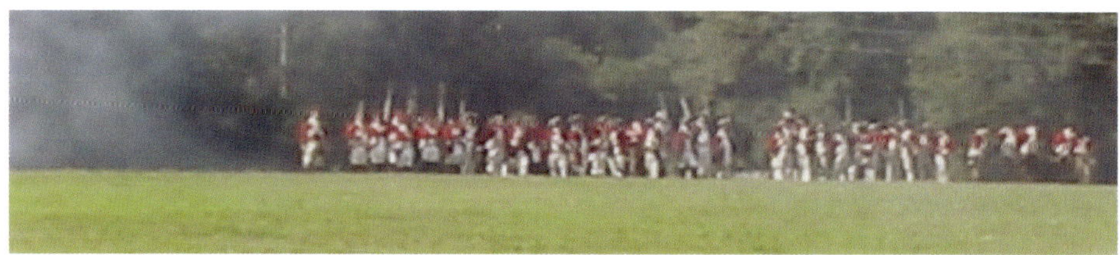

5. The British in line of battle. *Courtesy of Partisan Pictures and Historic Camden Revolutionary War Park.*

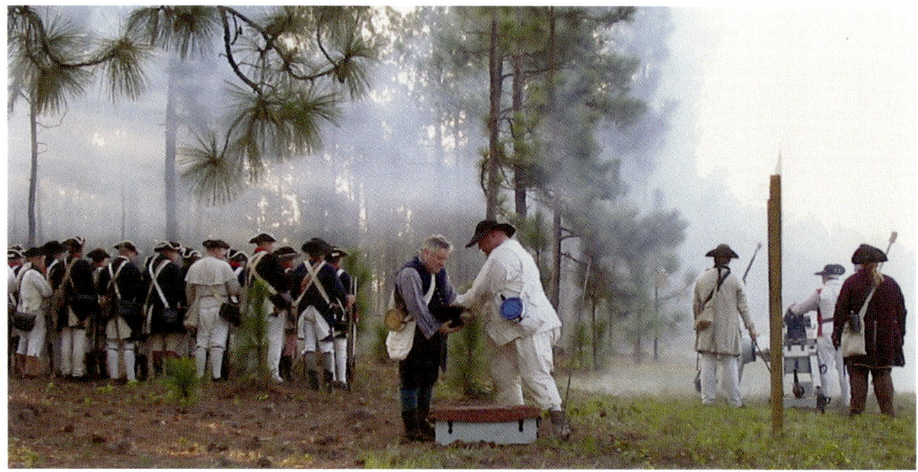

6. American artillery prepares to open fire. *Courtesy of Partisan Pictures and Historic Camden Revolutionary War Park.*

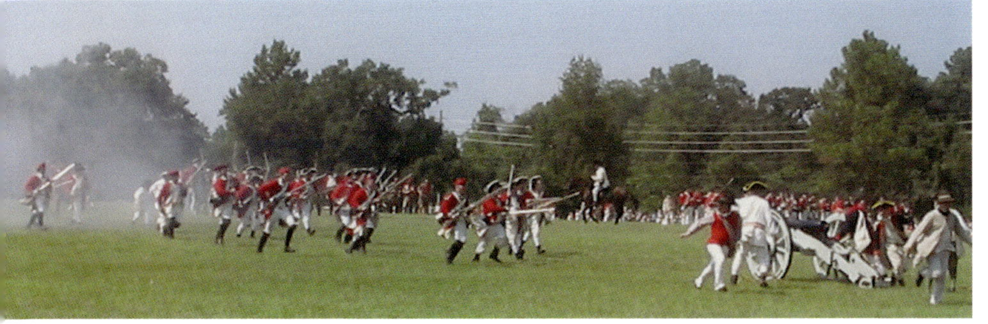

. British troops charge the American artillery. *Courtesy of Partisan Pictures and Historic Camden Revolutionary War Park.*

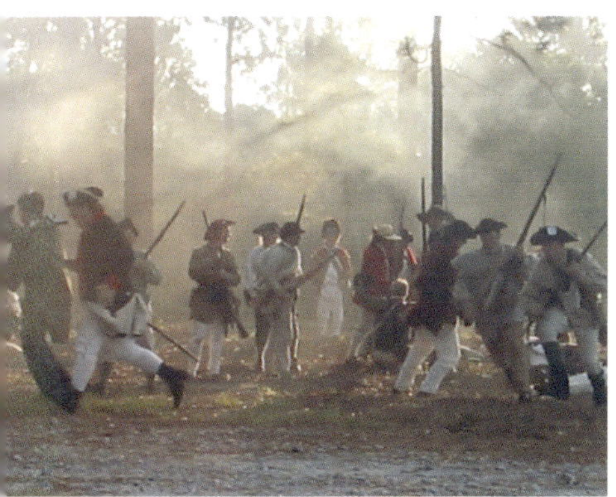

. American militia flee before the advancing British. *Courtesy of Partisan Pictures and Historic Camden Revolutionary War Park.*

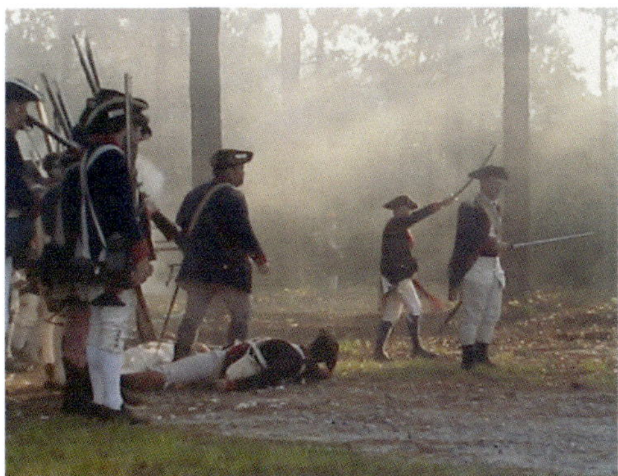

9. The American right wing under De Kalb advances against the British. *Courtesy of Partisan Pictures and Historic Camden Revolutionary War Park.*

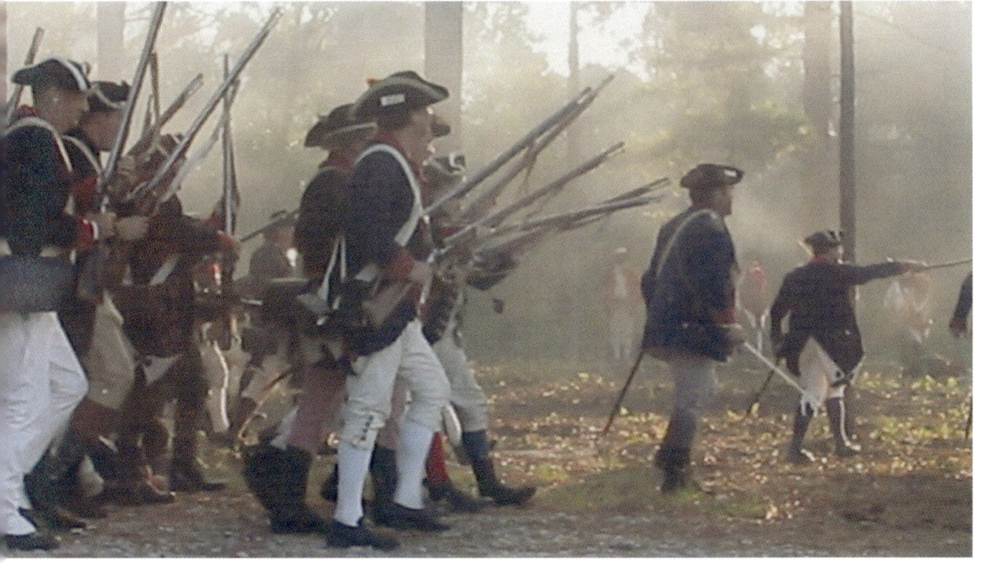

0. Another view of De Kalb's counterattack. *Courtesy of Partisan Pictures and Historic Camden Revolutionary War Park.*

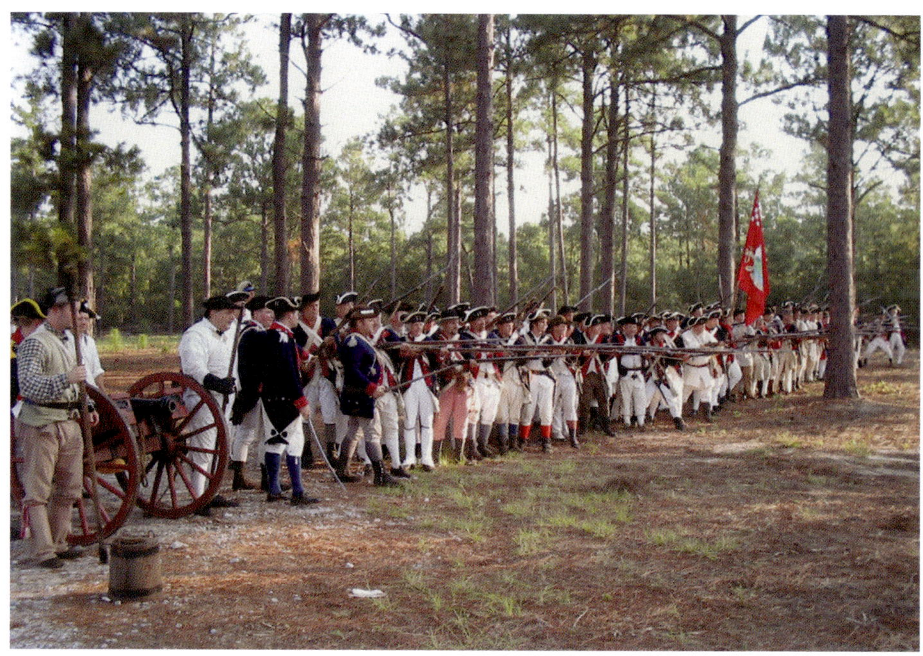

11. The Continentals move forward with fixed bayonets. *Courtesy of Partisan Pictures and Historic Camden Revolutionary War Park.*

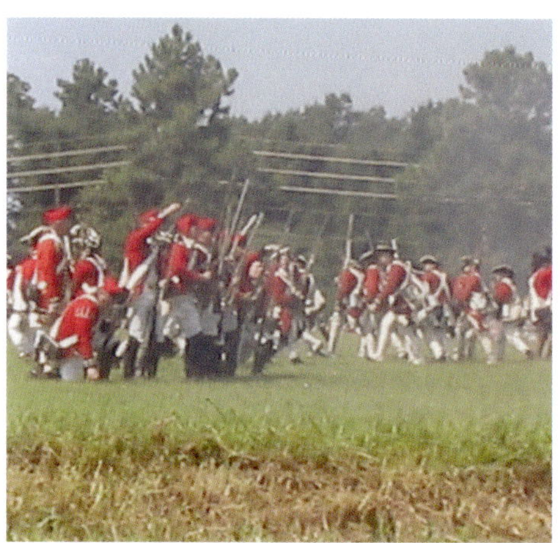

12. The British left falls back before the American charge. *Courtesy of Partisan Pictures and Historic Camden Revolutionary War Park.*

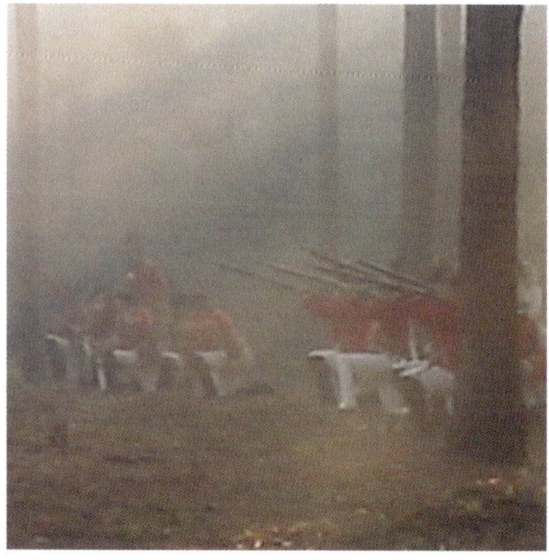

13. After dispersing the militia, troops on the British right attack the Continentals. *Courtesy of Partisan Pictures and Historic Camden Revolutionary War Park.*

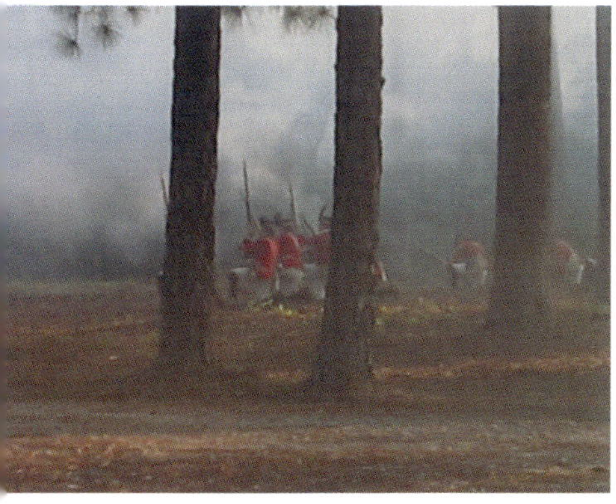

4. British troops fire at the Continentals. *ourtesy of Partisan Pictures and Historic Camden Revolutionary War Park.*

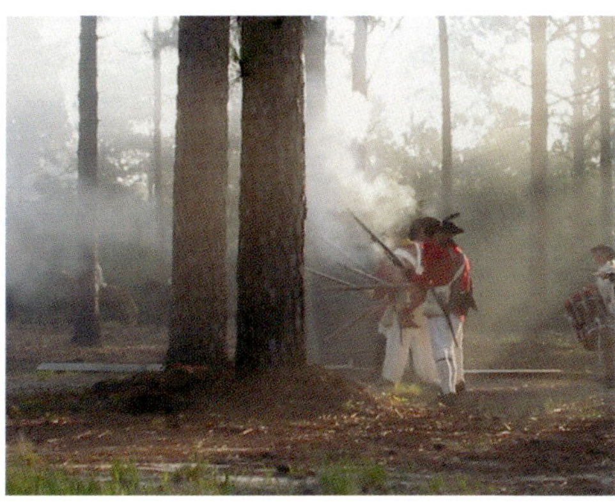

15. British musket volleys were intended to soften up the enemy so they would be vulnerable to a bayonet charge. *Courtesy of Partisan Pictures and Historic Camden Revolutionary War Park.*

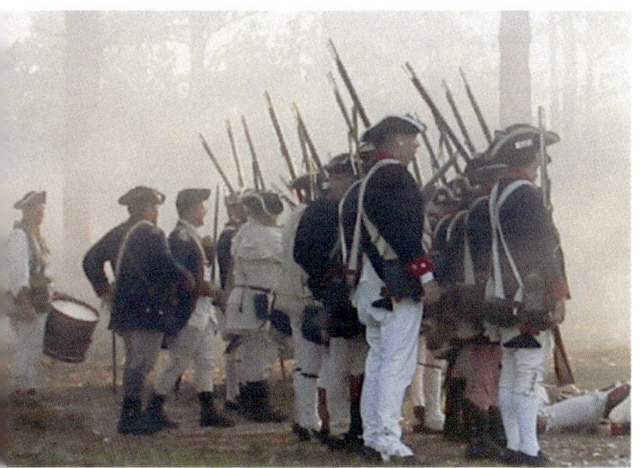

6. The Americans prepare to meet the British ttack. *Courtesy of Partisan Pictures and Historic amden Revolutionary War Park.*

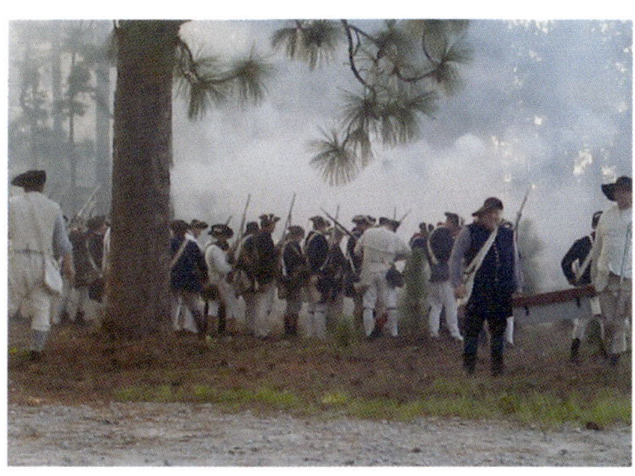

17. The Continentals reload between volleys. *Courtesy of Partisan Pictures and Historic Camden Revolutionary War Park.*

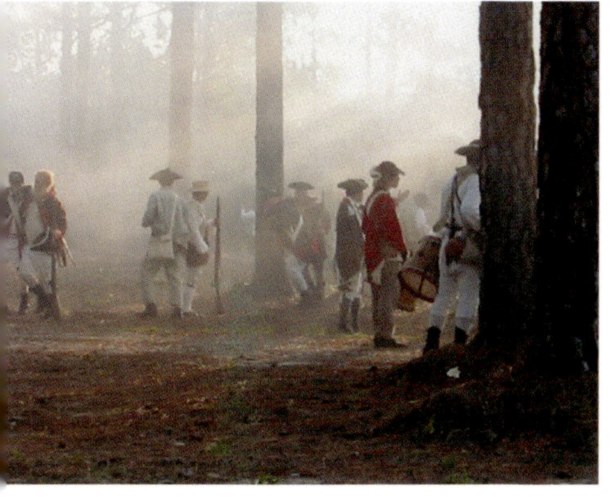

8. American wounded seek safety in the rear. *ourtesy of Partisan Pictures and Historic Camden evolutionary War Park.*

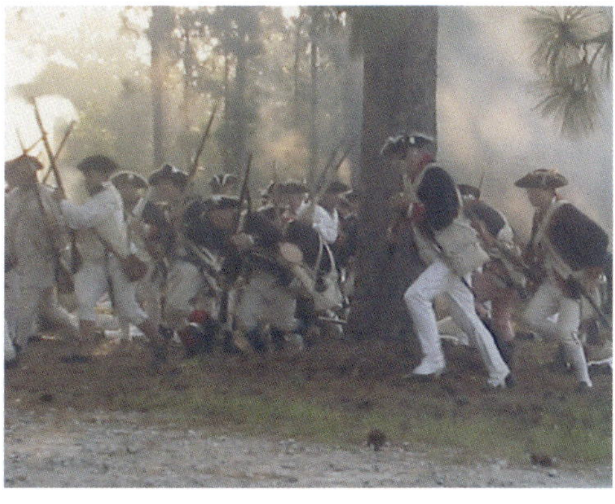

19. The outflanked Continental line begins to break. *Courtesy of Partisan Pictures and Historic Camden Revolutionary War Park.*

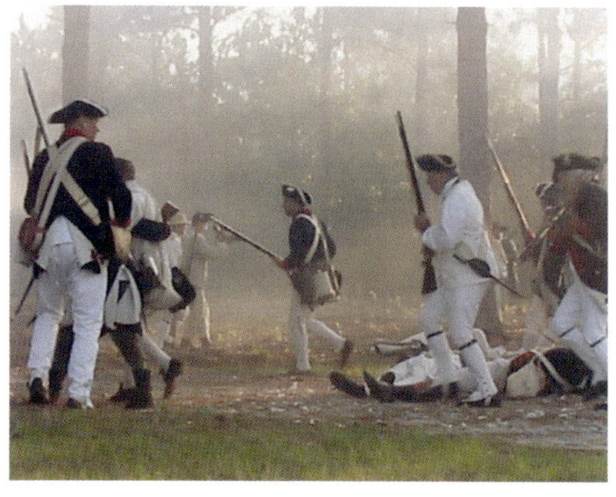

20. Some American troops tried to retreat in an orderly manner. *Courtesy of Partisan Pictures and Historic Camden Revolutionary War Park.*

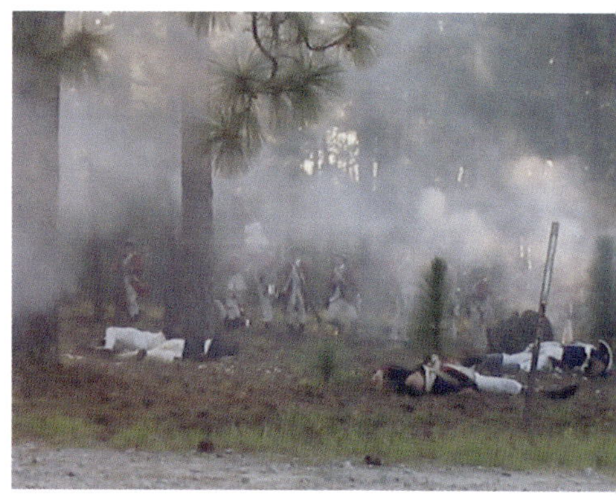

21. British troops reach the American position. *Courtesy of Partisan Pictures and Historic Camden Revolutionary War Park.*

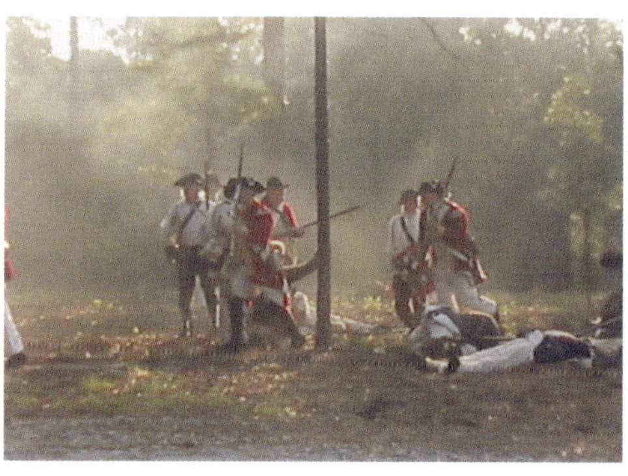

22. The British overrun the American line. *Courtesy of Partisan Pictures and Historic Camden Revolutionary War Park.*

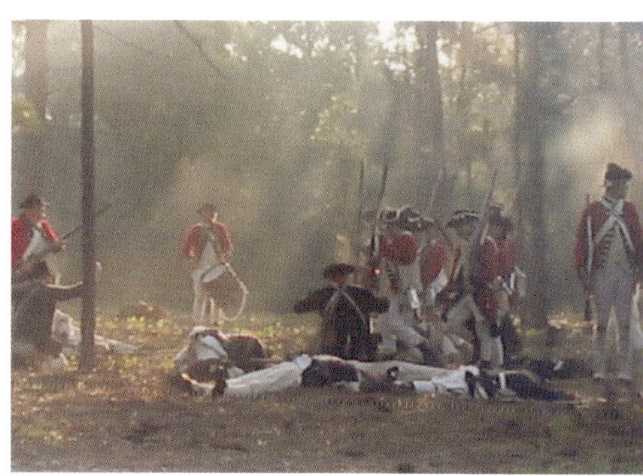

23. Numerous Americans are taken prisoner by the advancing British. *Courtesy of Partisan Pictures and Historic Camden Revolutionary War Park.*

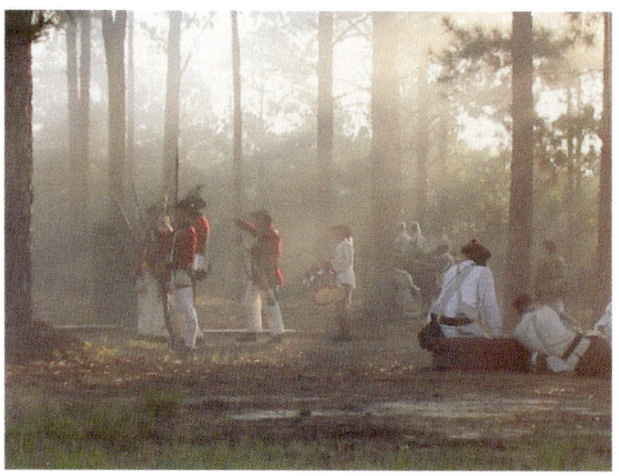

24. After securing the captives, British troops re-form and await further orders. *Courtesy of Partisan Pictures and Historic Camden Revolutionary War Park.*

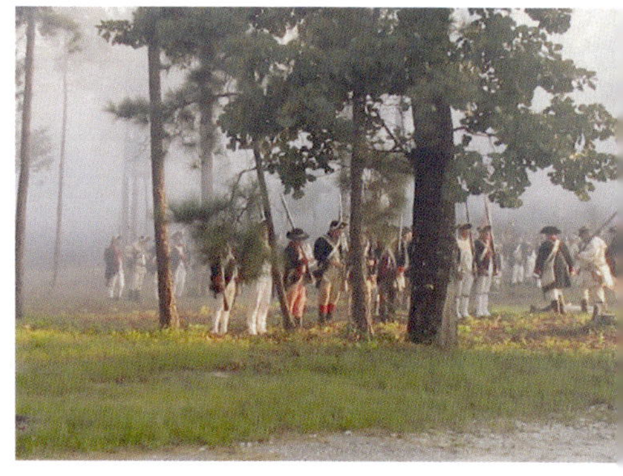

25. The Continentals try to re-form their line at a new position in the rear. *Courtesy of Partisan Pictures and Historic Camden Revolutionary War Park.*

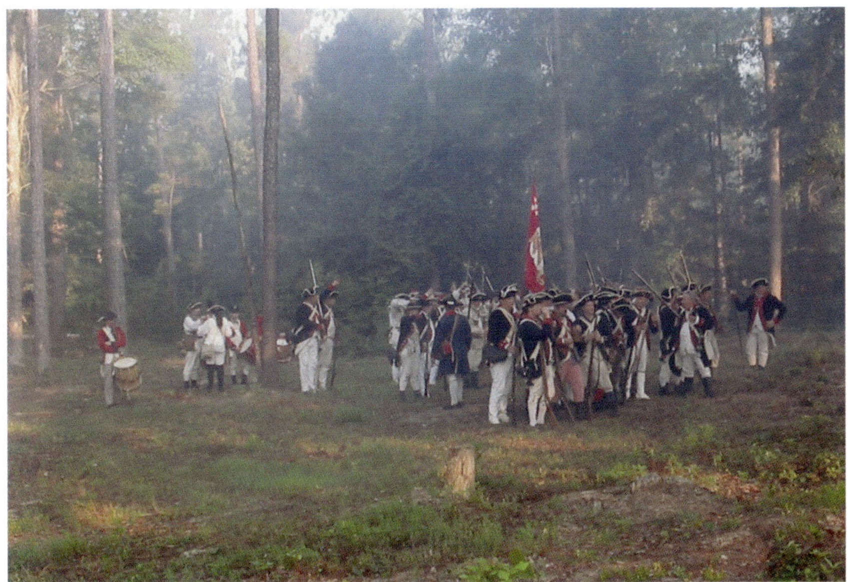

26. The handful of Americans still willing to resist were too few to oppose the British. *Courtesy of Partisan Pictures and Historic Camden Revolutionary War Park.*

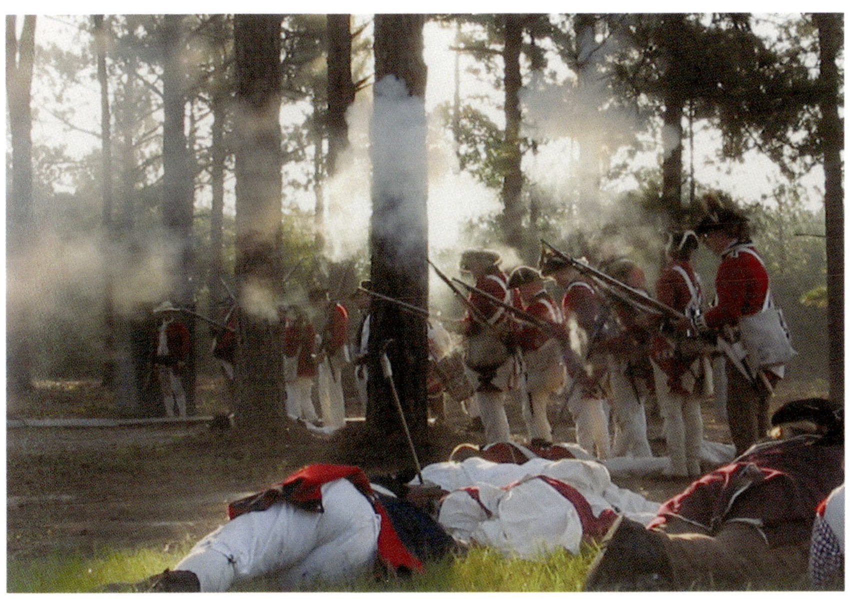

27. British troops fire at the re-forming Americans. *Courtesy of Partisan Pictures and Historic Camden Revolutionary War Park.*

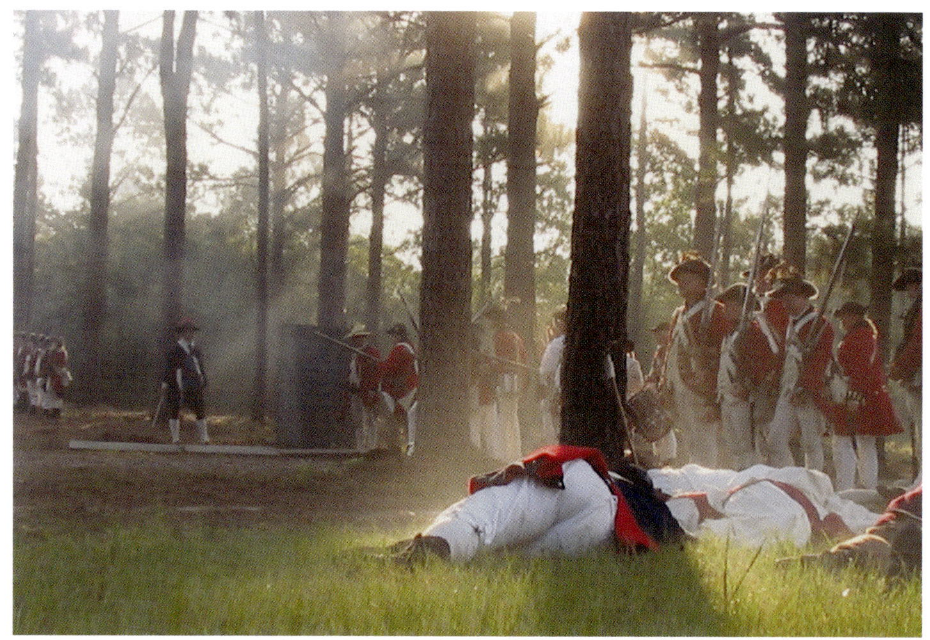

28. The victorious British re-form on the battlefield. *Courtesy of Partisan Pictures and Historic Camden Revolutionary War Park.*

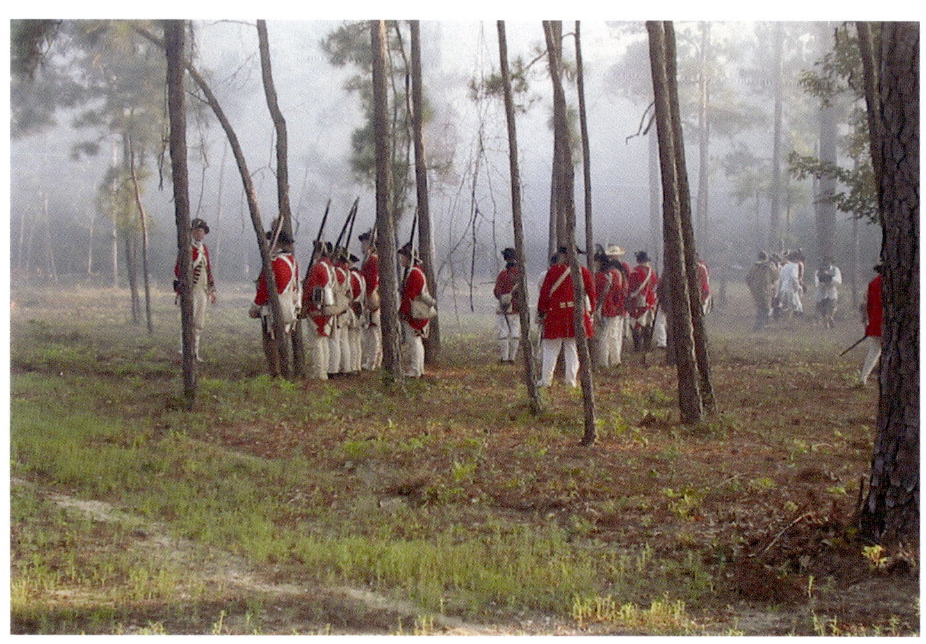

29. Cornwallis held his infantry on the field and sent the cavalry to pursue the Americans. *Courtesy of Partisan Pictures and Historic Camden Revolutionary War Park.*

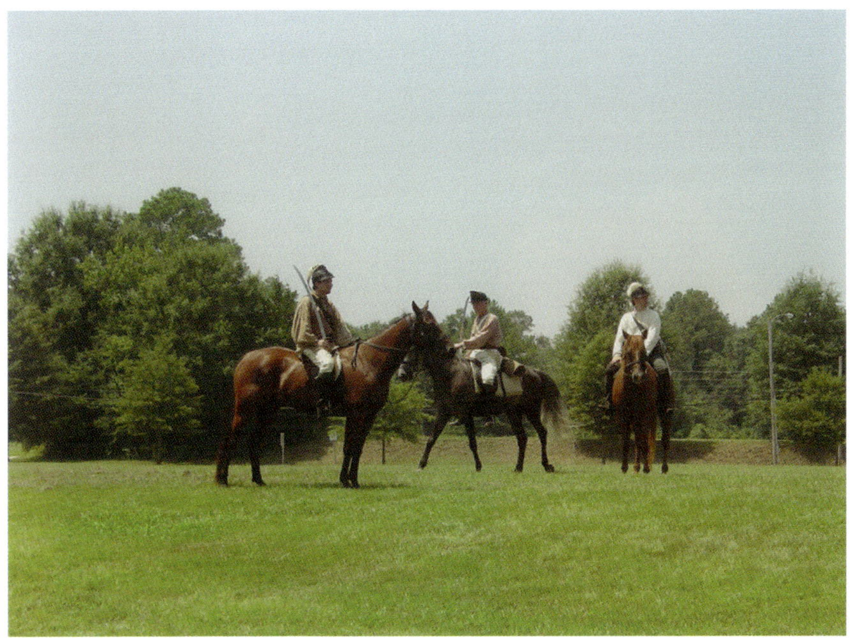

30. American dragoons. *Photo taken by R.G. Absher, courtesy of Historic Camden.*

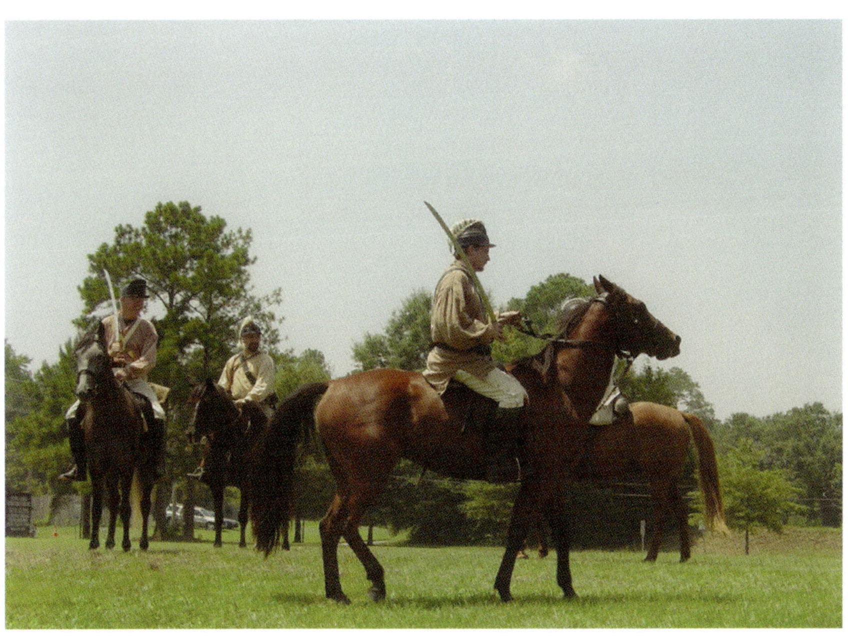

31. Dragoons like these were part of Armand's Legion. *Photo taken by R.G. Absher, courtesy of Historic Camden.*

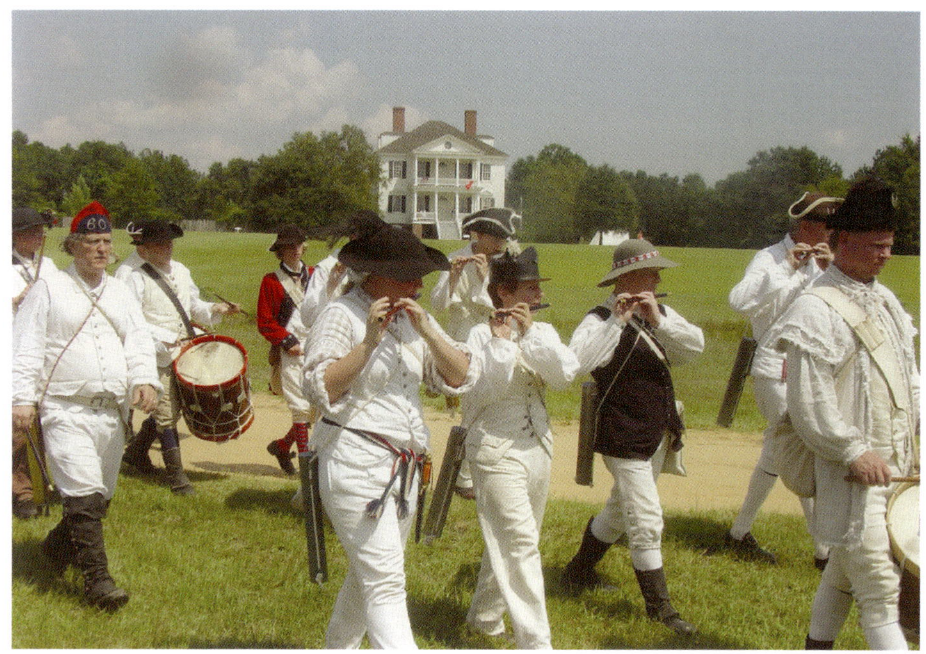

32. British troops drill on the Camden fields in front of the Joseph Kershaw House, which served as Lord Cornwallis's and Lord Rawdon's headquarters. *Photo taken by R.G. Absher, courtesy of Historic Camden.*

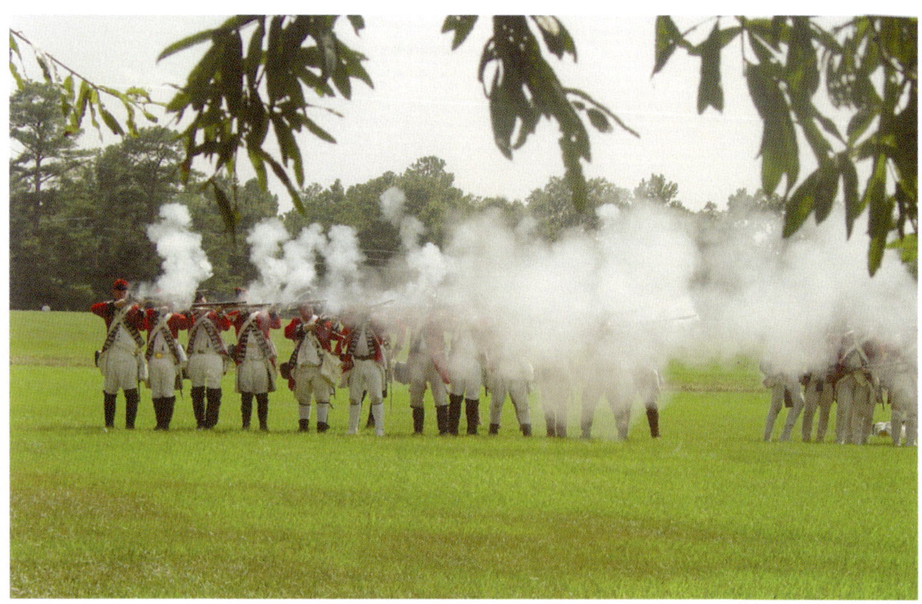

33. British troops drill with muskets in occupied Camden. *Photo taken by R.G. Absher, courtesy of Historic Camden.*

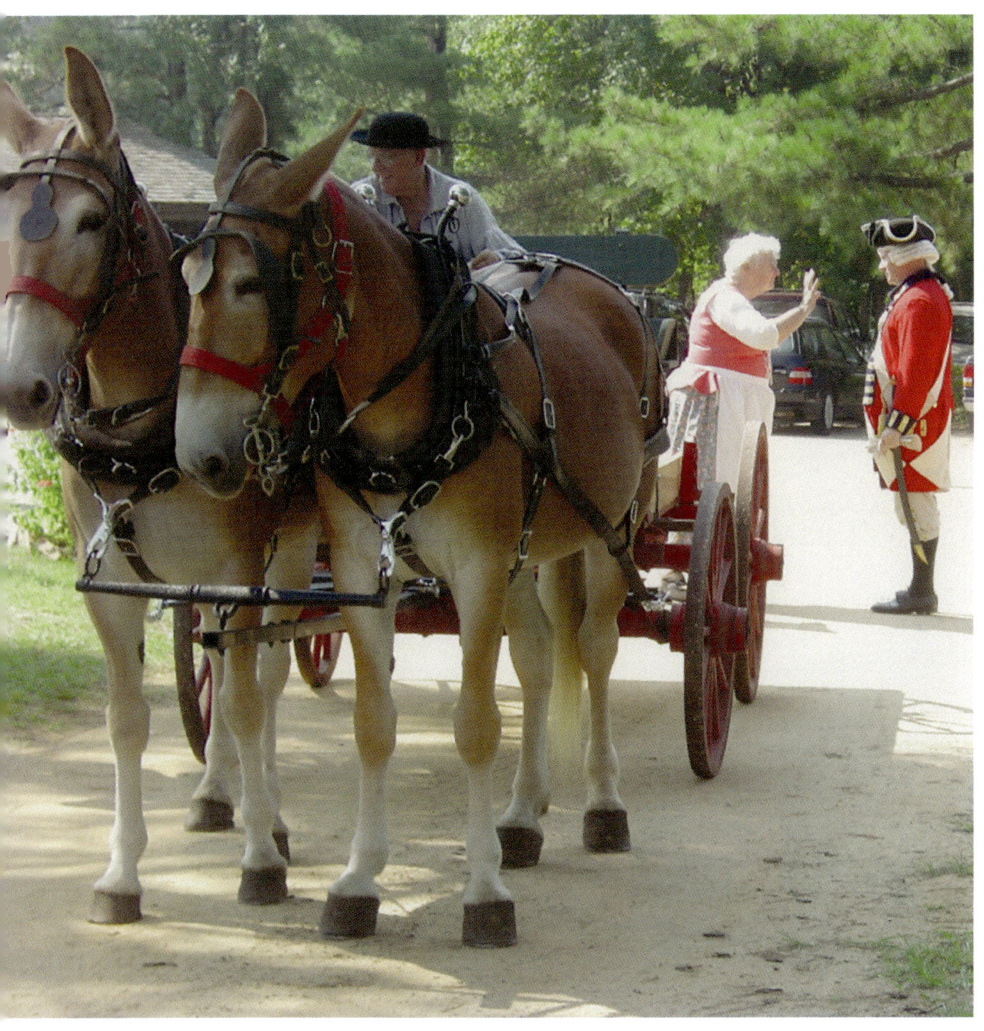

34. Wagons like these carried supplies for the British army. *Photo taken by R.G. Absher, courtesy of Historic Camden.*

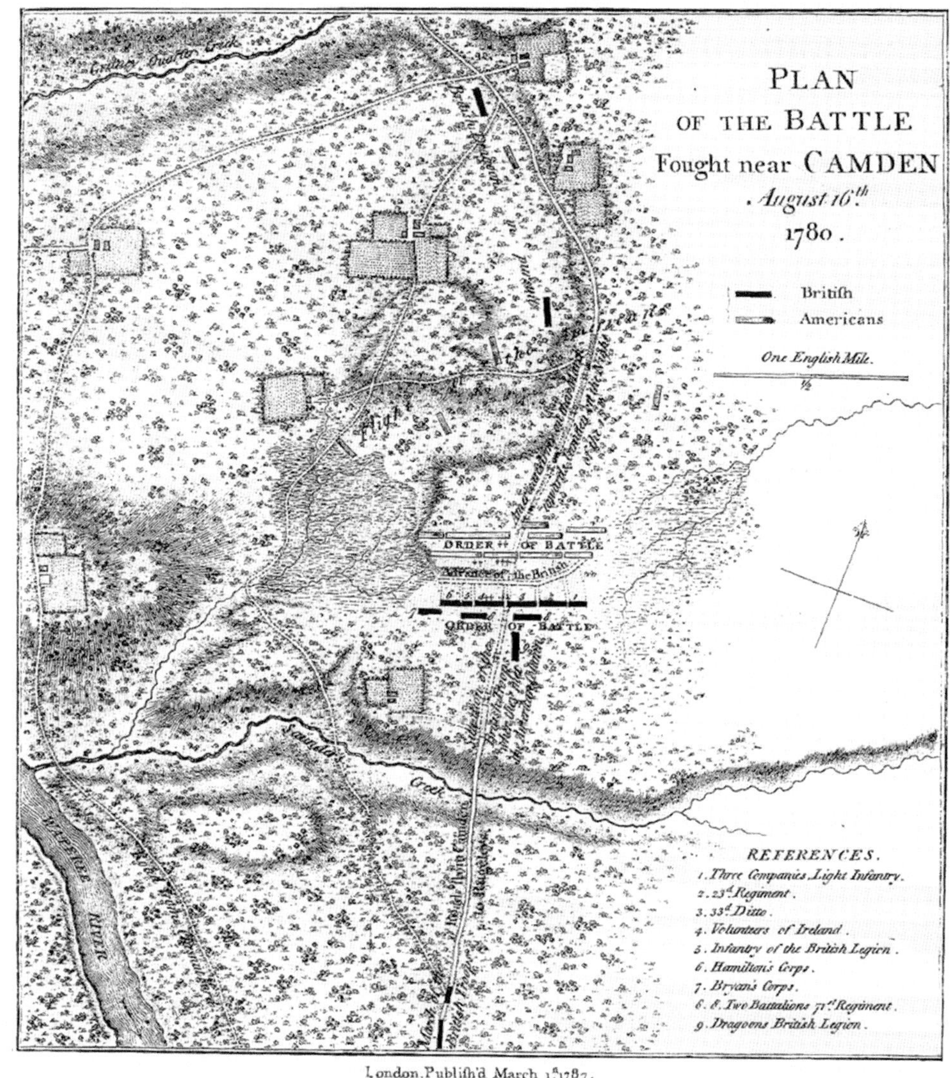


35. Map of the battle of Camden, from Tarleton's memoirs.

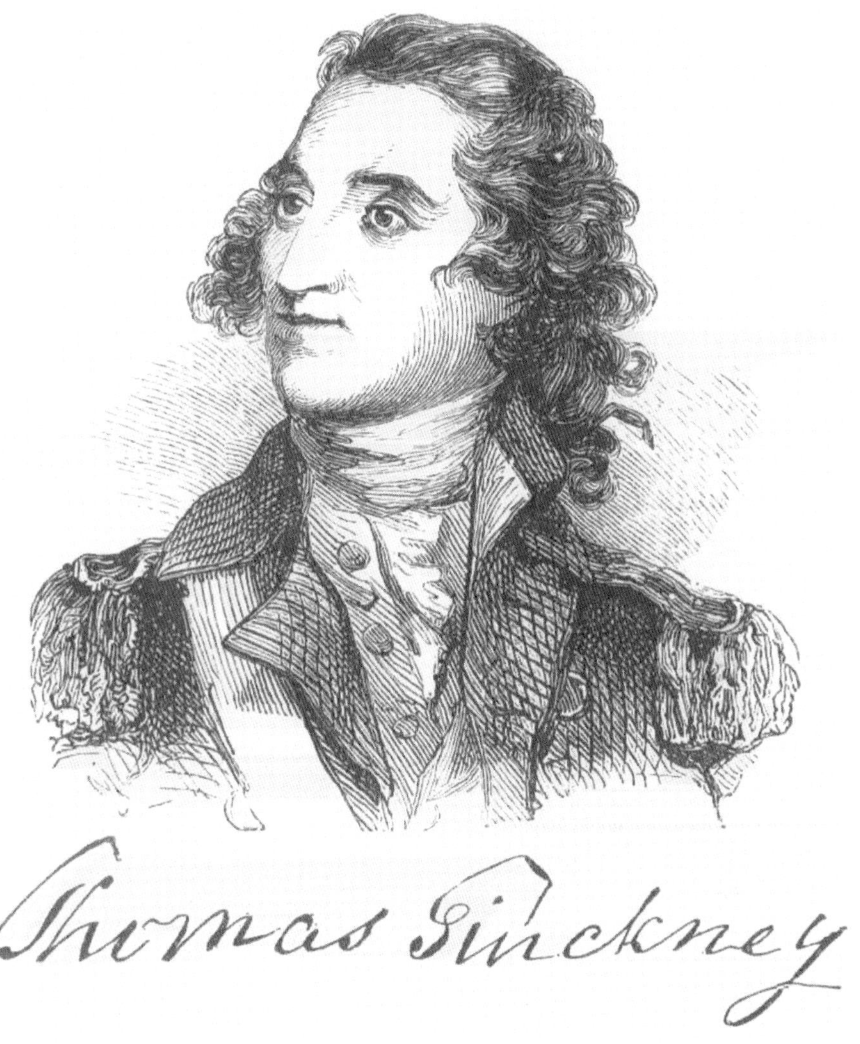


36. Major Thomas Pinckney, engraving by Benson J. Lossing.

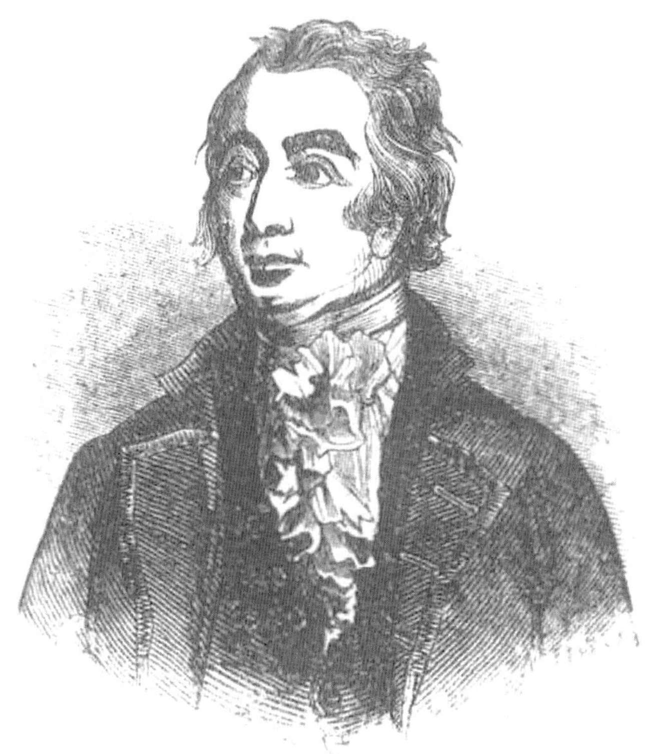

37. Francis, Lord Rawdon, engraving by Benson J. Lossing.

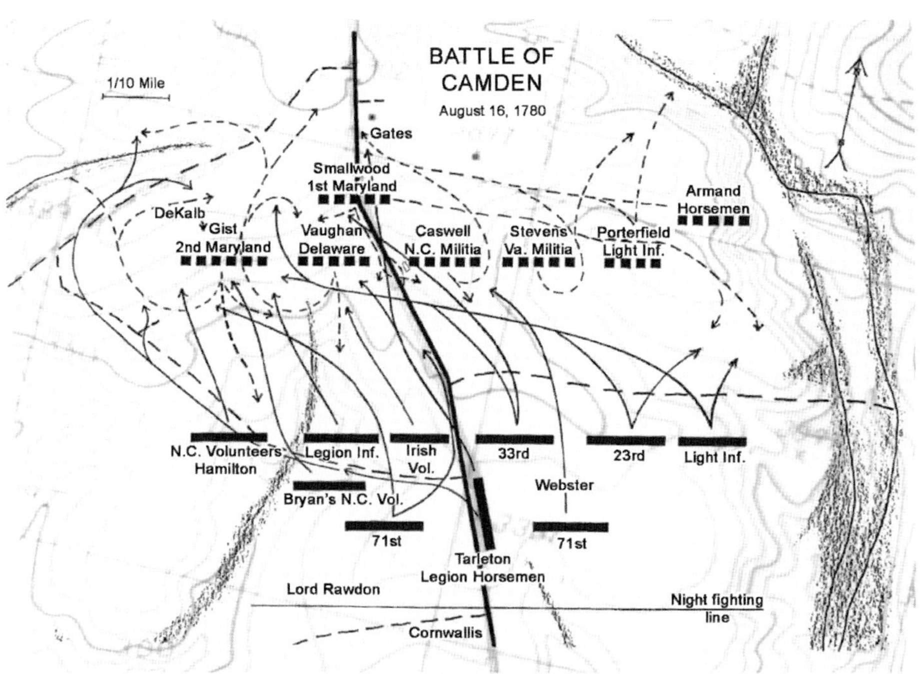


38. By Calvin Keys (1990). *From Christine Swager,* The Valiant Died, *Heritage Press, 2006. By permission.*

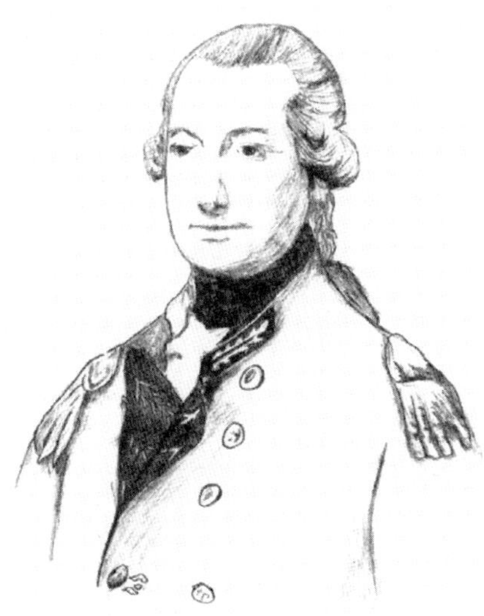

39. Lieutenant General Lord Cornwallis, pencil drawing by John Robertson Jr. from Gainsborough portrait, 1783. This is how he would have appeared during the Southern campaign of the American Revolution. *From* Come to the Cow Pens, *Christine Swager, Hub City Writers Project, 2002. By permission.*

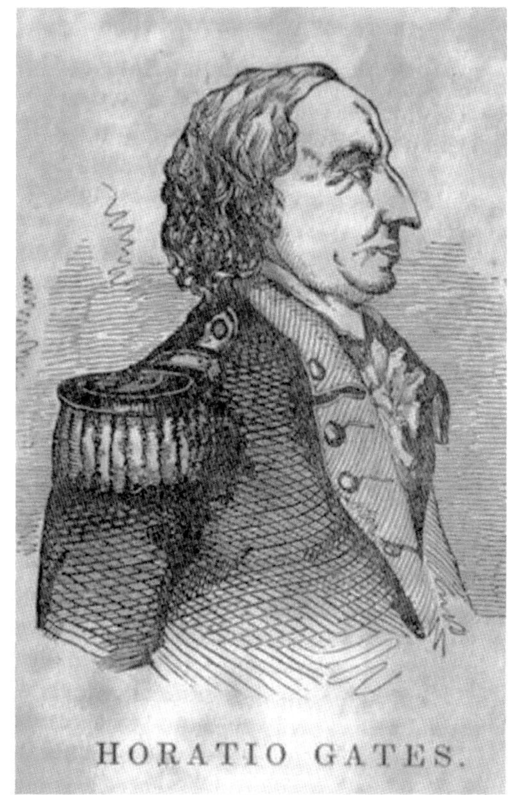


40. Major General Horatio Gates.

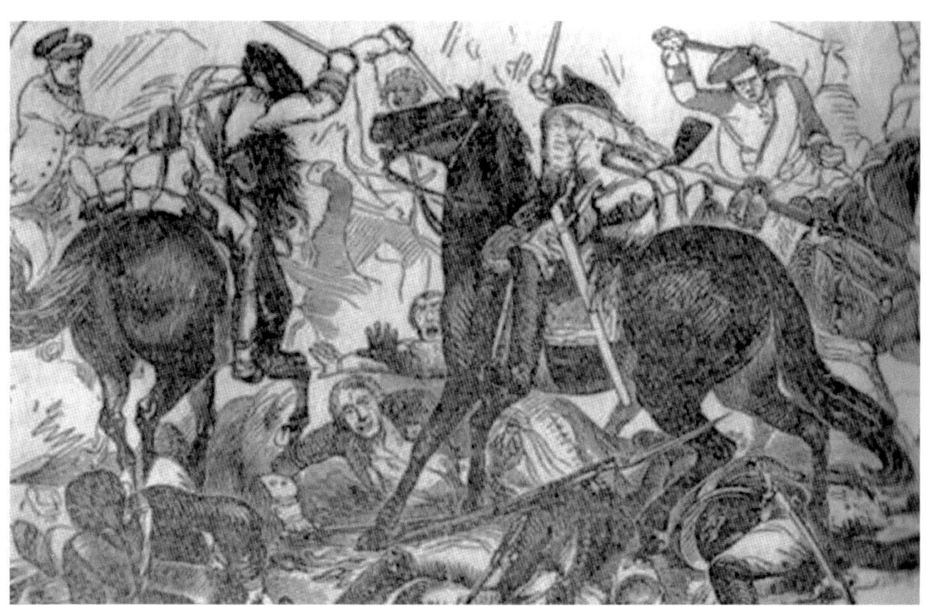

41. British dragoons overwhelm American troops in this somewhat fanciful depiction of the battle.

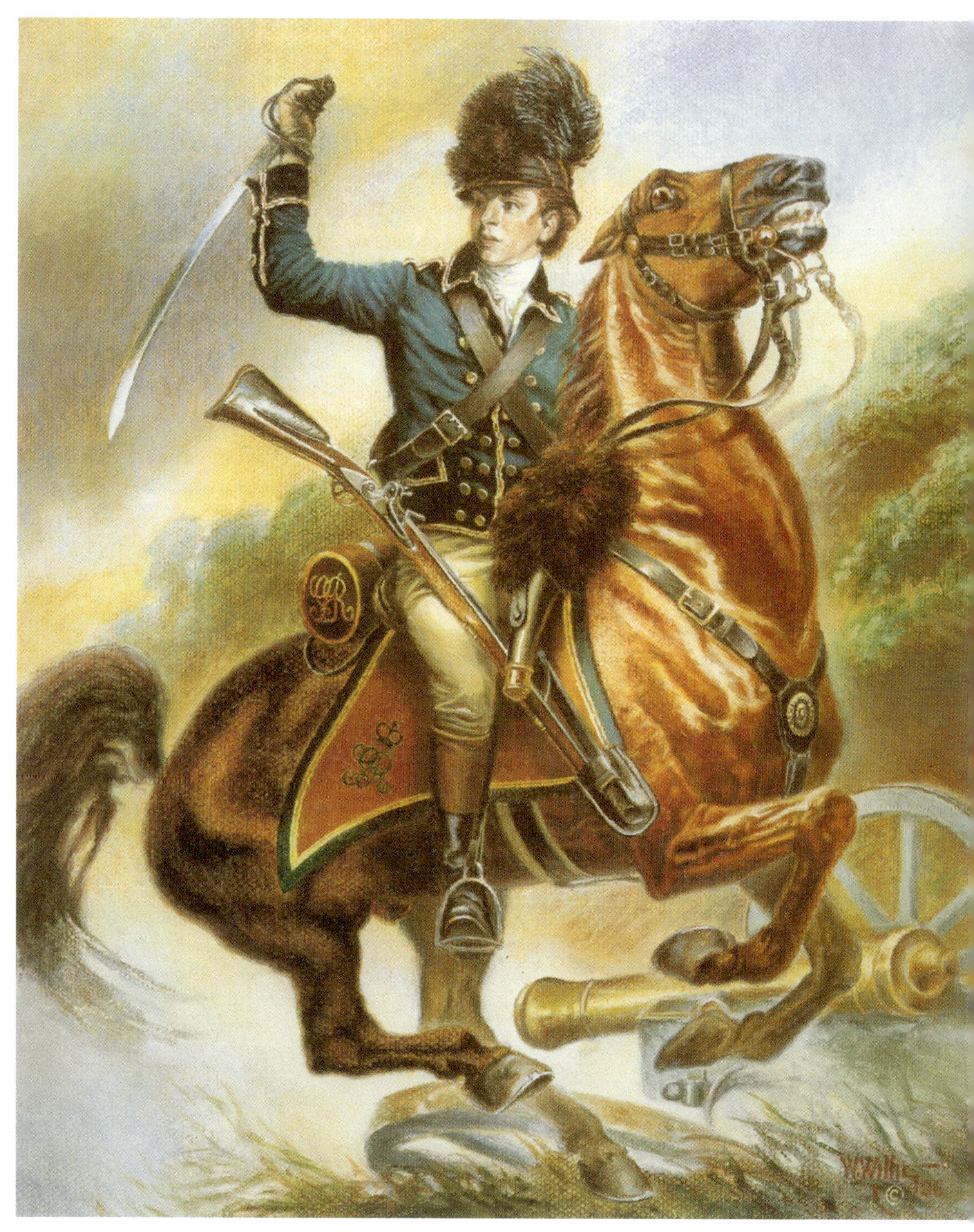

42. Lieutenant Colonel Banastre Tarleton. *Courtesy of the artist, Werner Willis.*

*the Americans were thrown into total confusion, and were forced to give way in all quarters. The continental troops behaved well, but some of the militia were soon broken. In justice to the North Carolina militia, it should be remarked, that part of the brigade commanded by general Gregory acquitted themselves well; they…kept the field while they had a cartridge to fire. Gregory himself was twice wounded by a bayonet in bringing off his men: several of his regiment, and many of his brigade who were made prisoners had no wound except from bayonets. About one thousand prisoners were taken, two hundred and ninety of which being wounded were carried into Camden, and more than twice that number killed…Almost all their officers were separated from their respective commands. The fugitives who fled on the common road, were pursued above twenty miles by colonel Tarleton's cavalry…Baron de Kalb…was mortally wounded, having exhibited great gallantry in the course of the action, and received eleven wounds; he was taken prisoner, and died on the next day of his wounds; we buried him in Camden with all the honors of war…*

*As in this engagement, I had the honor of carrying one standard of colours belonging to the 23d regiment, I was of course, near the centre of the right wing. I had an opportunity of beholding the behaviour both of the officers and privates; it was worthy the character of British troops…Lord Cornwallis's judgment in planning, his prompitude in executing, and his fortitude and coolness during the time of action, justly attracted universal applause and admiration. The earl of Moira, (then lord Rawdon, who was only twenty-five years of age) bore a very conspicuous part in the contest. Colonel Webster also ought to be particularly mentioned. His conduct was completely consistent with his general character in the army. Cool, determined, vigilant, and active; he added to a reputation established by long service the universal esteem and respect of the whole army, as an officer, whose experience and observation were equal to his personal bravery, and the rigid discipline which he maintained among the troops. Captain (now general) Champaigne,*[129] *who commanded the Royal Welch Fuzileers, also evinced the most perfect intrepidity and valor. Thus far I speak, not from the report of others, but from my own immediate observation.*

*…lord Rawdon was so well pleased with the conduct of his regiment (the volunteers of Ireland) that he ordered a silver medal to be struck off, and presented to several of his men who had signalized themselves in the action.*

*The author cannot conclude the account of this day's victory, without entreating pardon from the reader, while he remarks that three years…had elapsed since he was made prisoner at Saratoga by general Gates! He had at length, the satisfaction of seeing the same general to whom his majesty's forces, under Burgoyne surrendered, sustain a signal defeat. What were his feelings at that eventful moment! How did he bless that Providence which inspired him with the idea of effecting his escape, and preserved him to be a partaker of that triumph which the soldier feels, when his sovereign's troops are victorious over his enemies! More especially when that*

> *victory was obtained in the hard fought field over a general whose former success at Saratoga, had been trumpeted from one end of America to the other, and who had injured the British name, by charging the officers and privates with depredations that never existed but in his own imagination.*[130]

One soldier in the British Thirty-third Infantry Regiment, John Robert Shaw, settled in America after the war, and related his experiences at Camden in his memoirs.[131]

> *We remained at Monk's corner*[132] *until the capitulation of general Lincoln; after which we marched for Camden under the command of general Cornwallis and lord Rawdon, with 1500 effective infantry and 150 cavalry. When we arrived at Camden, a detachment was ordered to Ninety-six, but it fell to my lot to continue at Camden, where I fell sick…*
>
> *While we continued at Camden we fared pretty well; only general Gates advanced to disturb our repose; and having encamped at a place called Ruggles,*[133] *about thirteen miles from Camden, he sent us word that "he would eat his dinner in Camden, or in hell, the next day."*[134] *His force was vastly superior to ours, at least in numbers, being computed at 5000 or 6000 men; the greater number, however of these consisted of militia, on whom little dependence could be placed.*
>
> *Having received intelligence that general Gates had encamped in a bad situation, Lord Cornwallis, mustered his troops, and harangued them in words nearly to this effect: "Now, my brave soldiers, now an opportunity is offered for displaying your valour, and sustaining the glory of the British arms;—all you who are willing to face your enemies;—all you who are ambitious of military fame stand forward; for there are eight or ten to one coming against:—Let the man who cannot bear to smell gun-powder stand back, and all you who are determined to conquer or die turn out." Accordingly we all turned out except a few who were left to guard the sick and military stores. We marched out of Camden about ten o'clock at night, August 15, 1780; it being the intention of our general to surprise the enemy in their quarters at Ruggles; but in this he was disappointed, for general Gates had set out about the same hour, in hopes to surprise us at Camden. We came up with their advanced party, about seven miles from Camden, when the light troops and advanced guards on each side, necessarily engaged each other in the dark. In this blind encounter, the American cavalry being driven back on the van, occasioned some disorder in their ranks, and having thus repelled them, we were eager for a general engagement; but Lord Cornwallis finding that the enemy were on bad ground, was unwilling to hazard in the dark, the advantage which their situation would afford him in the light. We then lay on our arms until day break, when both armies formed their lines, and approached within 100 yards of each other, and the Americans gave the*

*first fire, which killed and wounded nearly one half of our number. We returned the fire, and immediately charged on them with the bayonet. The action became general along the lines, and was supported with great obstinacy. The haziness of the morning prevented the ascent of the smoke, which occasioned such a thick cloud, that it was difficult to observe the effects of a well supported fire on both sides. It was discoverable, however, that the British troops were pushing forward and the Americans giving way; and after an obstinate resistance, for about three quarters of an hour, the latter were thrown into confusion. We then opened to the right & left and let Tarleton's light horse pass through.—Victory declared in our favor.—We took 900 prisoners and more are said to have been killed and wounded; but the precise number was probably never ascertained…The whole body of the militia (which constituted, as I before observed, much the greater part of general Gate's force) with the exception of only one North-Carolina regiment, took to their heels the first fire, and though their general did all in his power to rally them, he could not persuade them to make a single stand, and so getting to the woods as fast as they could, they totally dispersed, leaving the continental regular troops to oppose the whole force of the British army. The continental troops indeed made a gallant stand, and merited the highest encomiums. It was a hard fought battle, and the victory not very cheaply purchased on the side of the British; for even in one regiment (the 33d to which I belonged) not less than 116 out of 240 were killed and wounded.*

5

# Contemporary American Observations and Reports

MANY MEMBERS of the Continental Congress in Philadelphia had expected Gates to repeat his success at Saratoga. Because news traveled slowly in the Revolutionary era, they were still expressing optimism about the campaign after the battle had been fought. South Carolina representative Thomas Bee, not knowing what had taken place at Camden, shared the latest news from the South with General Benjamin Lincoln[135] on August 18.[136]

> *Our Accounts from General Gates's Army, is, that he has now upwards of Ten Thousand Men with him, & has sent 5000 towards Camden & with the rest would move towards Pee Dee—there have been several smart Skirmishes between Advanced Parties.*

On August 25, nine days after the battle, Pennsylvania congressman Benjamin Rush sent John Adams a confident account of Gates's progress.[137]

> *General Gates who you know is used to creating Armies is doing wonders in the Southern states. We expect every day to hear of Lord Cornwallis being confined to the Sands of Charlestown.*

Perhaps the first report ever written about the battle was hurriedly composed by Colonel Benjamin Seawell of the North Carolina militia from his camp north of Camden. Addressed to militia General William Harrington, it was written at 3:00 a.m. on August 17.[138]

> *I have a few minutes ago rec'd intelligence by two of my light horse men whom I sent Express to M. Genl. Caswell but did not Get to head Quarters, that yesterday morng.*

*about 2 o'clock in the morng. a General Engagement between Our Army & that of the Enemy Commenc'd. Our Army was totally defeated & Put to flite, if this be true & I doubt not but that it is, Our Situation is truly deplorable. I cannot, give you any Particular acct. of the action & my light horse Only Seeing Colo. Exum*[139] *On his retreat who gave them their Information, Cannot satisfie me on this head. I shall be glad of your advice On this Subject. Pray come up with all Expedition as I shall wate to hear from you.*

The disaster at Camden had severe repercussions for Whigs in the Carolinas and Virginia. It crushed their hopes of quickly recovering South Carolina, while Rebels in North Carolina and Virginia feared that an invasion of their states was imminent. General William Moultrie of South Carolina, who had been taken prisoner at the surrender of Charleston, described the effects in his memoirs.[140]

*General Gates moved towards Camden, being possessed with a belief that the British intended, and were preparing to retreat; he therefore was determined to be near at hand, to prevent them, or to be close in their rear, to harrass them as much as possible…*

*Lord Cornwallis' army consisted of seventeen hundred infantry and three hundred cavalry; on the night of the fifteenth he marched out to attack the American army; at the same time General Gates put his army in motion, to take a position on Sander's-creek.*

*The American army was drawn up on the sixteenth of August…in the morning a general engagement took place: the British appeared at about two hundred yards distant, all drawn up in front of the North Carolina troops; the artillery was ordered to fire; and General Stevens to attack the column which was displayed on the right; he marched up with great bravery, and advanced with his brigade in good order, within fifty paces of the enemy, (who were also advancing) and called out to his men, "My brave fellows, you have bayonets as well as they, we'll charge them." At that moment the British infantry charged bayonet with a shout: the Virginians threw down their arms, and run off as fast as possible; the North Carolina militia followed their example, except a few of General Gregory's brigade, who halted a little longer; a part of Colonel Dixon's brigade fired a few rounds; but the greatest part of the militia run off, without firing a single shot: this dastardly behaviour of the militia, left the continentals to be attacked by the whole British infantry and cavalry: they fought bravely…and a great fire of musketry was kept up on both sides, with great obstinacy; at length, Lord Cornwallis ordered his cavalry to charge, which soon put an end to the contest: General Gates endeavored to rally the militia, to cover the retreat of the continentals, but in vain. The cavalry pursued the fugitive militia, upwards of twenty-five miles, and made a dreadful slaughter among them; the road on which they fled, was strewed with arms, baggage, the sick, wounded and dead…*

> *This victory over General Gates…occasioned great rejoicings and congratulations in Charlestown:*[141] *the troops were turned out and fired a fue de joye,*[142] *whilst the poor prisoners were quite dispirited at the total defeat of their army; they lost all hopes of ever recovering their country again: most of the officers who were taken at Camden and Fishing-creek, were sent to Haddrell's-point, upon parole with the officers taken in Charlestown, which gave us an opportunity of knowing many particulars relative to these two unfortunate affairs.*
>
> *The situation of America in the southern department was truly deplorable, their army dispersed and taken.*

William Dobein James, a soldier in Francis Marion's partisan unit, summarized the effect of the battle in a single sentence.[143]

> *The news of the defeat of Gen. Gates now became public, and repressed all joy upon this occasion; no event which had yet happened, was considered so calamitous.*

Moses Young, who was aboard a merchant ship bound for Portugal, heard a garbled story of the battle from the captain of another vessel. He relayed the account to South Carolinian Henry Laurens, who was imprisoned in London.[144]

> *Lord Cornwallis & Gen Gates happened both to make choice of the same piece of ground for Encampmt—about 14 Miles from Camden where both Armies arrived on the night of the 17th. August, when each d*[iscovered] *the other exchanged one fire and lay upon their Arms all night. Gen Gates had 7000 Men 1200 of which were continental troops Lord Cornwallis Army consisted of 2500. At Break of Day the Action began and the second fire from the Enemy broke our Militia who fled, the Continentals immediately charged and continued for ½ an hour the most bloody conflict that has happenned since the commencemt of the War which ended with the total Rout of our brave troops and the loss of about 400 Men… Previous to this engagement Gen Gates's Army consisted of 11,000 Men but he had detached 4000 of them in two Parties intending to cut off the Retreat of the Enemy from Camden.*

North Carolina Governor Abner Nash sent the unpleasant news of the defeat to his state's congressional delegates on August 23.[145]

> *Since our late defeat near Camden, I delayed writing till I could give you some certain account of that unhappy affair. The militia, except one North-Carolina regiment, commanded on the occasion by Colonel Dixon, of the regulars, gave way on the first fire, and fled with the utmost precipitation. The regulars and the regiment just*

> *mentioned, bravely stood, and pushed bayonets to the last...General Caswall has sent in a flag, and a surgeon to attend the wounded. As yet we have no particular account of the fate of the missing, except a few principal officers; among these is the Baron de Kalbe, said to be mortally wounded...General Caswall made a stand at Charlotte, near the boundary line, and called in upwards of one thousand fresh men. These he added to Colonel Sumpter's party of about seven hundred, and gave him the command of the whole, whilst he came here. I have ordered out three regiments from this district... so that I hope in a few days we shall be able to assume a tolerable good countenance.*

James Iredell, North Carolina's attorney general, discussed the battle with American officers and described their dissatisfaction with Gates in a September 28 letter to his wife, Hannah.[146]

> *Genl. Gates's conduct is much censured, and I am told by his officers in general, so that I fear there are too much grounds for it. The report is, that upon the Militia giving way, he immediately fled without sending any orders to the Continental troops to retreat, some of whom were pushing the enemy before them, and afterwards knowing nothing of the flight, were almost surrounded; whereas it is said, that if he had given them timely orders to retreat, they could have done it in good order, and at least saved all the Baggage and stores. But they would not retreat without orders until it appeared absolutely necessary, and even then they brought off 600 Men (one half their number) entire. Armand's Corps was almost cut to pieces, and he is gone to the northward, I am told, with violent exclamations against Gates. The Baron De Kalb was a quarter of a mile in advance of our army, when he was killed, pressing on with great success; and after he had received a musket shot, concealed it, and was animating his men in the most heroical manner, when a Cannon Ball gave him a mortal wound, of which he soon died.*

Virginians were also puzzled by Gates's conduct of the campaign. John Page, a prominent Whig, questioned Gates's decisions in a letter to Thomas Jefferson written on August 30.[147]

> *I most heartily condole you on the Defeat of our Troops under General Gates. Did not the General venture on too boldly, relying too much on a Continuance of his former good Fortune? I had no idea of his pushing on so rapidly towards Chas. Town. I conceived that no Operations would have been commenced in So. Carolina till Novr. However, Gates certainly knew better than I can pretend to know, what was best to be done, and may have only failed, by relying too much on Militia. May not this Affair at last turn out to our Advantage? May it not rouse up our Northern States to exert themselves more vigorously?*

Rather than dwell on the defeat, Jefferson preferred to focus on the future, as he told Governor Nash of North Carolina in a letter dated September 3.[148]

> *The misfortune we have met with is indeed matter of great grief to me, and the more so as the militia of this state bore so eminent a share in producing it. It remains however that we look forward, and consider what is to be done to re-establish our affairs.*

That same day, Jefferson wrote to George Washington explaining the steps that were being taken to rebuild the Southern army.[149]

> *As I know the anxieties you must have felt since the late misfortune to the South, and our later accounts have not been quite so unfavorable as the first, I take the liberty of inclosing you a state of this unlucky affair extracted from letters from General Gates, Gen. Stevens, and govr. Nash, and taken as to some circumstances from an officer who was in the action. Another army is collecting. This amounted on the 23d. Ult. to between four and five thousand men consisting of Porterfeild's corps, Armand's legion, such of the fugitive militia as had been reclaimed, and about 3000 N. Carolina militia are now embodied. We are told they will increase these to 8000…We are calling out 2000 militia who I think however will not be got to Hillsborough till the 25th. of October. About 350 regulars marched from Chesterfeild a week ago; 50 march tomorrow and there will be 100, or 150 more from that post when they can be cleared of the hospital. This is as good a view as I can give you of the force we are endeavoring to collect. But they are unarmed. almost the whole small arms seem to have been lost in the late rout. There are here on their way Southward 3000 stand of arms sent by Congress, and we have a few*[150] *still remaining in our magazine.*

Jefferson's enclosure provided Washington with a detailed account of the battle.

> *"A Narrative of the late disaster in South Carolinia Collected from the Most authentic Accounts which have been Received."*
>
> *On the 13th. of August Genl. Gates with the Maryland line the Artillery and North Carolina Militia arrived at Ridgeley thirteen miles from Cambden and took post there and was the Next day joind by Genl. Stevens with Seven hundred of the Virginia Militia. Col. Sumpter was then at the Waxsaws with four hundred South Carolinia Militia…The 15th. at day light Genl. Gates reinforced Col. Sumpter with three hundred North Carolinia Militia one hundred of the Maryland line and two three pounders. Col. Sumpter took possession of all the passes on the Wateree from Elkins's ford to Whiticars farm five Miles below Campden. At one of these he supprised the enemy's Guard killed Seven and took about thirty…and afterwards on*

*the Same day he took about Seventy prisoners, British, Six waggons, baggage & c. on their way from Ninety Six. At ten OClock Genl. Gates's Army Marched intending to take post on an advantageous Situation where was a deep Creek in front about seven Miles from Cambden…Between 12. and 1 oClock after Marching About Five Miles they Met with the enemy…who had Marched out from Cambden about Nine OClock of the Same Night intending to attack our Camp by supprise about day break. This Meeting was equally unexpected on both Sides and Occationed a halt of both Armies. The enemy's Cavalry then charged Col. Armands legion which was well supported on the flanks by Col. Porterfield's Corps who repulsed the Assailants, but Unfortunately Col. Porterfield himself had his leg broke in the first fire. The enemy's infantry then advancing with a heavy fire, the troops in front gave way to the front of the 1st. Maryland brigade and a Confusion ensued which took Some time to regulate. At length the Army was ranged in line of battle…Col. Armands Corps was ordered to the left to Support the left flank and oppose the enemy's Cavalry. Their infantry from a defect in Numbers were only a Single file five feet apart. In this Situation they remained till day break of the 16th. when our troops advanced in a line a few hundred yards. The enemy attacked and drove in our light party in front; and after the first fire charged the Militia with bayonets where upon the whole gave way, except Col. Dixon's regiment of N.C. Militia, and their cavalry continuing to harrass the rear. Such was the panic diffused through the whole that the utmost and unremitting exertions of the Generals Gates Stevens Caswell and others…to rally them…proved ineffectual. They ran like a torrent and bore all before them. This shamefull d*[e]*sertion of the Militia gave the enemy an opportunity of bending their whole force against the Maryland troops and Dixons Regiment…The Conflict was obstinate and bloody and lasted fifteen Minutes, Dixons Militia standing firm with their regular brethren and pushing bayonets to the last. Superior bravery was at length obliged to give way to superior Numbers, and this gallant Corps Compelled to retreat from the ground. They were then furisly charged by a party of British horse (their Numbers Not known) whom they Compleatly Vanquished, insomuch that not more than two of the party are said to have got off. These brave men suffered greatly, having lost as is believed one half of their number, and to their immortal honour made their retreat good…We lost 8 pieces of cannon…and nearly the whole muskets which were in the hands of the militia who basely threw them away. The numbers of the enemy are not certainly known; prisoners say they were 3500 regulars; Colo. Sumpter's intelligence on the 15th. made them 1200 regulars 1000 militia and a reinforcement of 500 regulars on their way, but whether these had joined or not is unknown. It is believed their loss was full 500 killed and wounded. They retreated immediately to campden…Generals Gates, Gist, Smallwood, Huger, Stevens, Butler and Gregory are safe. Generals DeKalb and Rutherford are missing, the latter a prisoner certainly, the former a prisoner and some accounts say mortally wounded, others that he is unhurt. Colo. Porterfield an inestimable officer, is said, we fear too truly to be dead of his wounds. About one third of his corps was lost.*

From his headquarters in New Jersey, Washington replied to Jefferson on September 11, describing the steps he was taking to restore the situation in the South.[151] He wrote that Jefferson's letter of September 3

*relieved me from much anxiety as, from Genl. Gates's letter of the 20h. Augt…there was the greatest reason to apprehend that the whole of the Maryland line and the troops which made a stand with them had been cut off. The stroke, as it is, is severe; but the total loss of the regular troops would have rendered the speedy assemblage of another Army extremely difficult.*

*The loss of the Arms, which were thrown away by the Militia, is a most disagreeable circumstance at this time…Immediately upon hearing of the disaster near Campden I directed the additional Regiment of Maryland which was on the march to join this Army to return and proceed to the southward. This Regiment is raised for the War*[152] *and by the last returns amounted to above 400 Men.*

While Washington, Nash and Jefferson worked to rebuild the Southern army, Colonel David Jameson of the Virginia militia told his friend James Madison in a letter dated September 13 that Gates had squandered the opportunity to regain South Carolina.[153]

*We are very anxious to hear something more from Chas. Town, should there be a French or Spanish Fleet there,*[154] *something may yet be done, but the defeat of Gen. Gates will in all probability prevent the speedy retaking the place and the capture of the whole british force there. had he proceeded with caution, as he would have been joined by Men from both South & No. Carolina, The Enemy must have retreated to Chas. Town And he would have found himself in a condition with a foreign aid to have compleated the Work.*

Colonel John Banister, who served with both the Virginia Continentals and the militia, expressed a more optimistic view of the situation when he wrote to fellow Virginian Richard Bland in September.[155]

*…we are certainly informed that the defeat was not so fatal as was apprehended. Instead of all the Maryland line being killed and taken, near five hundred are come in, with most of the officers…who were said to have been slain.*

*This veteran corps, after having sustained the attack of the enemy, with the assistance of only one regiment of North Carolina Militia, by a bold and well conducted attack on the enemy forced a passage through their main body and retreated…The militia are collecting at their places…and Gov. Nash informs me that the defeat is by no means so disastrous as was at first represented; and adds that in a few days they should be able to face about and confront their enemies, who have been severely handled in this action, and had not advanced from their post at Camden.*

Officials in Maryland and Delaware were deeply concerned over the fate of their states' troops who had fought at Camden. The slow pace at which news traveled, and the rumors of disaster, made the wait for accurate information excruciating. A September 2 letter from Maryland congressman John Henry Jr. to Governor Thomas Sim Lee recounts the suffering of families who had relatives in the battle.[156]

*The Fate of the Action on the morning of the 16th of Aug. you must have heard. It is a melancholy and distressing blow for Maryland, and a ruinous and destructive one to the Southern States. I wish it was in my power to give you the Fate of our gallant countrymen, and to relieve the pain and anxiety of those Distressed Families who wait with a sorrowful impatience to hear the Sacrifice of their dearest connections. But it is not in my power. Genl. Gates' Letter…gives no other information, than, that they were left by the Militia and himself on the first fire, surrounded by a Force infinitely their superior in Numbers…This account I suppose the General gives from the known and established valor of the Troops; it could not be from his knowledge of the Action, for he doesn't appear, by his Letter to have seen the regular Troops after two O'Clock in the Morning when the first skirmish took place. As the State of Maryland was deeply interested in this Action, I thought it my duty to move that the Letter should be published, but Congress determined and I now believe very wisely, that it should not: It must be known sooner or later, and when ever it is, you will join with me in pronouncing it a very extraordinary one. I shall forbear at present to make any observation lest my resentment should carry me beyond the bounds of propriety and Justice…*

*Reports…say that many officers fell…I trust this voluminous Catalogue will considerably diminish when we have a more accurate account; some of our officers will no doubt escape. Till then, or the return of a Flag sent in by General Gates we must remain in the dark.*

The three letters that follow, written by Delaware militia colonel Thomas Rodney to his brother, Governor Caesar Rodney, illustrate the process by which news of the battle spread across America, and how the information grew more accurate as time passed. The first was written on September 1.[157]

*Mr. A. Montgomery…Says he was informed…that General Gates had been Totally defeated near Camden and lists the greatest part of his Army Killed and Taken prisoners; That the enemy were forced to Action and Gates Attacked to disadvantage by Too hasty a pursute, and the Malitia Giving way his Regulars were overpowered… If This Account is True the Stroke is More Severe than that at Charles Town is Smallwood was killed but he could not learn Any particulars respecting the Delawares…As Mr. Montgomerys immagination is fertile in parroting I hope this affair will not Turn out altogether so bad but I fear Gates has suffered considerably and has no doubt been Obliged to retreat but I cannot yet believe he has been Totally defeated, as such accounts are always exaggerated on their first Transpiring…*

*P.S. Since writing the within Col. White*[158] *pas'd through this place from the Southward, and gives Some More particulars of the action—He Says when Genl. Gates drew near Camden Cornwallace Left it but fearing he Could not get of returned again That the same night Both Gates & Cornwallace formed a plan of Surprizing each other of Course both Armies being in Motion Met near Camden a little before or about daylight that after a smart action The British were obliged to retreat and being pursued too precipitately by the Malitia they got into disorder and the British Taking advantage of this Circumstance returned to the Charge routed the Malitia and bent their whole force around our Regular Troops; rushing upon them with fixed Bayonets where they were bravely Opposed in the same Manner Till over powered by Numbers—Some of the Line forced their way through them and the Genl. escaped with them—He adds that Gunby & Guest*[159] *is killed but does not know any thing particular of Our officers from whence I have hopes that none of them have fell…it is not unlikely but some of those said to be dead are only prisoners.*

Thomas Rodney sent his brother an updated report on September 5.

*I wrote you an Account of the Battle to the Southward as the inteligence came to hand… The Accounts at that Time were very Uncertain & I waited with great Anxiety to git a More perfect Account…knowing very well that the friends and relations of the Delawares would be greatly distressed on hearing the Wild and extravagant reports then Circulating—Since I wrote last Col. Ramsey*[160] *has been in this Town. Says he Saw Genl. Gates letter to Congress. That it Contain'd only a very Uncertain Account of the Action for when our Line Charged the Enemy with fixed Baynets (which was done by the Line with Such Success that they got several peices of the Enemies Artilery) the Malitia got into disorder and the Generl. retiring to Rally them the Brittish Horse took advantage of their confusion, broke through the line and Routed them & the Genl. being thus Seperated from the Army in the heat of Action was pursued by a party of Horse 24 or 25 Miles, which was the reason he Could give No certain Account How it Terminated But expected from the Circumstances Mentioned that they were Totally*

*Routed. Some Gentlman (said to be one of the Engineers)*[161] *has passed up since… who Says that there were only 900 of Our Regular Troops Engaged in the Action, that Some where between four and five hundred there were Killed and Taken prisoners, And that the rest Made a safe retreat and that in Killed the Brittish Suffered Much More than Our Army. That the remainder of the Army which was the greatest part… were in the rear 20 or 30 Miles, I have some hope the Delawares were among these but cannot learn particularly.*

On September 12, Thomas Rodney finally relayed more accurate information to his brother.

*I…Just Now have Seen the last paper in which is a full Acct. of the unlucky Action to the Southward…I will inform you as to the Delawares—They are in one respect very happy for there is not one officer among them Killed, wounded or Missing But eight of Them are Prisoners Vizt. Col. Vaughan, Major Patton, Captn: Rhoads Captn. Larmouth, Lt. Duff, Skillington Purvis & Ensign Roach, The Rest are among those who have fortunately escaped the perils of this disaster.*

New York Congressman James Duane also had difficulty obtaining information about the battle, as he informed his state's governor, George Clinton, on September 7.[162]

*On my way to Congress I had the Mortification to learn that our Southern Army under General Gates had met with a fatal Check near Camden in South Carolina. The particulars are involved in impenetrable obscurity. We wait impatiently for Authentic Information that we may lay it before the publick, and endeavour to repair our misfortune by a vigorous Effort suitable to so deplorable a Catastrophe in Appearance, for if it has the effect of animating Virginia to put forth her Strength and great Resources it may eventually prove a Benefit.*

Many American officers in the North were alarmed by the defeat at Camden and feared that it would seriously undermine the Americans' chances of winning the war. Major General Nathanael Greene of Rhode Island had just been appointed commandant at West Point when he learned of the battle. In a September 5 letter to William Greene, he worried that the demoralizing loss would make it difficult for the Americans to recover the South, little knowing that he would soon be appointed to replace Gates.[163]

*We have just received the disagreeable intelligence of General Gateses defeat to the Southward…The action happened on the 16th of last Month within a few*

> *Miles of Cambden…The two Armies met in the Night and a little skirmishing ensued, but the action was not serious until the morning. At daylight General Gates made the necessary disposition of his troops, consisting of between 800 and a 1000 regulars; and about 2000 Militia and some few horse. The Enemy had from 1200 to 1500 regular troops; and about 1000 Militia. Our Militia gave way the first fire; and left the Continental Troops to bear the brunt of the whole of the Enemies force; which they did with great spirit and bravery. General Gist who commanded one of the Maryland brigades repulsed the Enemy with charged Bayonets; but the Militia quitting their ground, let the Enemy into his rear. General Gates made several unsuccessful attempts to rally the Militia, but they were so pannick struck, it was all to no purpose; and the General was bore away in the croud, and had the mortification to leave the Maryland line bravely engaged without having it in his power to assist them, or even to tell what was their fate; but as the firing ceased after he had got Eight or ten Miles in the rear, he supposes they must have been cut to pieces; however this is not certain by any means…*
>
> *This is a great misfortune and the more so as that unfortunate Country was too discouraged before to make any great exertions. However it was beginning to recover itself and some few days before the action we had gained several advantages and taken several hundred prisoners.*

After replacing Gates in December 1780, Greene learned more about the battle from his subordinates who had fought at Camden. He shared his opinions with Alexander Hamilton in a letter dated January 10, 1781.[164]

> *The battle of Camden here is represented widely different from what it is to the Northward. Col Williams thinks that none of the General Officers were entitled to any extraordinary merit. The action was short and succeeded by a flight wherein every body took care of themselves as well Officers and soldiers. Not an officer except Major Anderson and one or two Captains that brought off the field of battle a single soldier. The Col also says that General Gates would have shared little more disgrace than is the common lot of the unfortunate notwithstanding he was early off, if he had only halted at the Waxhaws or Charlotte: the first about sixty, and the last about eighty miles, from the field of battle…The greater part of the loss of the Maryland line in the action of Cambden happened after they began to retreat: indeed this was the case with all the troops.*

Like Greene, Dr. James Thacher of Massachusetts was concerned with both the military aspects of the battle and its impact on Gates's reputation. A surgeon in Washington's army, Thacher recorded his impressions of the battle and its demoralizing effect on the Northern troops in his journal.[165]

*September.—Intelligence of an unpleasant and distressing nature, has just reached us from South Carolina. Our southern army, under the command of Major-General Gates, has been totally defeated, in a general action with Lord Cornwallis, on the 19th of August. General Gates…retreated with precipitation to the distance of eighty miles, to escape the pursuit of the enemy. This mortifying disaster gives a severe shock to our army, as it must be productive of the most important and serious consequences, as it respects the welfare of the Southern states…*

*This very unfortunate event has given an impression universally unfavorable to the character and conduct of General Gates, as he has disappointed the high expectations of the public. He is indeed a painful example of the vicissitudes of the fortune of war; but it ought not to be expected that an officer should be held accountable for the strokes of fortune; nor for the effects of superior force or address in the enemy. Considering the former high character and meritorious services of the general, we cannot justly suspect him to be chargeable with any deficiency in point of integrity or conduct, and time and investigation must decide how far he has been guilty of any culpable error.*

Another American officer, Lieutenant Colonel Eleazar Oswald, was primarily interested in the effect of the battle on Gates's reputation. He pondered Gates's actions in a September 15 letter to General Benedict Arnold.[166]

*You have no doubt 'ere this, heard of General Gates's Disaster near Camden, So. Carolina. He is severely censured by many, but how justly I cannot determine. Previous to the Scene of Carnage and Confusion, which from the best Intelligence we have been able to collect, terminated much to our Disadvantage, he displayed great Knowledge and Abilities in the "Art Militare," and a Spirit of Enterprise which did him Honor; but his subsequent Conduct bears, in my Opinion, evident Marks of Terror and Dismay. But as Accounts are variously related, and perhaps exaggerated, Censure or Applause cannot at present be directed to its proper Object. It is however obvious, and at the same Time to be lamented, that a few Sprigs of the Saratoga Laurels are withering in the Sun burnt Sands of Carolina.*

No one in the American army derived more joy from the news of Camden than Washington's staff officer, Alexander Hamilton. Because Hamilton considered Gates a rival to Washington, and also disagreed with Gates on the value of militia, he was glad to see Gates's reputation destroyed. Hamilton expressed his satisfaction with Gates's misfortune in a letter to James Duane, written on September 6.[167]

*I have heard since of Gates defeat, a very good comment on the necessity of changing our system. His passion for Militia, I fancy will be a little cured, and he will cease to think them the best bulwark of American liberty. What think you of the conduct of this great man? I am his enemy personally, for unjust and unprovoked attacks upon my character, therefore what I say of him ought to be received as from an enemy, and have no more weight than as it is consistent with fact and common sense. But did ever any one hear of such a disposition or such a flight? His best troops placed on the side strongest by nature, his worst, on that weakest by nature, and his attack made with these. 'Tis impossible to give a more complete picture of military absurdity. It is equally against the maxims of war, and common sense. We see the consequence. His left ran away and left his right uncovered. His right wing turned on the left has in all probability been cut off. Though in truth the General seems to have known very little what became of his army.*

*Had he placed his Militia on his right supported by the Morass, and his Continental troops on his left, where it seems he was most vulnerable, his right would have been more secure, and his left would have opposed the enemy; and instead of going backward when ordered to attack would have gone forward. The reverse of what has happened might have happened.*

*But was there ever an instance of a General running away as Gates has done from his whole army? and was there ever so precipitous a flight? One hundred and eighty miles in three days and a half. It does admirable credit to the activity of a man at his time of life. But it disgraces the General and the Soldiers. I always believed him to be very far short of a Hector, or an Ulysses.*[168] *All the world I think will begin to agree with me.*

*But what will be done by Congress? Will he be changed or not? If he is changed for God's sake overcome prejudice, and send Greene. You know my opinion of him. I stake my reputation on the events, give him but fair play.*

On the same day, Hamilton wrote to his fiancée, Elizabeth Schuyler, daughter of General Philip Schuyler. He combined a sarcastic jab at Gates with assurances that the defeat would not prove fatal to the Americans.[169]

*Most people here are groaning under a very disagreeable piece of intelligence just come from the Southward; that Gates has had a total defeat near Cambden… Gates however who writes to Congress seems to know very little what has become of his army. He showed that age and the long labors and fatigues of a military life had not in the least impaired his activity; for in three days and a half, he reached Hillsborough, one hundred and eighty miles from the scene of action, leaving all his troops to…get out of the scrape as well as they could. He has confirmed in this instance the opinion I always had of him.*

*This event will have very serious consequences to the Southward. Peoples imaginations have already given up North Carolina and Virginia; but I do not believe either of them will fall. I am certain Virginia cannot.*

Although General Philip Schuyler shared Hamilton's dislike of Gates and welcomed the humiliation of his rival, he worried more about the repercussions of the defeat, as he told Hamilton on September 10.[170]

> *I am very apprehensive the unhappy event…will draw very serious consequences in its train. It will certainly much embarrass us, and probably retard the termination of the war. It will however be attended with one good, the adherents in Congress to the Gallant commander will not have it any longer in their power to play him off against the General.*[171] *Gracious God! that any rational being should put two men in compe*[ti]*tion, one of which has commanded an army the other only been at the head of one, for I aver that when he was to the northward he never made a disposition of his troops. Indeed he was incapable, he never saw an Enemy except at a good distance and from places of perfect security. Indeed! Indeed, he has not lost a whit in my estimation by this last stroke of his.*

George Washington was not particularly well disposed toward Gates, but he was too responsible a commander to engage in petty criticism when events in the South demanded his attention. In a September 12 letter, Washington reassured the despondent South Carolina governor, John Rutledge, of his concern for the South, and urged Rutledge to work with other Southern governors to recruit more Regular troops in their states.[172]

> *I am fully impressed with the importance of the southern States, and of course with the necessity of making every effort to expel the enemy from them. The late unlucky affair near Camden renders the situation more precarious, and calls for every exertion to stop, at least, the further progress of the British army. It is to be wished, that our composition of force in this quarter, our resources, and the present situation of the fleet and army of our ally would admit an immediate and sufficient detachment, not only to answer the purpose I have just mentioned, but to carry on operations of a more serious and extensive nature. But this not being the case…let it suffice that your Excellency be informed, that our views tend ultimately to the southward.*
>
> *In the mean time, our endeavours in that quarter should be directed rather to checking the progress of the enemy by a permanent, compact, and well organized body of men, than attempting immediately to recover the State of South Carolina by a numerous army of militia, who, besides being inconceivably expensive, are too fluctuating and undisciplined to oppose one composed chiefly of regular troops. I would recommend to you, therefore, to make use of your influence with the States from Maryland southward, to raise without delay at least five thousand men, for the war if it can be effected, if not, for as long a time as possible. These, with the militia in the vicinity, would answer the*

> *purpose I have last mentioned, and would in proper time make a useful body, either to form a diversion in favor of, or to cooperate with, a force upon the coast.*

Washington also apprised his French ally, Admiral Luc Urbain de Bouexic, Comte de Guichen, of the situation in the South on September 12. He also hinted at the need for French naval assistance to drive the British from the region.[173]

> *Lord Cornwallis, with some seven or eight thousand men, is in complete possession of two states, Georgia and South Carolina; and, by recent misfortune, North Carolina is at his mercy. His force is daily increasing by an accession of adherents, whom his successes naturally produce in a country inhabited by emigrants from England and Scotland, who have not been long enough transplanted to exchange their ancient habits and attachments in favor of their new residence.*
>
> *...The enemy are now said to be making a detachment from New York for a southern destination. If they push their successes in that quarter, we cannot predict where their career may end. The opposition will be feeble, unless we can give succour from hence, which...must depend on naval superiority.*

The international ramifications of the battle extended far beyond the question of French cooperation in stopping Cornwallis from overwhelming the Southern states. News of the battle caused almost as much excitement in Europe as it had in America, since France and Spain were at war with Britain, while Holland was providing aid to the Americans. Thomas Digges, a Briton who supported the Americans, kept American diplomats Benjamin Franklin and John Adams informed of events in England. Digges recounted the effect that the victory at Camden had on British public opinion in an October 10 letter to Franklin.[174]

> *Last week & indeed until last night the general cry was "we are undone—we can never do any thing in America—the War must be given up—our armys will be Burgoined—our fleets beaten" &ca &a &a. Yesterday an officer arrivd Express from Cornwallis with an accot of a victory over Gates's Army at Cambden in So Carolina, and now they are all in the Skies again—The whole Southern America is theirs—Virginia will "come in" on a certainty—the Rebels will be beat every where—a few thousand more regulars sent over directly will insure the subjugation of America—let us persue the war vigorously &ca. &a—their folly is enough to make one sick.*

In Amsterdam, John Adams had received a similar letter from Digges, but the Massachusetts statesman remained undaunted, as he told Digges on October 14.[175]

*Cornwallis's and Tarletons Gasconade serves to diminish the Esteem of Mankind, for the People of England, by giving Fuel to their Passions, and making them throw off the Mask.*[176] *I dont believe that his Advantage is half so great, nor the Americans Loss half so much as they represent. Time you know is the Mother of Truth…Fighting is the Thing—Fighting will do the Business. Defeats, will pave the Way to Victories.*

Adams concealed his worries from Digges, but admitted them to Samuel Huntington, president of the Continental Congress, when he wrote on October 14 that Gates's defeat had made the Dutch reluctant to loan more money to the Americans.[177]

*I wish I could give you Hopes of speedy Success in this Business,*[178] *but I fear that Cornwallis's account of his Defeat of General Gates, whether true or false, will extinguish the very moderate Hopes which I had before, for a Time.*

French writer Antoine Marie Cerisier, a strong supporter of America, told Adams on October 17 that he believed that the Americans could learn from their experience at Camden.[179]

*I hope that the last action, which Lord Cornwallis has so pompously described, will have no bad consequences. But, will you give me leave to observe that this last battle appears to be a proof that undisciplined milices*[180] *are not a match for European regular troops?*

After the battle, a French cartographer drew a map depicting the terrain and positions of the units involved. It was accompanied by a "Relation Du Combat pour l'intelligence du plan." ("Account of the Battle for understanding the map.") The description of the battle was clearly taken from a British source.[181]

*The Americans…camped at the home of Colonel Rugeley twelve miles from Camden where they were joined by the Virginians.*

*The next day at two-thirty in the morning the advanced guards encountered one another and there was a brisk fire, which convinced the English General to wait for day to begin a general action.*

*At daybreak, the English army was in line of battle…*

*The Americans formed in two lines opposite and close to the English when a detachment under the orders of Lieutenant Colonel Webster began the attack with great vigor and a short time after that the action became general.*

*The English advanced with coolness, maintaining a constant fire, until they reached the bayonets of the Americans. After a brave resistance that lasted about an hour the courage of the latter was obliged to give way to British intrepidity seconded by discipline and experience. Soon confusion spread among them and our troops penetrated into their lines, the enemy then took flight in all directions. The rout was complete and the massacre that the English cavalry made of the fugitives that they pursued to a distance of twenty-two miles covered the country with the dead and dying.*

*One must concede that the Americans withstood the first shock with plenty of bravery and firmness, but they had made the mistake of taking position between two swamps, that penned in their line and gave the larger expanse to that of the English. Besides, General Gates, in positioning his troops, had not left a sufficient interval between the front and rear lines of his Army, in the middle of which when his front was thrown into disorder, there was no place to fall back and reform…without throwing the second line into confusion as well.*

Doctor Hugh Williamson of North Carolina had been sent into the British lines by his superiors immediately after the battle to treat that state's wounded soldiers who had been left behind and taken prisoner. Upon returning to North Carolina, Williamson described the sufferings of the wounded to Thomas Benbury, speaker of the state legislature; his letter was written on December 1.[182]

*After the Battle of the 16th of August, as soon as I overtook Genl. Caswell, he gave me a Flag to return to the Enemies Lines for the relief of our wounded; I was also instructed to ask for a return of the Prisoners.*

*This return*[183] *I have made to the present Commanding Officer…I wish I could say that our loss after the Battle, either by wounds or sickness, was inconsiderable; but we labored under many difficulties. It was our misfortune that the Countenance we showed immediately after the Battle was not calculated to Command that respect which is due to an army of the United States. The Enemy was disposed to neglect us, and a victory which they greatly overrated did not seem to increase their Humanity. For eight or ten days after the Battle our people suffered under great neglect. After the Bitterest Complaints and most urgent importunity our supplies became more liberal. We were also weak in Medical Help. Our Militia Surgeon disappeared after the Battle…It happened that one of the Continental Surgeons fell into the hands of the Enemy. It may be supposed that with his assistance, tho' he was indefatigable, I found it impossible to give the desired help to 240 Men, who Laboured under at Least 700 Wounds. After three weeks we were happily reinforced by Dr. Johnson, a Senior Surgeon of great skill & Humanity in the Continental Service…*

*The number of wounded brought into Cambden from the actions of the 16th and 18th of August was 240. Of this number 162 were Continental Troops, 12 were South Carolina Militia, 3 were of Virginia Militia, and 63 were of the Militia of this State, of whom the List is enclosed.*

*On the 7th of September 18 of our Militia, having recovered from their wounds, were sent to Charlestown; 9 of the Militia, having recovered, escaped at different times, and 10 of them remained in Cambden on the 13th of October chiefly well. We had the misfortune to lose 5 Privates, who died by their Wounds, 9 by the Small Pox, 1 by a Putrid fever, and 4 by the Flux;*[184] *2 Officers died by their Wounds and 2 by the Small Pox.*

*It will be observed that we paid a heavy tribute to the Small Pox. However…no means in our power were omitted by which we might avoid or palliate its dangerous effects…During the whole of our attendance on the wounded and Sick, we had occasion to remark That the most of our Prisoners were visited by the Flux, which prevailed in Cambden; we did not lose a single Man by that disease, unless of those who had broken thighs or Legs.*

*That small Boys suffered most by the Flux; That the sufferings of our men were greatly increased by the want of Sugar, Tea, Coffee, Vinegar,*[185] *and such other palatable antiseptic Nourishment as is best suited the Sick. The cry for these Articles was constant, while our supplies were so scanty as hardly to deserve the name, nor was any thing of the kind to be purchased for Money, unless in very trifling Quantities.*

Long after the war, Colonel William R. Davie of North Carolina, a highly successful partisan commander, wrote an account of the war in the South in which he harshly criticized Gates.[186]

*"Gates defeat—Observations."*

*The advanced situation of Caswells division, the ill-effect of a retrograde movement, and the situation of the country about Lynch's Creek appear to have impelled Genl Gates to move forward to Rugeleys mills—*

*This position taken by accident rather than choice was not so bad as has been generally represented, its neighbourhood contains the strongest ground in that part of the Country. From this place must be dated the error of the General and the misfortunes of the Army; When he determined to approach Camden as near as Saunders Creek, the Enemy being there within surprising distance. He ought to have pushed forward his light troops with 2 or 3 pieces of artillery and taken possession of that pass early in the day, at this place There is a wide boggy morass passable only by the causeway, and the ground rises considerably on the Northern side—Had the light troops been in possession of this post, their patroles must have given early notice of the Enemys advancing in force The cause way might have been disputed & the light troops supported or withdrawn at pleasure and arrangements for attack, keeping the enemy in check, or avoiding a general action could have been easily made.*

*As the recovery of the two Southern States and the security of the remainder depended upon the army then collected it was the grossest folly to stake the whole blindly upon one single throw of the die; the whole army were necessarily brought into action, the Enemys force was unknown, he might succeed but there was no certain data to calculate this success upon, the want of success was inevitably followed by a total defeat—nothing but the most desparate circumstances could warrant a General to stake so much upon a single Hazard.*

*Three fourths of this army were militia, these alone might have been a match for the royal army if properly fought under such advantages as a country covered with woods morasses and broken grounds almost every where affords. There never was a necessity to attack the British army at any particular point or place and the militia allways behaved well when served up by detachment, and under the impulse of attack.*

*The center and left of the front line were composed of militia, these could not be expected to wait the shock of a charge made by regular troops, otherwise discipline would be useless and military tacticks a farce. The consequence was this flank was immediately turned, the whole reserve could they have been brought up in time would not have filled this fatal interval between Gists Brigade and the swamp, DeKalbs Division on the right was of course instantly overwhelmed, and the reserves soon involved in their fate.*

*The Ground on which the armies met was not the choice of the general but the accident of the night, but being narrowed by swamps both on the right and left was particularly favorable to the inferior numbers of the royal army & leaving no advantage to the superior numbers of their opponents; and still too extensive and too open to fight the Militia to advantage.*

*General Gates had joined the army but a few days which time was employed in continual marches, he was entirely unacquainted with the character of the officers or the merits of the different corps which composed his army, and was ignorant of their numbers, having never received a return untill after the orders of the 15$^{th}$ were issued, the regular troops wanted rest and refreshment, the whole of the militia wanted arrangement and the ordinary preparation for a battle was intirely neglected among them, in Rutherfords Brigade there was scarce a cartridge made up, and their arms were generally in bad order; the consequence of continual marching & exposure. A man must have had more than ordinary good fortune to avoid a defeat under so many unfortunate circumstances.*

Henry Lee, the famed "Light Horse Harry" and father of Civil War general Robert E. Lee, led his famous legion throughout most of the Southern campaign. Lee arrived in the South several months after the battle of Camden, but discussed the battle in detail with officers who had participated. His account reflects their experiences and opinions as well as his own viewpoint.[187]

*The American general* [Gates] *soon after he entered South Carolina, directed his march toward Lynch's Creek…Lord Rawdon, unwilling that Gates should find him in Camden, where were deposited his stores, ammunition, and sick, advanced to a strong position, fifteen miles in front, on the southern bank of Lynch's Creek.*

*…Gates…moved to Lynch's opposite to Lord Rawdon; and the two armies remained for four days, separated only by the creek. Gates broke up from this ground inclining to his right, which putting in danger the British advanced post at Rudgely's mill, Lord Rawdon directed its evacuation, and fell back to Logtown, in the vicinity of Camden. Here, he became acquainted with the insurrection of the inhabitants on Black River, headed by Brigadier Marion…Gates, desirous of opening his communication with Sumter, continued to advance upon the north side of Lynch's Creek, and took post at Rudgely's mill…Gates weakened his army, though in striking distance of his foe, by detaching to Sumter four hundred men…with two light pieces. As soon as this detachment was put in motion, preparations were made to advance still nearer to Camden.*

*The evacuation of Rudgely's mill and the falling back of Lord Rawdon from Lynch's Creek, seem to have inspired General Gates with the presumption that his approach would drive the enemy from Camden. No conclusion more erroneous could have been drawn from a fair view of the objects and situation of the respective armies.*

*The British general was under the necessity of maintaining his position; for retreat yielded up that country which he was bound to retain, and encouraged that spirit of revolt which he was bound to repress. All the disposable force under his orders had been concentrated at Camden; delay would not thicken his ranks, while it was sure to add to those of his adversary. Every consideration urged the British general to battle; and no commander was ever more disposed than Lord Cornwallis to cut out relief from embarrassment by the sword. The foundation of the policy pursued by General Gates, was laid in error; and we ought not to be surprised at its disastrous termination. Had Gates not confidently presumed that a retrograde movement on the part of the enemy would have been the effect of his advance, he certainly would have detained Woolford's detachment, and ordered Sumter to join him: it being unquestionable that victory in the plains of Camden would give to him the British army, and with it all the posts in South Carolina except Charleston. To this end his means ought to have been solely directed; or, if he preferred the wiser course, to spin out the campaign, condensing his main body, and beating the enemy in detail, he should have continued in his strong position behind Lynch's Creek, ready upon Cornwallis's advance to have fallen back upon its head-waters…*

*No doubt General Gates was unfortunately persuaded that he had nothing to do but to advance upon his enemy, never supposing that so far from retiring, the British general would seize the proffered opportunity of battle.*

*Unhappily for America, unhappily for himself, he acted under this influence, nor did he awake from his reverie until the proximity of the enemy was announced by his fire in the night, preceding the fatal morning.*

*Lord Cornwallis…hastened to Camden…he found his army very much enfeebled; eight hundred being sick, his effective strength was reduced to somewhat less than two thousand three hundred men…he rated his enemy at six thousand; in which estimation his lordship was much mistaken, as…it appears that our force did not exceed four thousand, including the corps detached under Lieutenant-Colonel Woolford; yet there was a great disparity of numbers in our favor, but we fell short in quality, our Continental horse, foot, and artillery, being under one thousand, whereas the British regulars amounted to nearly one thousand six hundred.*

*Notwithstanding his diminished force, notwithstanding the vast expected superiority of his enemy, the discriminating mind of the British general paused not an instant in deciding upon his course.*

*No idea of a retrograde movement was entertained by him. Victory only could extricate him from the surrounding dangers; and the quicker the decision, the better his chance of success. He therefore gave orders to prepare for battle, and in the evening of the 15th put his army in motion to attack his enemy next morning in his position at Rudgely's mill…*

*"After Gates…prepared his army to move, it was resolved in a council of war to march on the night of the 15th, and to sit down behind Saunder's Creek, within seven miles of Camden. Thus it happened that both the generals were in motion at the same hour…with this material distinction, that the American general grounded his conduct in his mistaken confidence of his adversary's disposition to retreat; whereas the British commander sought for battle with anxiety, regarding the evasion of it by his antagonist as the highest misfortune…*

*Our loss was very heavy. More than a third of the Continental troops were killed and wounded; and of the wounded one hundred and seventy were made prisoners. The regiment of Delaware was nearly annihilated…The North Carolina militia also suffered greatly; more than three hundred were taken, and nearly one hundred killed and wounded…the Virginia militia, who set the infamous example which produced the destruction of our army, escaped entirely.*

*De Kalb…in his last resolute attempt to seize victory, received eleven wounds, and was made prisoner. His yet lingering life was rescued from immediate death by the brave interposition of Lieutenant-Colonel Du Buysson, one of his aids-de-camp; who embracing the prostrate general, received into his own body the bayonets pointed at his friend. The heroic veteran, though treated with every attention, survived but a few days…We lost, besides Major-General Baron de Kalb, many excellent officers; and among them Lieutenant-Colonel Porterfield, whose promise of future greatness had endeared him to the whole army…*

*In the dreadful gloom which now overspread the United States, the reflecting mind drew consolation from the undismayed gallantry displayed by a portion of the army, throughout the desperate conflict; and from the zeal, courage, and intelligence exhibited by many of our officers. Smallwood and Gist had conducted themselves with exemplary skill and bravery. Stevens and Caswell both deserved distinguished applause, although both were the mortified leaders of spiritless troops. Colonel Williams, adjutant-general, was conspicuous throughout the action; cheerfully risking his valuable life…and volunteering his person wherever danger called. Lieutenant-Colonel Howard demonstrated a solidity of character which, on every future occasion, he displayed honorably to himself and advantageously to his country. The general-in-chief, although deeply unfortunate, is entitled to respect and regard. He took decisive measures to restore the action, by unceasing efforts to rally the fugitive militia; and had he succeeded, would have led them to the vortex of battle. By seconding the Continental troops with this rallied corps, he would probably have turned the fortune of the day, or have died the hero of Saratoga.*

*None…can withhold applause from Colonel Dixon and his North Carolina regiment of militia. Having their flank exposed by the flight of the other militia, they turned with disdain from the ignoble example; and fixing their eyes on the Marylanders, whose left they became, determined to vie in deeds of courage with their veteran comrades…In every vicissitude of the battle, this regiment maintained its ground, and when the reserve under Smallwood, covering our left, relieved its naked flank, forced the enemy to fall back…*

*Major-General Gates assumed the command under the happiest circumstances. He was hailed as the conqueror of Saratoga; and our gallant troops, anticipating the future from reflecting on the past, proudly presumed that his skill, directing their valor, would liberate the South…*

*Considering the condition of the respective armies, this fond expectation will not appear chimerical. But…General Gates…seems to have acted under a conviction that it was only necessary to meet the foe to conquer…he rashly advanced toward the enemy; and persevered in the same precipitancy, until stopped by his adversary, moving to strike him in his camp. Let us suppose that he had conducted his operations on different principles; what would have been the probable result? Had he wisely taken with him the old regiment of dragoons under White and Washington,*[188] *as those brave officers in vain solicited, instead of a dastardly flight, an example of heroism would have been exhibited. The enemy would have been driven in; prisoners would have been made by, but none from, us; intelligence would have been shut to the enemy, but open to ourselves; and the dawn of day would have found our troops, emboldened by the example of the cavalry, panting for battle. He would, moreover, have been provided with a body of horse, more numerous and capable than that of his enemy; and would have carried his army, full of bodily strength and high in spirits, into the neighborhood of his foes. By falling back from Lynch's Creek, when Lord Rawdon retired to Logtown, he would have placed himself in a friendly, strong, and plentiful country; where, out of striking distance, he might have employed a week or ten days in training his militia, and infusing into them that self-confidence which doubly arms the soldier in the day of battle. While improving the condition of his army, he might by dispatching influential characters to the west of the Alleghany, have brought down one or two thousand of those hardy warriors to Charlotte,*[189] *to be used as an army of reserve, should events require it. What was of the highest importance, he must, by this delay, have ascertained with precision the intention of the enemy in time to elude or resist it; and would have drawn Cornwallis further from his point of safety; thus more and more exposing him to the harassing attacks of Marion and Sumter on his flanks and in his rear. All these advantages were within the general's grasp. The partial, though sure, game of destruction had commenced… Obvious as was this mode of operation, General Gates, with the "Veni, vidi, vici" of Caesar*[190] *in his imagination, rushed on to the fatal field, where he met correction, not more severe than merited.*

6

# Contemporary British Observations and Reports

Reports of Cornwallis's victory quickly reached British and Loyalist troops in the field and boosted their morale. Alexander Chesney, a South Carolinian serving in the Loyal militia, was operating with his unit against Rebel partisans when he heard the news.[191]

> *On the 16th we heard a heavy firing towards Camden, which kept us in the utmost anxiety untill the 18th when a letter was received…informing us that his Lordship had attacked & defeated Gates' Army had killed or taken 2,200 men 18 Ammunition Waggons and 350 waggons with provisions and other stores. This news made us happy as people in our situation could possible be.*

Pennsylvania Loyalist Charles Stedman accompanied the British expedition to Charleston and served as commissary in Cornwallis's army. He was probably with the army in Camden, and although he probably remained in town when Cornwallis marched to attack Gates, he later had the opportunity to hear many firsthand accounts from British participants, and incorporated them in his history of the Revolution.[192]

> *In the mean time the different corps of continental troops and militia…having formed a junction, entered the province of South Carolina. General Gates joined them on the twenty-seventh of July; and the whole…advanced by the main road towards Camden. In order to stop their progress, lord Rawdon moved forward, with the force under his command at Camden, and took a strong position about fourteen miles in front of it, upon the west branch of Lynche's Creek. General Gates advanced on the opposite side; and the two armies continued for several days opposed to each other, with the creek only intervening between their advanced parties. While the opposite armies lay in this situation, orders were sent to lieutenant-colonel Cruger to forward with all haste to Camden the four companies of light-infantry stationed at Ninety-six; and intelligence*

*being received of a movement made by the Americans towards their right, orders were sent to the British officer commanding at Rugeley's Mills, to evacuate his post, which was exposed on account of its advanced situation, and, after sending part of his detachment to join the army, to retire with the rest to Camden. By the evacuation of the post at Rugeley's Mills the road leading from Waxhaws to Camden was left unguarded; and lord Rawdon, fearing that general Gates might attempt to pass him by this road, and get into his rear, found it necessary to fall back from Lynche's Creek, nearer to Camden, and took a new position at Logtown.*[193] *By this time almost all the inhabitants between Black River and Pedee had openly revolted and joined the Americans; and, in other quarters, they seemed disposed to follow the example, whenever it could be done with security. Sumpter, with his force increased by a detachment of continental soldiers, was sent across the Wateree to favour the revolt of the inhabitants on the north-west side of that river, and to intercept the supplies and reinforcements on the road to Camden; and general Gates, in order to preserve a communication with Sumpter, moved to his right up the north side of Lynche's Creek, and took post at Rugeley's Mills, intending to advance from thence, by the Waxhaw road, to Camden. Information of these movements on the part of the enemy being regularly transmitted by lord Rawdon to Charlestown, Earl Cornwallis thought it necessary to postpone the completion of the civil arrangements in which he had for some time past been engaged, and to proceed to Camden, where the threatening aspect of affairs required all his immediate attention. He set out from Charlestown in the evening of the tenth, and arrived at Camden in the evening of the thirteenth, of August. The following day he spent in examining the condition of his own force, and in obtaining information of that of the enemy: Nearly eight hundred British troops were sick at Camden. The number of those who were really effective, amounted to something more than two thousand, including officers, of whom about fifteen hundred were regulars, or belonged to established provincial corps, and the rest, militia and refugees from North Carolina. The force under general Gates was represented to amount to six thousand men, exclusive of Sumpter's corps, which was estimated at one thousand…But almost the whole country seemed upon the eve of a revolt. The communication between Camden and Charlestown appeared in danger of being cut off by the enterprising movements of Sumpter, whose numbers were daily increasing by the junction of disaffected inhabitants. The safety of the army depended upon preserving a communication with the seacoast; and something was necessary to be done immediately for extricating it from its perilous situation. At this juncture a retreat to Charlestown might have been effected without much difficulty; but the sick must have been left behind, the magazines of stores either abandoned or destroyed, and the loss of the whole country would have necessarily followed, except indeed Charlestown, in which there was already a sufficient garrison…And where the motives for action so strongly preponderated, there was not much room for deliberation in the breast of an officer of so much enterprise as lord Cornwallis. Confiding in the valour and discipline of his troops, however inferior in number, he resolved to move forward and attack the enemy, whose present situation at Rugeley's Mills inclined him to execute his intention without delay. Meaning to attack them early in the morning of the sixteenth of August, and to point his attack principally against the continental regiments, whose position, from the information he had received, he knew to be a bad one, earl Cornwallis began his march towards Rugeley's Mills, at ten in the evening of the fifteenth of August, committing the defence of Camden to major McArthur, with some provincials, militia, convalescents of the army, and a detachment of the sixty-third regiment, which was expected to arrive during the night…It is not a little singular that the same night, nearly about the same time, and with a similar intention, general Gates should have left his encampment at Rugeley's Mills, and moved forward towards Camden. Both armies marching on the same road, in opposite directions, their advanced guards met and fired upon each other about two in the morning. Some prisoners were made on both sides; and from these the respective commanders became acquainted with the movements of the other: Both armies halted and were formed; and the firing soon afterwards ceased as if by mutual consent. The ground on which the two armies had accidentally met was as favourable for lord Cornwallis as he could have wished: A swamp on each side secured his flanks, and narrowed the ground in front, so as to render the superiority of the enemy in numbers of less consequence: He therefore waited with impatience for the approach of day; and as soon as it appeared made his last disposition for the attack…*

*The American army was also formed in two lines…*

*The opposite armies being thus ranged in order of battle, and some movement being observed on the left of the provincial line, as if a change of disposition had been intended, lord Cornwallis deemed this the critical moment for beginning the action, and gave orders to lieutenant-colonel Webster to advance and charge the enemy. The order was immediately executed with such alacrity, and the charge made with so much promptitude and success, that the Virginia militia, quickly giving way, threw down their arms and fled, and were soon afterwards followed by the greatest part of the militia of North Carolina. The American reserve was now brought into action; and general Gates, in conjunction with general Caswell, retiring with the militia, endeavoured to rally them at different advantageous passes in the rear of the field of action, but in vain; They ran at first like a torrent, and afterwards spread through the woods in every direction. Lord Rawdon began the action on the left with no less vigour and spirit than Webster had done on the right; but here, and in the center, against part of Webster's division, the contest was more obstinately maintained by the Americans, whose artillery did considerable execution. Their left flank was, however, exposed by the flight of the militia; and the light-infantry and twenty-third regiment, who had been opposed to the fugitives, instead of pursuing them, wheeled to the left and came upon the flank of the continentals, who, after a brave resistance for near three quarters of an hour, were thrown into total confusion, and forced to give way in all quarters. Their rout was completed by the cavalry, who continued the pursuit to Hanging Rock, twenty-two miles from the field of action. Between eight and nine hundred of the enemy were killed in the action, and in the pursuit, and about one thousand made prisoners, many of whom were wounded. Of this number, were major-general baron de Kalbe, and brigadier-general Rutherford. The former of these officers, at the head of a continental regiment of infantry, made a vigorous charge on the left wing of the British army, and when wounded and taken prisoner would scarcely believe that the provincial army had been defeated. He died of his wounds a few days after the action…General Gates, who retired with the militia to endeavour to rally them, finding all his efforts vain, gave up every thing as lost, and fled first to Charlotte, ninety miles from the place of action; and from thence to Hillsborough, in North Carolina, one hundred and eighty miles from Camden. General Gist alone, of all the American commanders, was able to keep together about one hundred men, who flying across a swamp on their right, through which they could not be pursued by the British dragoons, made good their retreat in a body. The loss of the British troops in this battle amounted to three hundred and twenty-five, of whom sixty-nine were killed, two hundred and forty-five wounded, and eleven missing. The weight of the action fell upon the thirty-third regiment on the left of Webster's division, and the volunteers of Ireland in the right of lord Rawdon's; and of course, by them the greatest loss was sustained, which amounted to two thirds of the whole. The road for some miles was strewed with the wounded and killed, who had been overtaken by the legion in their pursuit. The number of dead horses, broken wagons, and baggage, scattered upon the road, formed a perfect scene of horror and confusion; such was the terror and dismay of the Americans…Lord Cornwallis's judgment in planning, his promptitude in executing, and his fortitude and coolness during the time of the action, justly attracted universal applause and admiration. The lord Rawdon, who was only twenty-five years of age, bore a very conspicuous part in this day's action. Colonel Webster's conduct was consistent with his general character: Cool, determined, vigilant, and active in action, he added to a reputation established by long service, the universal esteem and respect of the whole army, as an officer of great experience and observation as well as bravery and rigid discipline. In a word, every British officer and soldier evinced in this day's action the most perfect intrepidity and valour. The American wounded were treated with the utmost humanity…*

*By the victory gained over general Gates at Camden, and the rout and total dispersion of his army, followed so soon after by the defeat and ruin of the corps under Sumpter, the provincial force to the southward seemed for a time entirely annihilated; and nothing prevented earl Cornwallis from proceeding immediately on his long-projected expedition into North Carolina, but the want of some supplies for the army, which were on their way from Charlestown.*

Colonel Robert Gray, a South Carolina Loyalist, commanded the Cheraw district militia in 1780. He was not present at Camden, but observed the consequences of the battle.[194]

> *...the approach of the* [American] *army seemed to be a signal for a general revolt in the disaffected parts of the back Country, but the speedy & successful issue of the action at Camden put an end to it immediately, and restored tranquillity to the Country.*
>
> *...A universal panic seized the rebels after the battle of Camden and had Lord Cornwallis had a sufficient army to have marched into North Carolina & to have established posts in his rear at convenient places to preserve his communication with South Carolina & to prevent the rebels from assembling in arms after he had passed along North Carolina would have fallen without a struggle, but the smallness of his numbers soon turned the tide against him.*

One week after the battle, Charleston newspapers described how Loyalists and British troops in town celebrated the victory.[195]

> *On Friday afternoon an officer arrived in town from Camden, with advices of a most complete and decisive victory being obtained on the 16th instant, by the Royal Army, commanded by the Right Honourable Lieutenant General Earl CORNWALLIS, over that of the rebels led by Major-General GATES. At sunset, the troops in garrison were paraded, the cannon in the batteries and a feu de joy fired, attended with the acclamations of the soldiers and numerous spectators; joy beamed in every countenance but those of the adherents of the late usurpation, whose lengthened visages denoted their inward grief. In the evening there was as general an illumination as the shortness of the notice could admit; but on the following one it was more universal, notwithstanding the badness of the weather.*

A subsequent newspaper article reported on the condition and attitude of the Continental prisoners taken at Camden. Even if the account is exaggerated, it indicates that the American troops had been badly demoralized by their defeat.[196]

> *On Friday night and Saturday morning about five hundred rebel prisoners, taken in the action of the 16th of August, arrived in town, escorted by a detachment of the 64th regiment, under Major Macleroth*[197] *and a party of Volunteers of the Charlestown militia, mounted for the service, under the command of Major Inglis.*[198]
>
> *It is worthy of remark, that of these two divisions, only four persons, Continental soldiers, who were taken in this town, and had made their escape from hence, shewed the least inclination to get away. On the contrary, they in general appeared highly satisfied with their situation, which many of them acknowledged vastly preferable to*

> *that they had recently been in. They were almost unanimous in execrating their late rulers, who by every means of force and deceit, had dragged them to the field against men represented in the most odious colours, but from whom they had experienced every attention that humanity and generosity could dictate.*
>
> *Gates is spoken of by the prisoners in the most disrespectful terms, saying that he fled in the beginning of the action, with every mark of trepidation and dismay. De Kalb and Smallwood are regarded in a very different light by them.*
>
> *It would really be matter of surprise, if the soldiers in the Congress service should be otherwise than dissatisfied. Their cloathing scarcely merits the name—their usage and food bad in the extreme—and their pay of so little value, that it required a month's to purchase a pint of Whiskey.*
>
> *We are informed by authentick accounts, that General Gates retreated with such expedition, that he was one hundred and fifty miles from the field of battle, on the Friday morning after the action, (which happened on the Tuesday) concealed in a cellar for fear of the Tories in North-Carolina, where he staid a few hours and proceeded with great haste towards Virginia, without a single attendant.*

The story of Gates hiding in a cellar was untrue, but Loyalist newspapers continued to print similar rumors. One account claimed that Gates had virtually conceded defeat in the South.[199]

> *We are well assured that when General Gates arrived at Philadelphia…he acquainted the Congress that unless an Army as numerous as that under the Command of General Washington was sent to the Carolinas immediately, all was over in that Quarter of the Continent.*

Gates had not gone to Philadelphia, but that error did not prevent the press from publishing another disparaging tale about the American general ten days later.[200]

> *We hear that Smallwood has the chief command of the Rebel forces in North-Carolina, Gates being under an arrest.*

A young British clerk, Robert Biddulph, was working for a merchant firm in Charleston when he informed his parents about the battle on August 27. His prediction of the dire consequences of an American victory reflected the fears aroused by Gates's advance.[201]

> *Ld. Cornwallis…was inform'd of a large Army under Genl. Gates, within a few Miles of him, and determined to fight them. On the 15th he heard they were*

*reinforced by 1500 Men. This did not incline him to change his resolution. He march'd on that Night, and met the Army coming to attack him. Both Parties formd without Interruption, and lay upon their Arms till daylight. The Action then commenced and lasted ab't an Hour, when the Rebells gave way. The Cavalry under Col. Tarleton chargd them, pursued their Remains for 22 Miles, killing great Numbers. The Number of Prisoners is not known, upwards of 1000 were left dead upon the field. This Victory, the greatest and most important to this Country, was obtain'd by 1800 Men over 6,400. Genl. Gates, finding the destruction of his Army inevitable, left the field with a few Officers before the Charge of the Cavalry. Genl. Du Kalb was taken wounded and since dead…The* [Rebel] *Army made no Doubt of Ld. C's retreating before them, or if he sh'd hazard an Action, of cutting him to Pieces—but good fortune and the Courage of British Soldiers have prevented this. Had they succeeded at Campden, this Town would in all Probability have been in their Possession, as our internal Enemies would have been as active as the external ones.*

Lieutenant Colonel Nisbet Balfour of the Twenty-third Regiment served as commandant of Charleston. Although he was pleased by the victory, he was also concerned by the large number of Americans who had violated the oaths they had recently taken to Britain when Gates approached. He denounced them in a letter to Sir Henry Strachey, a member of Parliament, written on August 30.[202]

*This comes by friend Ross…His news are worth bringing, if the saving this provence, Georgia, and the probability of gaining N. Carolina, is any object at present in England—If not, the military reputation Lord Cornwallis has gained is very high—and thats all—*

*In vain we expected, loyalty and attachment from the inhabitants—they are the same stuff as compose all Americans—freightned into oaths of allegiance, when we are the strongest but the moment they think that is not the case they are ready to fight against us, and usualy lay a plan to make of for their former bad behaviour to their countrymen.*

*In the present case, they conducted their matters as usual well, and with secrecy, they privately invited Gates' approach, and the moment he came near, revolted and joined him.*

*Luckily his folly, and Lord Cornwallis' decision, marred all their plans, and has again put them in our power, nor does his Lordship mean to let slip his advantage, but punished as they deserve.—*

*Gates had made a wonderful long march and getting into North Carolina raised all he could to bring at, in hopes of getting at us in detail before we were collected, being invited by his friends here—Lord Cornwallis, stripped of allmost any troops, and left bare by his Excelly.*[203] *had been obliged to detach very widely, but soon collected, and fortunately himself got to Camden just in time there he found Mr Gates within twelve miles of him with six thousand men, he having fourteen Hundred.*

*However there was no alternative, a retreat, and a defeat, were the same, and without hesitating, he determined to attack him, under these circumstances, and marching on the 15th. At light fell in with him just as he was marching to attack at Camden—what followed the gazette will fully informe you of, Lord Cornwallis and his little army gained immortal honor and the convention was revenged—*

*From the compleatness of the business I think this…province and Georgia secured, and N. Carolina possessed…the difficulty of a march to the southward*[204] *must secure us, if His Excelly. Does not mean to guard the North river, with twenty thousand men,*[205] *it is to be hoped we will see some of his troops without their General, & if so, Virginia will also be allarmed But I fear his aversion, and Jealousy to us, will prevent any good…for never was a hatred as marked and so strong, except that to our friend at whose name he yet turns pale.*[206]

On August 26, a Hessian officer in Charleston named Von der Malsburg described the battle's importance in a letter to his commander, Lieutenant General Wilhelm von Knyphausen, who was in New York. The Hessians were German troops whose rulers had hired them out to the British government to serve in North America.[207]

*Much depended on the victory Lord Cornwallis has just gained. If he had been beaten, the whole of this province would have again fallen into the enemy's hands; our whole army would have been enclosed in Charlestown, and been entirely cut off from all fresh provisions; nay, we should probably have had to put up with being besieged by General Gates. Now we are not only insured against such a disaster for some time to come, but we shall even invade North Carolina in all probability as soon as the hot weather permits of it, so as to bring that province to obedience too.*

An unnamed Hessian officer in the Charleston garrison recorded news of the victory celebrations, along with a satirical advertisement, in his regiment's journal.[208]

*On the 18th August the gratifying news was received from Lord Cornwallis that he had totally defeated General Gates with his whole army at Cambden. In celebration of this victory the garrison lighted a bonfire and towards evening the town was splendidly illuminated. The newspaper here published the following announcement regarding the same.*

*"The following is said to be a Copy of an Advertisement stuck up at the public Places in Philadelphia on the late arrival there of General Horatio Gates.*

*"Millions! Millions! Millions! Reward, strayed, deserted, or stolen from the Subscriber on the 16th of August last near Cambden in the State of South Carolina a whole Army, consisting of Horse, foot, and Dragoons, to the amount of near 10,000 as has been said—with all their Bagage, Artillerie, Waggons and Camp Equipage. The subscriber has very strong Suspicions from Information received, from his aid de Camp, that a certain Charles Earl Cornwallis was principally concerned in carrying off the said Army with their Bagage etc. Any Person or Persons civil or military, who will give information either to the Subscriber, or to Charles Thompson Esq. Secretary to the Continental Congress, where the said Army is, so that they may be recovered and rallied again, shall be entitled to demand from the Treasure of the united States the sum of three Millions of Paper Dollars as soon as they can be spared from the public funds, and another Million for apprehending the Persons principally concerned in taken the said Army of*[209]*—proper Passes will be granted by the President of the Congress to such Persons as incline to go in search of the said Army—and as a further Encouragement, no Deduction will be made from the above Reward on account of any of the Militia who composed Part of the said Army—not being to be found or heard of, as no Dependence can be placed on their services and nothing but the most speedy flight can ever save their Commander.*

*"Horatio Gates, M.-General and late Commander-in-Chief of the Southern Army."*

Loyalists and soldiers in New York joined in celebrating the victory and lampooning the vanquished. The New York newspaper published the first news of the battle on September 9, consisting of an article reprinted from an American source supplemented by other reports from South Carolina.[210]

*From the New-Jersey Paper, Chatham, September 6.*

*By intelligence from the southward, we learn that our army in South-Carolina, under the command of General Gates, had lately been repulsed with the loss of* UPWARDS *of* ONE THOUSAND MEN *killed and taken prisoners, and that General Gates with difficulty escaped sharing the fate of the latter. That Baron de Kalb, who commanded the Maryland line of continental troops, was wounded & taken; that the two armies met one another in the night, both endeavouring to gain a certain piece of ground; that to the pusillanimous behaviour of the militia the disaster may be attributed.*

*The action, said to be about 6 miles from Camden, commenced before day-break; the militia were posted to secure a pass leading to an eminence which was the object of the opposing Generals; upon the British charging the militia, the latter gave way, and fell back on their main army, which was instantly attacked and defeated. Col. Tarleton, having been detached round to the rear of the rebels, most of those who escaped the Bayonnet in front, were sacrificed to the broad swords of his mounted British Legion.*

*Further particulars respecting Earl Cornwallis's victory over the rebel army lately commanded by Mr. Horatio Gates.*

*Of eight continental regiments, consisting in seven from Maryland, and one from the lower counties,*[211] *(all of whom were inlisted to serve during the war) eight hundred and ninety three were absolutely killed and left dead on the spot; as the loss of the militia is for political causes, never mentioned in the enemy's returns of killed, wounded and missing, they on this occasion have suppressed the heavy sufferings of that part of their army, it would aggravate their disaster & dispirit their constituents. Mr. Gates went off the field with only forty or fifty men.—*

*Their Generals, Smallwood and Guest are missing, and as the line of Maryland troops was almost entirely killed, it is conjectured themselves shared the same fate: After Mr. Gates had been pursued one hundred miles, his panic carried him another hundred distance from the field of action, into Virginia. Six pieces of cannon and two howitzers, all the ammunition, baggage, provisions, tents, stores, &c. &c. fell into the hands of the Conquerors. The rebel army consisted of 3500 men at the beginning of the action, and their private accounts acknowledge their loss to be from 2,400 to 3,000.*

Four days later, the New York paper reprinted the following story from the September 6 *Pennsylvania Gazette*, along with printer James Rivington's comments.[212]

*We are assured, by good authority, that on the 16th inst, at two o'clock A.M. a bloody battle was fought within 8 miles of Camden, South Carolina, between his Excellency General Gates, at the head of about 3000 men, nine hundred of whom were regulars, and the British forces under Earl Cornwallis, consisting of 1800 regulars, and 2400 refugees, &c. The contending armies engaged each other with the greatest fury, and the prospect for some time, was extremely favourable to the American troops, who charged bayonets on the enemy, which obliged them to give ground, and leave some of their artillery in the possession of our advancing troops. But unfortunately, at this critical moment the premature flight of the militia terminated the* [battle] *in favour of the enemy—an event which has proved fatal to many of our brave countrymen of the regular troops; 4 or 500 of them having been killed and taken—amongst them are several valuable officers. The enemy's loss hath been much more considerable. Lord Cornwallis, or some other British General, it is conjectured, is amongst the slain. Notwithstanding this misfortune, General Gates, whose head-quarters are at Hillsborough, is collecting a force much superior to his late army, and appears resolved to try the fortune of another day.*

Rivington then inserted his own observations.

*The Printer hopes soon to give the public an accurate and official detail of this victory, for the present he communicates the following illustrations just come to hand, and as they are freely confessed by the enemy, he trust's they may be deemed genuine.—Instead of halting and collecting a force at Hillsborough in North-Carolina, General Gates's flight was rapidly continued three days into Virginia, one hundred and ninety miles from the field of action; it was effected upon a celebrated horse, the son of Colonel Baylor's Fearnought, own brother to his Grace of Kingston's famous Careless, purchased of a General officer of the first distinction. All that Horatio Gates (after the defeat of his troops) knew of the British army, and its noble commander, was their having in a short time become pre-eminently triumphant.—Why then is it presumed, by this Printer,*[213] *to assert the loss of the British was much more considerable than the rebels. Mr. Gates declares (concerning that great field day) that no part of his army could be accounted for, but himself, and an Aid de Camp, his attendant—The following dish we just now learn has been hashed, and served up at Mr. Washington's head quarters,—Imprimis, the killed, wounded, and prisoners taken of the* CONTINENTALS *amount to five hundred;—But (as we have already predicted) no mention is made of a single* MILITIA MAN *nor of the* MISSING *of the rebel army—*FOUR HUNDRED BAGGAGE WAGGONS *laden with every necessary for an army, with a most complete park (including many of the artillery taken at Saratoga) with six hundred stand of arms and accoutrements, for as many recruits, are part of the trophies…*

*We are assured from the rebel accounts, that the noble commander of the British troops, had from the latest advices advanced a considerable way into the province of North Carolina, from which every happy event may be presaged.*

*Mr. Gates was, at the above disastrous crisis, in an indifferent state of health, his complaint a Diarrhoea, his person was disguised in the retreat. It is said his officers have certainly, sent a request to the Rebel Board of War at Philadelphia, desiring a Court Martial may be held upon their commanding officer on the ever memorable, but calamitous 16th of August.*[214]

More than a month after the battle, an official account was finally published in New York with the approval of General Clinton.[215]

*The following accounts of the different actions which have lately happened in this province, we now publish by Authority.*

*Lord* CORNWALLIS *having received intelligence that General Gates had arrived at Deep Creek, in North-Carolina, the 24th of last month, and taken upon him the command of the troops which had been collecting there since the surrender of Charlestown, and that he was putting them in motion, set out for Camden on the evening of the 10th, and arrived there early in the morning of the 14th instant. General Gates had already penetrated into this province, and was advanced as far as Rugely's, about twelve miles distance from Camden. His Lordship having informed himself of the strength and position of the rebels, resolved to attack them, altho' they had been joined upon the 15th by about 1500 militia under General Scott,*[216] *from Virginia; and accordingly, about ten in the evening of that day, the army began their march, and after they had proceeded about eight miles, the advanced guards of both parties fell in with each other, and a skirmish ensued, in which several were killed and wounded on both sides: Col. Porterfield of the rebels had his leg broke, and afterwards fell into our hands, as also did an ammunition waggon, which they left upon the field. From the prisoners and deserters Lord Cornwallis was informed, that the whole rebel army was upon the march to attack him; in order to avoid the confusion of an action in the night, his Lordship halted on ground which was favourable for his small numbers, and in the mean time took measures to oblige the rebels to fight him on it. At day-break in the morning he formed his army into one line, with a reserve, and the cavalry behind the reserve…About twenty minutes after day, finding the rebels formed very near him, his Lordship ordered their left to be attacked, and the action soon became general. After a sharp conflict, which was sustained about three quarters of an hour, the rebels were thrown into total confusion, and gave way, when they lost a great number of men. The cavalry were ordered immediately to fall upon them, which they did with great slaughter. The pursuit was continued for upwards of twenty two miles, and many men were killed in the course of it. Seven pieces of brass cannon, and all their ammunition, were taken in the field. The baggage of their General officers, and all their other baggage and camp equipage, were taken in the pursuit by the cavalry, together with one brass field piece, the carriage of which was damaged in the skirmish in the night, and, with the seven before-mentioned, was the whole they had with them. A General Gregory was killed in the field, and General De Kalb (who is since dead of his wounds) and General Rutherford, who is also wounded, were made prisoners. Upwards of nine hundred officers and men were killed in the field and the pursuit, and about nine hundred were made prisoners, many of whom are wounded—The loss sustained by the royal army, in killed and wounded, amounts to 320 men, including ten officers, three of which were killed, and two more dangerously wounded.*

The same edition of the newspaper also included several related news items.[217]

*We are informed, from very good authority, that Lord Cornwallis's army consisted of no more than 1400 regular and provincial troops, and 500 militia, when his Lordship attacked the rebels under Mr. Gates.*

*General Gates is coming on with 800 men, at Cheraw-Hill.*

*Upwards of 1000 Rebels were found dead, on or near the field of battle, and interred—Major-General de Kalb is since dead of his wounds.*

| *STRENGTH of Major-General GATES'S ARMY, found in General Kalb's Pocket.* | |
|---|---|
| *Maryland and Delaware Line,* | *1500* |
| *Caswell's Militia,* | *2000* |
| *Virginia,* | *1500* |
| *Rutherford's,* | *1500* |
| *Armand's Horse,* | *100* |
| *Porterfield's,* | *300* |
| | *6,900* |
| *Deduct for Desertion, &c.* | *500* |
| | *6,400* |

*The Readers of this Gazette will be pleased now to remark that the Printer's predictions in last Wednesday's Paper have proved real, since the Lost HORATIO, as well as Clerk CHARLES THOMSON have totally suppressed the Returns both of their Continental privates, as well as those poor Devils the Militia, in the total rout of their army on the 16th ult.*

On September 27, 1780, Rivington's *Gazette* published this satirical poem about the battle. The author is unknown.[218]

*A Pastoral Elegy, Set to Music by Signora Carolina,*
*Jonathan: Isaac.*
*Isaac: O wherefore, brother Jonathan,*
*So doleful are your features?*
*Say, are you rather poorly, man,*
*Or have you lost your creatures?*
*Jonathan: Ah, wou'd to Heaven that were all!*
*But worse I have to mention,*
*For Gates, our gallant general*
*Has made a new convention.*[219]
*Isaac: Then Jonathan prick up your ears;*
*Why don't you smile and caper?*
*Why, we'll enlist the Regulars,*
*And pay them with but paper.*[220]
*Jonathan: The regulars prescribed the terms,*
*Nor staid for long orations;*
*They forc'd our troops to ground their arms*
*And eke their corporations.*

*Isaac: Oh! that is grievous! I mistook,*
*Tho' your lank phiz did bode ill,*
*How pert will ev'ry Tory look—*
*And sneer at Yankee-doodle!*
*Jonathan: A thousand slaughter'd friends we've lost,*
*A thousand more are taken;*
*Horatio's steed, which gallop'd post,*
*Has sav'd his rider's bacon.*
*Isaac: Now mourn, with sackcloth cover'd o'er,*
*Our Israel forsaken!*
*So many slain—while such a Boar*
*As Gates shou'd save his bacon.*

Even though the animosity between Clinton and Cornwallis grew worse after the war, in his memoirs Clinton could not help praising Cornwallis for the victory at Camden.[221]

*Lord Cornwallis was now hurried away from Charleston by intelligence from Lord Rawdon that the rebel forces under Gates, having penetrated into South Carolina, were advanced to within a small distance of Camden. And two days after His Lordship joined the King's army he obtained a most complete victory over the enemy, whose militia had very early in the action flung away their arms; and every other corps was so broken and dispersed that their Commander in Chief had scarcely a single attendant to accompany his flight to Charlottetown, from whence he posted with the utmost precipitation to Hillsboro. This very brilliant success against so great a superiority of numbers was almost beyond hope. But Lord Cornwallis' conduct certainly merited it, nor can too much be said in praise of His Lordship's ready decision to meet rather than wait the enemy's attack under his then circumstances, as well as the presence of mind and promptitude with which he availed himself of General Gates' injudicious attempt to change the disposition of his army at the moment of coming into action—a maneuver which must have been extremely hazardous with the best troops but, with such militia as the chief of his was composed of…nothing but ruin could be expected. That officer was consequently punished for it as he deserved.*

*The victory of Camden and the entire dispersion of Sumter's corps two days after by Lieutenant Colonel Tarleton had certainly greatly humbled the disaffected in South Carolina, and seemed to promise a restoration of tranquillity to every part of that province. And, indeed, there is every reason to believe this might have been the case could Lord Cornwallis have attended somewhat longer to that alone…But His Lordship was, of course, desirous of extending the consequences of his success as far as and as expeditously as possible.*[222]

As adjutant general of the Hessian troops, Carl Leopold Baurmeister was responsible for keeping his sovereign, the Landgrave of Hesse-Cassel, informed of events in North America. In a letter dated October 6, Baurmeister provided his sovereign with a detailed if occasionally inaccurate account of the campaign.[223]

> *On the 17th of last month General Clinton finally received a report from Lord Cornwallis, for which he had been waiting very anxiously, for the rebels had received news about an engagement as early as the 5th of said month. General Clinton issued no detailed report, which seems all the stranger to many of us, since on the 22nd of September, simultaneously with the festivities commemorating the King's coronation day, a feu de joie was fired at six o'clock in the evening by the New York garrison, the entire city militia, and the surrounding forts. Previously this has been intentionally omitted at public rejoicings in spite of all advantages over the rebels.*
>
> *I have collected only the following facts:…*
>
> *At the beginning of April Congress had detached the two Maryland brigades and the Continentals of the Delaware district under the command of General de Kalb from Washington's army to Philadelphia. Immediately after the reduction of Charleston these troops were ordered to proceed to Hillsboro, North Carolina, under the command of this general. He set out on the march with fifteen hundred men and reinforced his troops with as many more in Virginia. How difficult a march this was may be gathered from the fact that this region as far as the other side of the Roanoke is uninhabited and barren and that the troops carried no provisions. Advancing in small troops, they nevertheless made their way through this wasteland, ever searching for food, arrived at the place of rendezvous, and finally reached Hillsboro at the end of June.*
>
> *There they found fifteen hundred North Carolinians and one hundred horse under Colonel Armand. Quite unexpectedly, General Gates came with seven hundred Virginians under Brigadier General Stevens and took over the chief command of these forces, which had been lying quiet for a whole month, since provisions were entirely lacking. General de Kalb was eager to surrender the command.*
>
> *In this unpleasant situation General Gates listened to no one but himself, and on the 13th of August he marched to the Pedee*[224] *as far as Claremont, thirteen English miles from Camden, following the impatient Brigadier General Caswell. On the 14th he reinforced Colonel Sumter with four hundred men, intending to become master of all the passes along the Wateree. Thus communication with Camden was cut off, and the British, if attacked and put to flight, would find as many men in their rear as they had in front. The entire situation seemed favorable for General Gates.*
>
> *On the 15th of August he could proudly rejoice at seeing the British posts withdraw from Cheraw Hill to Camden. It was only with great difficulty that the British remained masters of both sides of the Wateree Ferry, for the post on the west*

*bank was fiercely attacked by a superior force, which inflicted a loss of seven men killed and some twenty men and Lieutenant Colonel Cary taken prisoners. They were captured while making a futile attempt to save thirty-eight wagons full of flour and rum. The entire garrisons from Forts Rutledge and Charlotte*[225] *were surrounded and captured on the road to Camden.*

*Lord Cornwallis joined the army late in the evening of the 14th of August, if indeed a force of less than two thousand men can be called an army. He did not think of rest, but formed his plans before the following morning, communicated them to Lord Rawdon and Colonel Webster, and began his movements on the 15th...*

*After a march of barely seven English miles, the advance guards of both armies engaged. General Gates, after having brought all his baggage up to the Waxhaws region, lost no time in meeting Lord Cornwallis...This was a force of 6,500 men, all of them under the strictest orders. For example, no officer, although accustomed to being attended by orderlies, was permitted to take a single man from the ranks.*

*General Gates had not expected to meet with the slightest delay in reaching the place where he meant to give battle, which was seven miles from Camden. There he would have had a creek on his right front and an elevation on his left wing, and his army could have occupied the entire field. However, Lieutenant Colonel Tarleton was familiar with the roads leading to this place, and Lord Cornwallis, lying in ambush, routed the vanguard, which caused so much confusion in the first Maryland brigade that it could not be re-formed.*

*General de Kalb then stationed his troops, as well as the woodland permitted...*

*Lord Cornwallis, who was quicker in forming his troops, drove the rebel volunteers away from the front and then, with his light infantry supported by the Volunteers of Ireland, rushed the enemy's left wing, thus silencing their cannon and routing the North Carolina troops and Colonel Armand's cavalry. The 23rd Regiment broke through the center of the Virginia militia, and then the Marylanders could no longer maintain themselves. They were the only ones who fought like men. Finally, they also were compelled to leave their places on the right wing.*

*Pursued by Lieutenant Colonel Tarleton, they pushed through dense and dark woods and were not safe even after retiring twenty miles, so close did our cavalry follow upon their heels. The enemy had eight hundred killed and twelve hundred taken prisoners, most of whom were wounded. General de Kalb and Brigadier Gregory were killed, and many commissioned officers wounded...*

*The English loss in killed and wounded was somewhat more than 350 men. Among them were three officers killed, two severely wounded, and five slightly wounded...*

*Lord Cornwallis has not yet advanced beyond Camden.*

Hessian Lieutenant John von Krafft recorded the victory celebrations at New York in his journal on September 22.[226]

> *At 3 P.M. the whole garrison of New York, English, Hessians and Militia, had to turn out and form a line on the North River (in honor of the victory of Lieut. Gen. Cornwallis in South Carolina over the Rebels, by whom tents, flags and guns, besides many dead, wounded and prisoners were left to our side,) and fired three rounds of joy, at a signal of 7 rockets from the ramparts of Bonkershill and their guns, besides the shouts of joy.*

Perhaps no one in Britain was happier to receive news of the victory at Camden than Lord George Germain. After years of indecisive fighting, Cornwallis's success, coming on the heels of the surrender of Charleston, seemed to indicate that Germain's strategy was finally working, and that the war was on its way to a successful conclusion. Germain expressed his pleasure in a November 9 letter to Cornwallis.[227]

> *My Lord, I had the very great pleasure to receive from Captain Ross who arrived in London on the 9th of last month your lordship's dispatches Nos. 1 and 2, which I immediately laid before the King who read with the highest satisfaction the account contained in the latter of the very glorious and complete victory obtained by your lordship over the rebels near Camden on the 16th of August.*
>
> *The great superiority of the enemy in numbers over the forces under your command, His Majesty observed, distinguished this victory from all that have been achieved since the commencement of the rebellion; and though it might have been expected that the long continuance of the war would have increased the military skill and discipline of the enemy, your lordship's complete success is a brilliant testimony that the spirit and intrepedity of the King's troops will always triumph over them, and that however they may exceed in numbers, the vigour and perseverance of the British soldiers will overcome all resistance when led on by an able and determined commander seconded by gallant and judicious officers. It is therefore particularly pleasing to me to obey His Majesty's commands by signifying to your lordship his royal pleasure that you do acquaint the officers and soldiers of the brave army under your command that their behaviour upon that glorious day is highly approved by their Sovereign and you will particularly express to Lord Rawdon, Lieutenant-Colonels Webster and Tarleton, His Majesty's approbation of their judicious and spirited conduct. The latter indeed has a double claim to praise for his great alertness in overtaking General Sumpter's detachment before they were apprised of Gates's defeat and by their destruction rendering the victory at Camden still more decisive.*

The success at Camden also alleviated Germain's worries about the security of Georgia. British civil government had been restored in that province, but Governor Sir James Wright had complained that Rebel partisans harassed the Loyalists there. On November 9, Germain informed Wright that Cornwallis's victory would end all threats to British control of Georgia.[228]

> *The glorious success of Lord Cornwallis at Cambden over the whole body of the southern rebel forces on the 16th of August, and so instantly followed by the destruction of Sumpter's detachment, of which you must have heard soon after your dispatches were sent off, will have removed all apprehensions of further disturbance from the rebel troops and must crush every hope in the secret abettors of the rebellion of again subverting the King's authority in South Carolina or Georgia.*

On October 11, Lord George Townshend, master-general of the ordnance, expressed his joy at the victory in a letter to Germain's deputy, William Knox.[229]

> *I was just ordering some Game to be pack'd up for you for the late Charles Town Success—When your Gazette from Lord Cornwallis arrived & hath filled us all with joy.—The very masterly, decided, & persevering conduct of my noble Relation has made This family compleatly happy.—Would to God—It did every one in the Country—We should no longer contend about preservation or loss of Territory we can never abandon without being perfectly insignificant—*
>
> *Accept Dear Sir, my usual small Tribute whenever favorable Events occur & allow them to contribute to a chearful Glass to our worthy friend in Carolina.*

# EPILOGUE

CORNWALLIS'S VICTORY at Camden, along with Tarleton's destruction of Sumter's partisan corps two days later, meant that the British effort to retake the Southern colonies could continue. The biggest obstacle, Gates's army, had been removed; it would be months before that crippled force could resume effective operations. A rapid advance into North Carolina promised to be a fatal blow to the Whigs there, the Loyalists would rally to the king's standard and Virginia, too, might be invaded. If George Washington detached a large force southward his own army might be weakened enough to allow Clinton to resume the offensive in the North. In the immediate aftermath of the battle of Camden, final British victory loomed close over the horizon.

But Cornwallis did not advance quickly. He could have, as he demonstrated in January 1781 after Tarleton's defeat at the battle of Cowpens, when he drove the American army all the way to Virginia. Instead, however, Cornwallis paused to accumulate supplies and allow his sick troops to recover. Not until September 8 did he begin his northward march, and he did not reach Charlotte until September 26.

The delay gave the Americans time to recover. Every day that Cornwallis waited, Whig morale improved. Sumter rebuilt his corps and returned to action. Marion continued to harass Loyalists in northeastern South Carolina. Continentals who had escaped capture at Camden made their way back to the army. More North Carolina militiamen turned out to defend their state. The British advantage was rapidly slipping away.

This became painfully clear in early October. When Cornwallis began his offensive, he ordered Major Patrick Ferguson, inspector general of the Loyal militia, to advance into western North Carolina to cover the flank of the main army. Ferguson and his one thousand militiamen reached Gilbert Town, North Carolina, on September 12. He was busy organizing Loyalists there when he received word that a large force of Whigs from the settlements west of the Appalachians was advancing to attack him. Retreating to a strong position on

King's Mountain just south of the border between the Carolinas, Ferguson sent messages to Cornwallis asking for assistance.

What Ferguson intended is unclear, but it appears from his earlier operations that he hoped to induce the Rebels to attack him, so that while they were engaged they could be attacked in the rear by the reinforcements he had requested from Cornwallis. But the earl, however skilled he was in battlefield tactics, had limited abilities when it came to coordinating the operations of widely separated units.[230] He sent no aid to Ferguson, who was only forty miles away. On October 7, the Whigs surrounded and attacked the Loyalists, killing Ferguson and 130 of his men and capturing the rest. The victory inspired the Whigs, demoralized the Loyalists and forced Cornwallis to abandon Charlotte and retreat to South Carolina. The advantage Cornwallis had won at Camden was now completely lost, and British fortunes began to dim.

It soon became evident that the Americans had gained more in the long term from the Camden campaign than the British had. The most important effect was that Gates's advance had rekindled the fire of resistance in South Carolina. Since the British invasion of Georgia, many Southern Whigs had believed that the Northern states were not doing enough to assist them. In the weeks after the fall of Charleston, most South Carolinians expected Congress to abandon them to their fate, and made their peace with the British. By advancing quickly and calling the people to arms, Gates had demonstrated that Congress and the Whigs in the North were committed to driving the British from the South. Recruits flocked to the partisan bands, and their constant attacks kept the Loyalists on the defensive and forced Cornwallis to send detachments of Regular troops roving across South Carolina to keep the raiders in check. As Lord Rawdon explained more than two months after the battle: "The approach of General Gates's Army unveiled to Us a Fund of disaffection in this Province, of which we could have formed no Idea; And even the dispersion of that force, did not extinguish the Ferment which the hope of its support had raised."[231] Loyalist casualties in the many engagements their militia fought against the partisans were substantial, and while British casualties were much lower, the losses whittled away at Cornwallis's strength.

Camden also provided the final lesson for American commanders in the proper use of militia. Poorly trained farmers could be effective as partisans, taking advantage of surprise to strike the enemy at weak points and retreating quickly afterward, but they were a liability in open field combat against British Regulars. After Camden, American leaders developed new tactics to maximize the militia's effectiveness when fighting alongside Continental troops. Daniel Morgan first employed these tactics at the battle of Cowpens in January 1781. He placed his militia in the front line, and deployed his Continentals in a second line in the rear. Morgan ordered the militiamen to fire two shots and then withdraw behind the Continentals. The plan worked perfectly. The militia's fire inflicted losses on the advancing British troops, and the militia withdrew before they were overrun.

Rallying behind the Regulars, they returned to outflank the British troops engaged with the Continentals and delivered the crushing blow. Nathanael Greene used the militia in a similar manner at the battle of Guilford Court House, North Carolina, in March 1781. Although Greene was defeated, it was because Cornwallis's troops overwhelmed Greene's Continentals, not because the militia failed to do its duty.

These benefits did not come without cost, however. The Continental army lost hundreds of veteran soldiers at Camden. Baron De Kalb's death deprived the army of an outstanding officer; his behavior at Camden had been heroic, and such leadership was vitally needed in the Southern campaign. Camden also cost the army the services of William Smallwood. With De Kalb dead and Gates in disfavor, Smallwood expected Congress to appoint him commander of the Southern army. When Greene was chosen instead, the angry Smallwood returned to Maryland. In addition to the losses in officers and men, the British capture of so much military equipment was severely felt, since the cash-strapped Congress could not easily replace it.

One of the most significant casualties of Camden was the military career of Horatio Gates. His contributions were forgotten. He had inspired South Carolina's Whigs to rejoin the rebellion and had lured his old Saratoga comrade, Daniel Morgan, out of retirement. When Congress had not promoted him to brigadier general, Morgan was enraged and returned to his Virginia home. It was Gates who pressed Congress to promote Morgan and then talked his friend into returning to duty. Morgan arrived too late for Camden, but he was the architect of the American victory at Cowpens.

Had Gates remained on the battlefield, his reputation might not have suffered. Washington had kept the confidence of Congress and the public despite a string of disastrous defeats in New York and Pennsylvania. Gates, however, had the misfortune of getting caught in the tide of retreating militia when he tried to rally them, and was swept off the field. Had he extricated himself and returned to the action, or retreated no farther than Charlotte, he might have escaped criticism. But his decision to go to Hillsborough to reorganize the army, even if justifiable, and the speed with which he went proved fatal to him. No general could leave a battlefield during the fighting and travel 180 miles from the scene of action in three days without expecting censure. Gates's enemies seized on his flight to imply that he was a coward. As a result, Gates became an object of ridicule, and went home in disgrace after Greene replaced him. Although Congress forgave him and ordered him back to duty in 1782, Gates still suffers at the hands of historians who have frequently portrayed him as incompetent.

Cornwallis, on the other hand, received praise from both his contemporaries and historians for his victory at Camden. Yet in an ironic twist of fate, it was the courageous, talented British earl who marched his army to Yorktown, Virginia, and a defeat that insured American independence, while Gates, whose advance to Camden sparked a revolt that eventually sent a frustrated Cornwallis off to seek victory in Virginia, remains a discredited figure.

# Appendix

On the afternoon of August 15, Horatio Gates issued the following orders for the march of his army.[232]

*After Orders.*

*The sick, the extra artillery stores, the heavy baggage, and such quarter-master's stores as are not immediately wanted, to march this evening under a guard to Wacsaws: To this order the general requests the brigadier generals to see that those under their command pay the most exact and scrupulous obedience.*

*Lieutenant-Colonel Edmonds,*[233] *with the remaining guns of the park, will take post, and march with the Virginia brigade, under General Stevens; he will direct, as any deficiency happens in the artillery affixed to the other brigades, to supply it immediately; his military staffs, and proportion of his officers, with forty of his men, are to attend him, and wait his orders.*

*The troops will be ready to march precisely at ten o'clock, in the following order, viz. Colonel Armand's advance, cavalry commanded by Colonel Armand: Colonel Porterfield's light infantry on the right flank of Colonel Armand, in Indian file,*[234] *two hundred yards from the road; Major Armstrong's light infantry in the same order as Colonel Porterfield's, on the left flank of the legion; advanced guard of foot, composed of the advanced pickets, first brigade of Maryland, second brigade of Maryland, division of North Carolina, Virginia division; rear-guard volunteers, cavalry on the right and left of the baggage equally divided. In this order the troops will proceed this night. In case of an attack by the enemy's cavalry in front, the light infantry on each flank will instantly march up, and give, and continue the most galling fire upon the enemy's horse; this will enable Colonel Armand not only to support the enemy's charge, but finally rout them: The colonel will therefore consider the orders to stand the attack of the enemy's cavalry, be their numbers what they may, as positive: General Stevens will immediately order one captain, two lieutenants, one ensign, three serjeants, one drum, and sixty rank and file, to join Colonel Porterfield's infantry. These men are to be taken from the most experienced woodsmen, and men every way fittest for the service.*

*The general will likewise complete Armstrong's light infantry to their original number; those must be immediately marched to the advanced post of the army. The troops will preserve the profoundest silence on the march; and any soldier who offers to fire, without the command of his officer, must be instantly put to death.*

*When the ground will admit of it, and the near approach of the enemy renders it necessary, the army will, when ordered, march in columns; the artillery at the head of their respective brigades, and the baggage in the rear. The guard of the heavy baggage will be composed of the remaining officers and soldiers of the artillery. One captain, two subalterns, four serjeants, four drums, and sixty rank and file, and no person whatever is to presume to send any other soldier upon that service.*

*All batmen, waiters, &c.*[235] *who are soldiers taken from the line, are forthwith to join their respective regiments, and act with their masters, while they are upon that duty.*

*The tents of the whole army to be struck at Tattoo.*

British officers prepared this "Field return of the troops under the command of Lieutenant-general Earl Cornwallis, on the night of the 15th of August, 1780."[236]

*Royal artillery. 2 lieutenants, 2 serjeants, 15 rank and file.*

*Light companies. 2 captains, 3 lieutenants, 1 ensign, 1 adjutant, 11 serjeants, 1 drummer, 129 rank and file.*

*23d regiment. 3 captains, 6 lieutenants, 1 adjutant, 13 serjeants, 8 drummers, 261 rank and file.*

*33d regiment. 1 lieutenant colonel, 5 captains, 4 lieutenants, 2 ensigns, 1 adjutant, 1 surgeon, 1 mate, 14 serjeants, 1 drummer, 209 rank and file.*

*1st battalion, 71st regiment. 2 captains, 4 lieutenants, 1 ensign, 1 adjutant, 1 quarter master, 1 mate, 14 serjeants, 6 drummers, 114 rank and file.*

*2d battalion, ditto. 1 captain, 3 lieutenants, 3 ensigns, 9 serjeants, 94 rank and file.*

*Volunteers of Ireland. 1 colonel, 4 captains, 4 lieutenants, 6 ensigns, 1 mate, 23 serjeants, 11 drummers, 253 rank and file.*

*British legion cavalry. 1 lieutenant colonel, 1 major, 2 captains, 3 lieutenants, 2 cornets, 1 adjutant, 1 surgeon, 12 serjeants, 2 trumpeters, 157 rank and file.*

*British legion infantry. 4 captains, 4 lieutenants, 9 serjeants, 3 drummers, 106 rank and file.*

*Royal North-Carolina regiment. 1 lieutenant colonel, 1 major, 5 captains, 6 lieutenants, 4 ensigns, 1 adjutant, 1 quarter master, 1 surgeon, 16 serjeants, 8 drummers, 223 rank and file.*

*Pioneers, 2 lieutenants, 3 serjeants, 23 rank and file.*

*Volunteer militia. 1 lieutenant colonel, 1 major, 3 captains, 5 lieutenants, 4 ensigns, 8 serjeants, 300 rank and file.*

*Total. 1 colonel, 4 lieutenant colonels, 3 majors, 31 captains, 46 lieutenants, 23 ensigns, 6 adjutants, 2 quarter masters, 3 surgeons, 3 mates, 133 serjeants, 40 drummers, 1944 rank and file.*

After the battle, Cornwallis's officers compiled a "Return of the killed, wounded, and missing…in the battle fought near Camden."[237]

*Royal artillery. 1 lieutenant, 2 rank and file, wounded.*
*Light infantry. 1 serjeant, 6 rank and file, killed; 1 ensign, 5 rank and file, wounded.*
*23d regiment. 6 rank and file killed; 1 captain, 17 rank and file, wounded.*
*33d regiment. 1 captain, 17 rank and file, killed; 1 lieutenant colonel, 1 captain, 2 lieutenants, 1 ensign, 4 serjeants, 72 rank and file, wounded; 1 rank and file missing.*
*1st battalion, 71st. 1 lieutenant, 4 rank and file, killed; 1 captain, 1 lieutenant, 1 serjeant, 22 rank and file, wounded.*
*2d battalion, ditto. 1 serjeant, 4 rank and file, killed; 1 serjeant, 8 rank and file, wounded.*
*Volunteers of Ireland. 17 rank and file killed; 1 lieutenant, 2 ensigns, 2 serjeants, 1 drummer, 64 rank and file, wounded.*
*Legion cavalry. 4 rank and file killed; 1 serjeant, 3 rank and file wounded; 2 rank and file missing.*
*Legion infantry. 1 rank and file killed; 1 lieutenant, 1 serjeant, 10 rank and file, wounded; 2 serjeants, 3 rank and file, missing.*
*Royal North-Carolina regiment. 3 rank and file killed; 1 lieutenant colonel, 1 lieutenant, 1 ensign, 3 serjeants, 8 rank and file, wounded.*
*Pioneers. 2 rank and file killed; 1 lieutenant wounded.*
*Volunteer militia. 2 rank and file wounded; 3 rank and file missing.*
*Total. 1 captain, 1 lieutenant, 2 serjeants, 64 rank and file, killed; 2 lieutenant colonels, 3 captains, 8 lieutenants, 5 ensigns, 13 serjeants, 1 drummer, 213 rank and file, wounded; 2 serjeants, 9 rank and file, missing.*

In the confusion following their rout, American officers were never able to calculate their army's exact losses. They did, however, prepare a "List of the continental officers killed, captivated, wounded, and missing, in the actions of the 16th and 18th of August, 1780," on August 29.[238]

The document named five officers known to have been killed, six wounded and thirty who had been taken prisoner, some of whom had also been wounded. Another five officers were listed as missing. The report noted that "Seven hundred non-commissioned officers and soldiers of the Maryland division have rejoined the army."

After the last American survivors had made their way to Hillsborough, Otho Holland Williams estimated the losses of the Maryland and Delaware troops by deducting the number of men then present from the totals recorded before the battle.[239]

> *The numbers* [of Maryland soldiers] *which were killed, captured and missing, since the last muster, could not, with any accuracy, be ascertained. The aggregate was, three lieutenant colonels, two majors, fifteen captains, thirteen subalterns, two staff officers, fifty-two non-commissioned officers, thirty-four musicians, and seven hundred and eleven rank and file. These, at least a very great majority of these, and all of them for aught I know, fell in the field, or into the hands of the enemy, on the fatal 16th of August. It is extremely probable, that the number killed much exceeded the number taken prisoners.*
>
> *…Eleven commissioned officers, and thirty-six privates of the Delaware regiment, fell into the hands of the enemy.*

British officers prepared a "Return of the Prisoners taken…at the Battle fought near Camden," that provides the most accurate account of the number of Americans captured.[240]

> *Continentals:*
>
> *Delaware: 1 lieutenant colonel, 1 major, 2 captains, 2 lieutenants, 6 serjeants, 64 privates*
>
> *Maryland: 1 major, 7 captains, 4 lieutenants, 1 ensign, 25 serjeants, 4 drummers, 304 privates*
>
> *Virginia: 1 lieutenant colonel, 9 privates*
>
> *South Carolina: 3 privates*
>
> *Armand's Legion: 2 captains, 1 lieutenant, 12 privates*
>
> *Artillery: 2 lieutenants, 4 drummers, 49 privates*
>
> *Militia:*
>
> *Virginia: 1 lieutenant colonel, 1 captain, 2 lieutenants, 3 serjeants, 38 privates*
>
> *North Carolina: 1 colonel, 1 lieutenant colonel, 1 major, 5 captains, 3 lieutenants, 8 serjeants, 124 privates*
>
> *Total: 1 colonel, 4 lieutenant colonels, 3 majors, 17 captains, 14 lieutenants, 3 ensigns, 42 serjeants, 8 drummers, 603 privates*
>
> *"General Officers & Staff*
>
> *1 Major General Since dead of his Wounds*
>
> *1 Brigr. General*
>
> *3 Aids de Camp*
>
> *1 Major of Brigade*
>
> *2 Commissarys*

This "Return of ordnance and military stores taken…at the battle fought near Camden" tallied the equipment captured by the British.[241]

> *Brass Field Pieces.*
> *Six pounders, 4; three pounders, 2; two pounders, 2. Total, 8.*
> *(Abandoned by the enemy, and brought from their camp, Lynche's creek.*
> *Iron Field Pieces.*
> *Three pounder, 1; two pounder, 1; swivels, 3. Total, 5.)*
> *Ammunition waggons, covered, 22; travelling forges, 2; fixed ammunition for six pounders, 160; ditto for three pounders, 520; stand of arms, 2000; musquet cartridges, 80,000.*

The day after the battle, Cornwallis congratulated his troops on their valorous performance.[242]

> *Lord Cornwallis's Orders.*
>
> *My sense of gratitude and admiration for the behaviour of the troops, which I had the honour to command in the action of yesterday is so great, that words cannot express my feelings. The determined intrepidity with which every soldier fought in that glorious field, proved his sincere affection to his King and country, and his resolution to maintain their rights, and revenge their injuries.*
>
> *My thanks are particularly due to Lord Rawdon, and Lieutenant Colonel Webster, for the great assistance which I received from them, and for the courage and ability which they shewed in conducting their respective divisions. The spirited exertions of the commanding officers of the different corps of infantry, deserve my warmest praise and acknowledgement.*
>
> *I am much indebted to Lieutenant Colonel Tarleton, who commanded the cavalry, and Lieutenant M'Leod who commanded the artillery, for the great service they performed on that important day.*
>
> *I must likewise express my obligations to Lieutenant-Colonel Hamilton, and have no doubt that the ardour which was shewn by the young troops under his command, will in future, be productive of the best consequences to the cause of Britain.*
>
> *I feel most sensibly the advantages I received from the zeal and good conduct of my Aide de Camps, Captain Ross, and Lieutenant Haldane, and of Major of Brigade England, acting as Deputy Adjutant General, and the Majors of Brigade, Manly and Doyle.*

On September 19, 265 Loyalists in Charleston signed an address congratulating Cornwallis on his victory at Camden.[243]

*"To the Right Honourable Charles Earl Cornwallis…The humble* ADDRESS *of divers Loyal Inhabitants of Charlestown."*

*We his Majesty's dutiful and loyal subjects, inhabitants of Charlestown…take this opportunity…of tendering to your Lordship, our joyful congratulations on the total defeat and dispersion of the Rebel army, by his Majesty's forces under your command.*

*When we reflect on the desolation and ruin with which this Province was threatened, by the unrelenting cruelty of a formidable and menacing enemy, we think ourselves fortunate that we had no idea of our danger, until we were effectually relieved from it by the glorious victory obtained by your Lordship, wherein the interposition of a protecting Providence is evident; which inspires us with gratitude to the Supreme Ruler of the Universe; and, at the same time, excites in our minds, a due sense of the manifold obligations we have to your Lordship, for your distinguished conduct and courage, so eminently conspicuous in the accomplishment of that great event; which has rescued this Province from impending destruction, and is no less advantageous to our most gracious Sovereign and the British Empire, than honourable to your Lordship; and which Fame will transmit to the latest posterity, with that tribute of praise and admiration your Lordship has so justly merited on this important occasion.*

*Although a prevailing Faction subverted our excellent constitution, and established a democratick*[244] *kind of government in its stead; yet, as that arbitrary system of rule was annihilated by the surrender of this capital, and submission of the country, every member of the community had an indubitable right to consult his own happiness; and as the People in general, induced by their predilection and veneration for the old Constitution,*[245] *have made an explicit declaration of their allegiance, and availed themselves of the protection of that Government under which they formerly enjoyed the highest degree of civil and political liberty, as well as security in their properties, we cannot but consider the late attempt of Congress to subjugate the freemen of this Province to their tyrannical domination, as an additional proof of their restless ambition, and of the wicked machinations of the contemptible remains of that expiring Faction, who have so recently exercised a despotick and lawless sway over us; and, we trust, that every other hostile experiment, by the goodness of God, and your Lordship's vigilance and animated endeavours, will be rendered equally futile.*

*"His Lordship's* ANSWER *To the Loyal Inhabitants of Charlestown"*

*Gentlemen,*

*It gives me great pleasure to be assured by you, that my conduct has merited the approbation of the loyal inhabitants of Charlestown. I shall always endeavour, to the utmost of my abilities, to contribute to the honour and prosperity of my King and Country, and to the release of His Majesty's loyal subjects in America, from the cruel and oppressive tyranny under which they have so long and so severely suffered.*

*…Cornwallis.*

*Charlotte-Town, N. Carolina, October 3d, 1780.*

# Notes

## Chapter 1

1. "The Southern Campaign 1780: Letters of Major General Gates," *Magazine of American History* 5, no. 4 (October 1880): 302–04.
2. "Line" refers to Continental soldiers, the well-trained professional troops who formed the backbone of the American army.
3. The plantation of Loyalist militia colonel Henry Rugeley.
4. Colonel Thomas Sumter of the South Carolina militia had organized a partisan corps after the fall of Charleston to resist the British occupation. On July 30 he attacked the British post at Rocky Mount, but was repulsed. Sumter then assaulted the British troops at Hanging Rock on August 6, inflicting heavy casualties before he was forced to withdraw.
5. Artillery pieces were classified by the weight of the projectile they fired. A three-pounder fired a solid iron cannon ball weighing three pounds. These guns could also fire grapeshot, shells containing small iron balls that dispersed when fired.
6. Ninety Six was the most important town in the South Carolina Backcountry. The British post there protected the many Loyalists in the area and served as a base for the Loyal militia.
7. A "legion" was a mixed force of infantry and cavalry. Armand had brought his own small legion from the North and absorbed the remnants of another legion originally commanded by Polish Count Casimir Pulaski.
8. Lieutenant Colonel Charles Porterfield commanded a unit of Virginia State Troops, who were better trained and served for longer terms than the militia.
9. Light infantry were troops capable of moving quickly and fighting in loose order. They were especially suitable for screening the movements of the army, hit and run attacks and pursuing a fleeing enemy.
10. Cavalry.
11. A flag of truce.
12. Thomas Jefferson.
13. "Southern Campaign 1780," 308–09.
14. Supporters of the Revolution commonly referred to Loyalists as "disaffected," and the Loyalists and British often applied the same term to Rebels. The numerous Loyalists in North Carolina had repeatedly urged Cornwallis to bring his army to assist them in driving the Rebels from that state.
15. On August 18, Lieutenant Colonel Banastre Tarleton attacked and routed Sumter's force at Fishing Creek, South Carolina.

16. "Extract of a Journal concerning the Action of the 16th August, 1780," *Magazine of American History* 5, no. 4 (October 1880): 275–78.
17. Charlotte, North Carolina.
18. Colonel James Carey, who commanded the Loyal militia in the Camden area.
19. Sanders' Creek.
20. Pioneers were troops who cleared obstructions, repaired roads and bridges and performed related work.
21. "Huzza" was a cheer used by troops of that era.
22. Griffith Rutherford, Isaac Gregory and John Butler.
23. Harold C. Syrett, ed., *The Papers of Alexander Hamilton* (New York: Columbia University Press, 1961), 385–88.
24. The name of a tavern and farm near the battlefield.
25. After the battle many Loyalists, and some Whigs who wished to ingratiate themselves with the British, captured some of the fleeing Continentals and militiamen and turned them over to Cornwallis.
26. Otho Holland Williams Papers, Maryland Historical Society, Baltimore.
27. Williams's horse.
28. The legendary horse of Alexander the Great.
29. Artillery fire.
30. William Johnson, *Sketches of the Life and Correspondence of Nathanael Greene, Major General of the Armies of the United States, in the War of the Revolution* (Charleston: A.E. Miller, 1822), 485–502.
31. Francis Marion and his partisans were assisting Gates by raiding supply lines and harassing Loyalists in the region east and southeast of Camden.
32. Rugeley's Mills.
33. Lieutenant Colonel Thomas Woolford, commander of the Fifth Maryland Regiment, led the detachment that reinforced Sumter.
34. Gates's orders for the night march on August 15 are found in the appendix.
35. Armand's comment is puzzling, since the army was marching in column, not deployed in line of battle, and it was customary for cavalry to precede marching infantry to screen them from the enemy. Cornwallis also placed his cavalry at the head of the British column when he marched that night.
36. On these occasions troops usually received a special issue of rum to fortify them for the tasks ahead.
37. Five ounces.
38. Williams is politely stating that the food gave many soldiers diarrhea.
39. Anthony Singleton of the First Continental Artillery Regiment.
40. Colonel Henry Dixon.
41. John Gunby of the Seventh Maryland and Archibald Anderson of the Third Maryland.
42. Benjamin Ford of the Fifth Maryland.
43. John Eager Howard of the Fifth Maryland Regiment and Robert Kirkwood of Delaware.
44. Every army had a considerable number of women with it. Called "camp followers," these women have often been considered prostitutes. However, while some camp followers did engage in prostitution, most were wives or friends of soldiers and they provided valuable services to the troops, such as laundry, cooking and caring for the sick and injured. For this reason, officers in both the American and British armies provided camp followers with rations from government stores.

45. William Lemar, or Lamar.
46. A glass container.
47. A reference to cockfighting, a popular sport at the time, and one that provided Thomas Sumter's nickname, the "Gamecock."
48. William R. Davie of North Carolina.
49. The Catawbas were the only Southern Indian nation to ally with the Americans. The Cherokees, Creeks, Choctaws and Chickasaws supported the British.
50. Robert Scott Davis Jr., "Thomas Pinckney and the Last Campaign of Horatio Gates," *South Carolina Historical Magazine* 86, no. 2 (April 1985): 84–97.
51. A redoubt was an earthwork fortification surrounded by a ditch, usually open in the rear. An abatis was a tangle of branches designed to obstruct an approaching enemy.
52. Gates had given Brigadier General William Harrington of the South Carolina militia command of the militia in the northeastern portion of the state and instructed him to operate against the British and Loyalists there.
53. The War of 1812, in which Pinckney served as a major general.
54. Major General Nathanael Greene, who succeeded Gates.
55. The paper currency issued by Congress was worth only a fraction of its face value, and few people were willing to accept it.
56. Charles Magill.
57. Lieutenant Christopher Richmond.
58. "Extract of a Journal," 278–79.
59. *Maryland Historical Magazine* 49, no. 2 (January 1954): 124.
60. Thomas J. Kirkland and Robert M. Kennedy, *Historic Camden: Part One, Colonial and Revolutionary* (Camden, SC: Kershaw County Historical Society, 1994, reprint edition), 189–90.
61. Ibid.
62. Both sides often released captured officers on parole; that is, the officer promised not to return to duty until exchanged for a prisoner of equal rank.
63. Horatio Gates Papers, New York Historical Society, New York.
64. *Delaware Archives: Military* (Wilmington: Public Archives Commission of Delaware, 1911), 622–23.
65. In the eighteenth century, captured officers were expected to pay for their own support.
66. The source of this letter is unknown. It was discovered by Charles Baxley and transcribed by John Robertson.
67. New York *Royal Gazette*, October 4, 1780.
68. Julian P. Boyd, ed., *The Papers of Thomas Jefferson* (Princeton, NJ: Princeton University Press, 1951), 558–59.
69. Walter Clark, ed., *The State Records of North Carolina* (Wilmington, NC: Broadfoot Publishing Company, 1993, reprint edition), 560.

## Chapter 2

70. Charles D. Ross, ed., *Correspondence of Charles, First Marquis Cornwallis* (London: J. Murray, 1859), 54–55.
71. An express was an urgent message delivered by courier.
72. K.G. Davies, ed., *Documents of the American Revolution 1770–1783* (Dublin: Irish University Press, 1978), 144–48.
73. Cross Creek is now Fayetteville, North Carolina.

74. Archibald McArthur with the Seventy-first Regiment was then posted at Cheraw Hill.
75. George Turnbull, commander of the Loyalist New York Volunteers.
76. Turnbull chose to unite with Major Patrick Ferguson, who was inspector general of militia.
77. Banastre Tarleton, *A History of the Campaigns of 1780 and 1781, in the Southern Provinces of North America* (London: T. Cadell, 1787), 128–35.
78. This was the area where Marion was operating.
79. Loyalists who had left their homes to join the British.
80. John McLeod of the Royal Artillery.
81. Isaac Gregory of the North Carolina militia, although wounded and taken prisoner, survived the battle.
82. Alexander Ross and Henry Haldane.
83. Major Richard England of Cornwallis's staff and Captains John Manley of the Thirty-third Regiment and John Doyle of the Volunteers of Ireland.
84. Former North Carolina Governor Josiah Martin had previously served as an officer in the British army.
85. Sir Guy Carleton Papers, Vol. 25, microfilm, Library of Congress.
86. Cornwallis Papers, PRO 30/11/63, microfilm, Library of Congress.
87. Henry P. Johnston, "De Kalb, Gates, and the Camden Campaign," *Magazine of American History* 8, no. 7 (July 1882): 496–97.
88. Chevalier Du Buysson.
89. Arthur Aspinall, ed., *The Correspondence of George, Prince of Wales* (New York: Oxford University Press, 1967), 192–97.
90. Rugeley's.
91. Tarleton, *History of the Campaigns*, 102–10.
92. George Hanger, Tarleton's second-in-command.
93. Davies, *Documents of the Revolution*, 139–43.
94. Clinton's June 3 proclamation had been intended to conciliate the Americans by releasing all of the militiamen from their paroles. However, many South Carolinians considered themselves absolved from their pledge not to bear arms and joined Rebel partisan units.
95. Martin erroneously believed that Caswell's maneuvers were intended to cover the advance of the main American army.
96. The Twenty-third Regiment, known as the Royal Welsh Fusiliers.

## Chapter 3

97. *Pennsylvania Magazine of History and Biography* 9 (1885): 454–56.
98. The drum signaling the end of the day's activities.
99. Officers with the rank of major or above were called field officers; those of lower rank were called line officers.
100. Joseph Brown Turner, ed., *The Journal and Order Book of Captain Robert Kirkwood of the Delaware Regiment of Continental Line* (Wilmington: Historical Society of Delaware, 1910), 11.
101. David Vaughn and John Patten of the Delaware Continentals.
102. William Seymour, *Journal of the Southern Expedition, 1780–1783* (Wilmington: Historical Society of Delaware, 1896), 5–7.
103. A purgative drug.
104. Guilford Dudley, "A Sketch of the Military Services Performed by Guilford Dudley, Then of the Town of Halifax, North Carolina, During the Revolutionary War," *Southern Literary Messenger* (March–June 1845): 144–48, 231–35, 281–87, 370–75.

105. Thomas H. Drew.
106. An advance scout.
107. Artillerists.
108. Gold and silver coins.
109. Between two and three hundred yards.
110. John C. Dann, ed., *The Revolution Remembered: Eyewitness Accounts of the War for Independence* (Chicago: University of Chicago Press, 1980), 194–95.
111. Henry Dixon of the North Carolina militia.
112. Petition of Samuel Dinwiddie, Landon Carter and other Amherst County Militiamen, Virginia State Library, Richmond.
113. Pension Application W326.
114. Pension Application S30831.
115. George Alexander.
116. Pension Application S2905.
117. Possibly Lieutenant Colonel Armand.

## Chapter 4

118. New York *Royal Gazette*, September 20, 1780.
119. Lieutenant Hugh Gillespie and Ensigns David Whatley and John Thomson.
120. Ensign Thomas Flyn.
121. New York *Royal Gazette*, September 20, 1780.
122. New York *Royal Gazette*, September 23, 1780.
123. Whig militia from Halifax, North Carolina.
124. New York *Royal Gazette*, September 23, 1780.
125. Gates's proclamations urged those who had taken the oath of allegiance to Britain to recant and join the American forces.
126. Cornmeal.
127. Roger Lamb, *An Original and Authentic Journal of Occurrences During the Late American War, From Its Commencement to the Year 1783* (Dublin: Wilkinson & Courtney, 1809), 302–06.
128. Porterfield.
129. Captain Forbes Champagne.
130. Both generals accused their opponents of killing and mistreating prisoners. Lamb believed that Gates's accusations were unjustified.
131. John Robert Shaw, *A Narrative of the Life & Travels of John Robert Shaw, the Well-Digger, Now Resident in Lexington, Kentucky. Written by Himself* (Lexingon, KY: Daniel Bradford, 1830), 49–52.
132. Also known as Monck's Corner, on the Cooper River about thirty-five miles from Charleston.
133. Rugeley's.
134. This rumor, although false, may have circulated among the British troops.

## Chapter 5

135. After Charleston's surrender, British commander Henry Clinton allowed Lincoln to go to Philadelphia on parole to report to Congress.
136. Thomas Bee Papers, South Caroliniana Library, Columbia.
137. Gregg L. Lint, ed., *The Papers of John Adams* (Cambridge, MA: Belknap Press, 1996), 92.

138. Clark, *State Records of North Carolina*, 406.
139. Benjamin Exum, a Continental officer commanding North Carolina militia.
140. William Moultrie, *Memoirs of the American Revolution* (New York: David Longworth, 1802), 231–36.
141. It was the Loyalists and British troops who celebrated, not the Whigs.
142. A feu de joie was a salute with cannon and musket fire.
143. William Dobein James, *A Sketch of the Life of Brig. Gen. Francis Marion and a History of His Brigade from its Rise in June 1780 until Disbanded in December, 1782* (Charleston: Gould and Riley, 1821), 49.
144. David R. Chesnutt and C. James Taylor, eds., *The Papers of Henry Laurens* (Columbia: University of South Carolina Press, 2000), 440–41.
145. Tarleton, *History of the Campaigns*, 149–50.
146. Don Higginbotham, ed., *The Papers of James Iredell* (Raleigh: North Carolina Division of Archives and History, 1976), 172.
147. Boyd, *Papers of Jefferson*, 576.
148. Ibid., 592.
149. Ibid., 593–97.
150. About three thousand. A stand of arms consisted of a musket, bayonet and cartridge box.
151. Boyd, *Papers of Jefferson*, 638–39.
152. The recruits had enlisted to serve until the end of the war, rather than for a specified number of years.
153. William Hutchinson and William M.E. Rachal, eds., *The Papers of James Madison* (Chicago: University of Chicago Press, 1962), 83.
154. Throughout the autumn of 1780, rumors circulated that a French fleet was off the Southern coast, ready to strike the British. Although widely believed, the reports proved false.
155. Clark, *State Records of North Carolina*, 65.
156. Helen Lee Peabody, ed., "Revolutionary Mail Bag: Governor Thomas Sim Lee's Correspondence," *Maryland Historical Magazine* 49, no. 2 (June 1954): 123–24.
157. Rodney Collection, Box 6, Folder 18, Historical Society of Delaware, Wilmington.
158. Anthony White, a cavalry officer, did not take part in the battle.
159. Gist.
160. Probably Nathaniel Ramsey.
161. Apparently Colonel Senf.
162. James and George Clinton Collection, Library of Congress, Washington, D.C.
163. Richard K. Showman, ed., *The Papers of General Nathanael Greene* (Chapel Hill: University of North Carolina Press, 1991), 257–58.
164. Ibid., 89–90.
165. James Thacher, *Military Journal, during the American Revolutionary War* (Plymouth, MA: privately published, 1823).
166. Miscellaneous Manuscripts, Oswald, New York, Historical Society.
167. Syrett, *Papers of Hamilton*, 420–21.
168. Two legendary heroes of the Trojan War.
169. Syrett, *Papers of Hamilton*, 422.
170. Ibid., 425.
171. Washington.
172. Jared Sparks, ed., *The Writings of George Washington; Being His Correspondence, Addresses, Messages, and Other Papers, Official and Private* (Boston: Russell, Odiorne, and Metcalf, 1835), 201–02.

173. Ibid., 197–98.
174. Barbara B. Oberg, ed., *The Papers of Benjamin Franklin* (New Haven, CT: Yale University Press, 1997), 400.
175. Lint, *Papers of John Adams*, 10:266-267.
176. Many Britons claimed they wanted reconciliation with America, but Adams believed that their celebration of British victories in the South proved that they wanted to punish the Americans for revolting.
177. Lint, *Papers of Adams*, 270.
178. Adams's effort to secure a loan from the Dutch.
179. Lint, *Papers of Adams*, 274.
180. Militia.
181. "Affaires Etrangeres," microfilm, Library of Congress. Translated by Jim Piecuch.
182. Clark, *State Records of North Carolina*, 166–68.
183. The document listed a total of 17 officers and 148 enlisted men of the North Carolina militia who had been taken prisoner at Camden.
184. Flux was an eighteenth-century term for dysentery that was often accompanied by hemorrhaging.
185. At the time, these items were believed to have medicinal value.
186. Blackwell P. Robinson, ed., *The Revolutionary War Sketches of William R. Davie* (Raleigh: North Carolina Department of Cultural Resources, 1976), 16–18.
187. Henry Lee, *The Revolutionary War Memoirs of General Henry Lee*, ed. Robert E. Lee (New York: Da Capo Press, 1998, reprint edition), 178–87, 190–92.
188. Lieutenant Colonels Anthony White and William Washington had led their cavalry units in the Charleston campaign, where they had been badly cut up by Tarleton's dragoons. Gates had ordered them to refit while he advanced southward with the main army.
189. Here Lee refers to the settlers west of the Appalachians, the so-called "overmountain men," who defeated Patrick Ferguson's Loyalists on October 7, 1780.
190. Julius Caesar's famous remark, "I came, I saw, I conquered."

## Chapter 6

191. E. Alfred Jones, ed., "The Journal of Alexander Chesney, a South Carolina Loyalist in the Revolution and After," *The Ohio State University Bulletin* 26, no. 4 (October 1921): 13.
192. Charles Stedman, *The History of the Origins, Progress and Termination of the American War* (London: J. Murray, 1794), 204–13.
193. A settlement just north of Camden.
194. Robert Gray, "Colonel Robert Gray's Observations on the War in Carolina," *South Carolina Historical and Genealogical Magazine* 11, no. 3 (July 1910): 141–42.
195. *South Carolina and American General Gazette*, August 23, 1780.
196. *South Carolina and American General Gazette*, September 6, 1780.
197. Robert MacLeroth.
198. Alexander Inglis.
199. *South Carolina and American General Gazette*, October 4, 1780.
200. *South Carolina and American General Gazette*, October 14, 1780.
201. Violet Biddulph, ed., "Letters of Robert Biddulph, 1779–1783," *American Historical Review* 29, no. 1 (October 1923): 94–95.
202. Sir Henry Strachey Papers, Library of Congress.

203. General Henry Clinton. When Clinton left Charleston at the beginning of June, he took most of the troops with him. Cornwallis told him that the number left in South Carolina was sufficient, but later complained that Clinton had not given him enough troops.
204. By troops from Washington's army.
205. The Hudson River in New York. Balfour is implying that Clinton is not using the troops at New York effectively.
206. Here Balfour refers to the bitter feud between Clinton and Cornwallis, and implies that Clinton is refusing to assist Cornwallis out of personal animosity.
207. "Military Reports and Accounts Concerning the Operation of the Hessian Corps in the American War," Hessian Documents of the American Revolution, 1776–1783, Item Z; Transcripts and Translations from the Lidgerwood Collection at Morristown National Historical Park, New Jersey.
208. "Journal of the Honorable Garrison Regiment von Huyn, later von Benning, from the year 1776 to the middle of November 1783," Hessian Documents, Item T.
209. Off.
210. New York *Royal Gazette*, September 9, 1780.
211. Delaware.
212. New York *Royal Gazette*, September 13, 1780.
213. The printer of the *Pennsylvania Gazette*.
214. Gates did complain of illness after the battle, but did not disguise himself to escape. Congress authorized Gates's successor, Nathanael Greene, to hold an inquiry into Gates's conduct, but Greene took no action on the matter.
215. New York *Royal Gazette*, September 20, 1780.
216. The Virginia militia was commanded by Edward Stevens. Another Virginian, General Charles Scott, had commanded the Virginia Continentals and was taken prisoner with them when Charleston surrendered.
217. New York *Royal Gazette*, September 20, 1780.
218. New York *Royal Gazette*, September 27, 1780.
219. Convention refers to the surrender agreement Gates entered into with Burgoyne after Saratoga. Under its terms, British prisoners were to be allowed to return to Britain and not participate in the war again until exchanged. Congress repudiated the agreement and held the captives as prisoners of war.
220. A reference to the nearly worthless American paper money.
221. Henry Clinton, *The American Rebellion, Sir Henry Clinton's Narrative of His Campaigns, 1775–1782, With an Appendix of Original Documents*, ed. William B. Willcox (New Haven, CT: Yale University Press, 1954), 224–25.
222. Clinton is implying that Cornwallis should have used the time after the battle to suppress the partisan warfare that Gates's advance had sparked in South Carolina, rather than invading North Carolina.
223. Bernard A. Uhlendorf, ed. and trans., *Revolution in America: Confidential Letters and Journals of Adjutant General Baurmeister of the Hessian Forces, 1776–1784* (New Brunswick, NJ: Rutgers University Press, 1957), 378–83.
224. The Pee Dee River is actually in northeastern South Carolina, a considerable distance from Camden.
225. The British had no garrisons at either of these places. Charlotte had never been under British control, and Fort Rutledge on the South Carolina frontier had been abandoned at the request of Britain's Cherokee Indian allies after the Whigs surrendered it.

226. Thomas H. Edsall, ed., *Journal of John Charles Philip von Krafft, Lieutenant in the Hessian Regiment von Bose, 1776–1784* (New York: privately printed, 1888), 120.
227. Davies, *Documents of the Revolution*, 225.
228. Ibid., 227. Germain's prediction proved incorrect; in September Whig partisans attacked Augusta in the Georgia Backcountry.
229. William Knox Papers, William L. Clements Library, Ann Arbor, Michigan.

## Epilogue

230. Cornwallis demonstrated this same shortcoming during the January 1781 Cowpens campaign, when he promised to cooperate with Tarleton and then failed to do so.
231. Rawdon to General Alexander Leslie, October 24, 1780, George Germain Papers, Vol. 13, Clements Library.

## Appendix

232. Tarleton, *History of the Campaigns*, 142–44.
233. Elias Edmonds of the Continental Artillery.
234. Single file.
235. Officers' servants. Many officers assigned soldiers to be their personal attendants.
236. Tarleton, *History of the Campaigns*, 136–37.
237. Ibid., 137–39.
238. Ibid., 151–53.
239. Johnson, *Life of Greene*, 505.
240. Carleton Papers, Vol. 25.
241. Tarleton, *History of the Campaigns*, 139–40.
242. New York *Royal Gazette*, September 20, 1780.
243. *Royal South-Carolina Gazette*, October 14, 1780.
244. Loyalists and Whigs both equated democracy with mob rule.
245. The British Constitution.